When War Dawns

Based on Historical Events

DAVID LEE CORLEY

DEDICATION

To the men and women that fought for their country.
Your sacrifices will not be forgotten.

&

To my great aunt, Patty Thomas who toured with Bob Hope as a dancer and choreographer in three wars – World War II, Korean War, and Vietnam War. She had an indomitable spirit, boundless energy, and loved cheering up "The Boys".

Table of Contents

PROLOGUE

Just after the Geneva Conference in 1954, Air Force Colonel Edward Lansdale arrived in the newly formed nation of South Vietnam. Reporting directly to the CIA Director, Allen Dulles, Lansdale had been sent as the Deputy Director of the Office of Special Operations to execute a clandestine operation codenamed "Nautilus."

Nautilus was a series of ongoing raids by South Vietnamese commandos and their American CIA officers against the North Vietnamese. The raids were both propaganda missions and paramilitary operations. The propaganda missions were designed to demoralize the communists. As a former advertising executive, Lansdale had become a master of wartime propaganda. The paramilitary operations were designed to "gum up the works" in North Vietnam and often involved blowing up railyards, bridges, ports, and other transportation infrastructure. Dozens of raids were successfully carried out under Lansdale's command.

After Lansdale was promoted to general and sent to the Pentagon, the Nautilus teams were transferred from the CIA to the Department of Defense. The generals of MACV were the new commanders and came up with a new plan of operation codenamed "OPLAN 34a." The plan would include all of the original mission profiles under the CIA but would be expanded to include naval intelligence gathering.

As part of the expanded duties, the US Navy set up

a base of operation in Da Nang and staffed it with US Navy SEALs, Naval Intelligence officers, and guerrilla warfare specialists. The clandestine naval unit included Nasty-class PT boats, a recommissioned submarine, and electronically equipped minesweepers. The focus of the naval missions changed to assaults on North Vietnamese coastal installations and proving Soviet and Chinese involvement in supplying weapons and supplies to the Viet Cong through electronic intelligence gathering.

After a few close calls from North Vietnamese gunboats threatening the defenseless minesweepers, the US Navy assigned a detachment of electronically equipped destroyers to replace the minesweepers. In response, the North Vietnamese Navy deployed heavy gunboats and torpedo-equipped frigates to watch over the American Naval operations. This powder keg would eventually develop into the Gulf of Tonkin Incident…

BIRTH OF A DRAGON

Mekong Delta, South Vietnam

The afternoon downpour had ceased and steam was rising from the ever-present heat. As nightfall approached, binoculars surveyed the rice fields and groves of mangroves around a South Vietnamese hamlet. The evening cooking fires had already created a thin layer of grey smoke over the village. The hamlet was part of a network of hamlets throughout the Mekong Delta. It was the best rice-growing region in the world and the breadbasket of South Vietnam. Rice was life in Vietnam and without the Mekong's fields, the people in the south would starve.

The fortified hamlet had been built by the government on a hill slightly higher than the surrounding fields. The additional height gave the lookout on the platform a good view and prevented the village from being flooded during the monsoon season. The villagers had been trained on how to use the weapons the government had given them when they were forced to move from their old village into the hamlet and replant their new fields. Government troops had burned their old village to the ground so none would return. The villagers wailed and cried. For most of them, it had been their home since birth and held the bones of their ancestors.

The rice plants were already turning from vibrant green to yellow, a sign that the harvest was not far off. It would be the first rice harvest of the year and the villagers were hopeful that it would plentiful. Unlike the other southeast Asian countries, Vietnam had been blessed with not one or two, but three rice harvests each year. The villagers thanked the gods by leaving fresh fruit and rice wine in front of statues sitting on stands around the village.

Watching through his binoculars, Rene Granier focused his attention on the possible avenues of approach the Viet Cong would use if they were to assault the hamlet. After almost two decades of fighting in Vietnam, he knew the enemy well. All seemed still and peaceful. He didn't trust it. But then again… trust was never Granier's strong suit. He knew the Viet Cong were out there somewhere and just because he couldn't see them didn't mean anything. The VC were sneaky bastards. When dealing with the Viet Cong, letting one's guard down was a death sentence for him, his team, and the hamlet he was watching. Knowing that kept him focused and alert.

Granier was a creature of habit and didn't like change. As a commander of one of the MACV paramilitary teams in South Vietnam, Granier needed to control his team and plan their missions. Change made his job more difficult. How does a commander plan a mission when everything is in flux?

His team's current mission was intelligence gathering on Viet Cong activity in Mekong Delta. In his opinion that was a waste of talent and training. Granier and his team were overqualified. The MACV generals clearly did not understand what the paramilitary teams were originally designed to do under the CIA– blow shit up and create mayhem. He liked the original mission, especially the creating mayhem part. It gave him and his men a lot of latitude.

Operating in the middle of chaos was exciting. It pushed him to his limits. It made him better.

Their surveillance mission on that night was to watch a strategic hamlet from afar. Intercepted radio communications indicated that the Viet Cong were going to attack the hamlet that evening. ARVN forces were hidden nearby but did not want to move into position before the attack. They wanted to trap the Viet Cong, not scare them off. American-piloted warplanes were also on standby to support the ARVN.

Granier brought Tom Coyle, a CIA pilot, along so he could analyze the air assaults on VC forces. Coyle had not been the same since his girlfriend Bian had been killed in Saigon a month earlier. His mind wandered unable to focus. Under normal circumstances, Coyle was probably the best pilot in all of Vietnam. But these weren't normal circumstances. This was a good mission for Coyle. It did not require flying under difficult conditions such as combat. Granier was not sure it was safe to fly with Coyle at the moment. He wanted his friend back. Friend. That's a word Granier didn't use much. Coyle was probably his only friend. And that's the way Granier wanted it. Friends were a pain in the ass. He wasn't sure why, but he had made an exception with Coyle. As of late, he was questioning that decision.

The strategic hamlet they were observing was an island surrounded on all sides by a sea of rice fields. It had a twelve-foot-deep moat filled with punji sticks with one end buried in the ground. The steep slope on the village side was also covered with punji sticks giving it a porcupine look. A ten-foot-high fence made of wooden spears surrounded the entire village. There was only one way in – the main gate – which was protected by a light machine gun encased in sandbags. It was a typical setup for a strategic hamlet and would discourage enemy assault. But not this village. The Viet Cong were coming that night.

Once dark, the Viet Cong would begin their assault. The VC would probably use a company-sized unit. They wanted to overwhelm the hamlet's defenses and strike fear into the villagers. Their objectives would most likely be raiding and recruitment. Although North Vietnam sent supplies to the Viet Cong, the shipments were not always reliable, especially since the American SOG with their Montagnard allies had stepped up their efforts to cut off the Ho Chi Minh Trail. A raid on a village usually solved that problem. But as more and more villages became strategic hamlets, the risk of assaults grew. But even if the VC were to end their supply raids, they could not hope to survive without recruits. The ARVN had been executing successful assaults against the VC base camps. At times, the VC were taking heavy losses and needed replacements. Recruits were the lifeblood of the Viet Cong and the villages were the best places to find them even if a bayonet was required to encourage the new volunteers.

Granier and his team had strict orders not to participate in the battle. They were allowed to defend themselves, if necessary, but Granier didn't see that as a very real possibility. He and his team were experts at dissolving into the landscape. It was unlikely the VC would ever find them. For this reason, Granier had only brought the American part of the team – four veteran soldiers that he could depend on in any circumstance. And, of course, Coyle who was just about worthless at the moment.

While Coyle stayed with him, the rest of the team had set up a defensive position at the edge of a grove of trees. If anything turned bad during their reconnaissance, Granier and Coyle could fall back to the team. No matter what, they would be there waiting… ready to fight.

As the sun disappeared below the horizon and twilight faded, Granier and Coyle had left their observation position and set out across the rice fields that surrounded the hamlet. They needed to get closer to observe the battle but still far enough away not to be detected. Granier had his sniper rifle slung across his back just in case. Keeping their heads below the earthen berms, they crouched down as they crossed the muddy water peppered with yellowing rice plants. When they came to a berm that they needed to cross, they belly-crawled. They did not want the VC to see their silhouettes against the night sky.

After a half-hour, Granier and Coyle took up a position behind a massive tree stump where four earthen berms met in a cross. Normally, all tree stumps would have been removed or burned out by the farmers, but the tree stump in the middle of the berms was huge. It had been easier to just build the berms around it. Shoots of small green leaves sprang from the trunk as if it were resurrecting the former tree. The stump offered Granier and Coyle good cover and was close enough to the hamlet to give them a suitable observation point. Once in position, there was nothing to do but wait and see what developed. They both kept their eyes surveying the surrounding area. "This is a stupid mission," whispered Granier.

"How's that?" whispered Coyle.

"We're supposed to observe an enemy assault on

the hamlet. But the ARVN have already been warned of the attack and have already moved up their troops in preparation. The US Air Force knows the attack is going to happen and already have their planes in the air. It's not realistic."

"It's like Heisenberg's Uncertainty Principle."

"What the hell is that?"

"You cannot observe something without affecting it."

"Yeah, like that. But without the fancy name."

"I see what you're doing."

"Yeah. What's that?"

"You're trying to get my mind off Bian."

"Is it working?"

"No."

"You've gotta move on, Coyle."

"I will when I'm ready."

"And when might that be?"

"Shut up, Granier."

"Suits me. I ain't much of a talker."

They fell silent for several minutes, then… "I had a dream last night," said Coyle.

"Bian?" said Granier.

"No. McGoon."

"Oh yeah. How is the ole' boy?"

"Dead, Granier. McGoon is dead."

"I know that. So, what did he say?"

"He was pissed that I hadn't found his two whores."

"Seems strange he'd still be worried about them."

"Yeah, well… he was. I made him a promise to watch out for them right before he died. I haven't done that."

"Well, now maybe you'll have the time."

"Maybe. It's not good to have a ghost angry at you."

"Especially one the size of McGoon."

"Yeah."

"So, when was the last time you saw his whores?"

"Hanoi, just before the end of the Indochina War."

"That was like ten years ago."

"Yeah, just about."

"Hell, they could be dead for all you know."

"I doubt it. McGoon wouldn't be hounding me if they were dead. He'd be preoccupied."

"Yeah, I suppose he would be. So, what are you gonna do?"

"Find 'em."

"That ain't gonna be easy."

"Yeah, well… it's like you said, I got the time now."

"If you see him again, tell 'em I said hello."

"It's a dream, Granier. I ain't gonna remember that."

"You might."

Coyle looked past Granier and made a hand signal to keep quiet, then pointed to something behind Granier. Granier slowly looked over his shoulder and saw the silhouette of a man holding a rifle moving toward the hamlet along the edge of a berm. The VC scout moved on without noticing the two Americans. Granier turned away from the hamlet and saw a skirmish line of one hundred Viet Cong fighters heading straight for him and Coyle. Granier motioned for Coyle to stay still. He unslung and slowly chambered a round in his rifle. Coyle removed his sidearm and slowly chambered a round in his pistol. If seen, their weapons would matter little against the overwhelming odds. They watched motionless as the line of VC moved closer. Granier motioned for Coyle to face back toward the hamlet in the same direction as the VC were looking. It was dark and difficult to see any detail beyond a silhouette. With luck, the VC would think Granier and Coyle were their own troops already in position.

Coyle's mouth was dry from fear. He could hear his heart pounding and thought it might give them away. He dared not even blink.

Granier readied himself for the fight. He would not go down without taking some of the VC with him. His eyes scanned both sides of their position without moving his head.

Several VC moved up to a position a few yards away from Granier and Coyle. They waited for their comrades to catch up, then belly-crawled across the berm and into the next rice paddy between them and the village. A straggler moved up from behind Granier and Coyle. He edged up next to Coyle and whispered something in Vietnamese. Keeping his face turned away from the VC, Coyle grunted in response. Granier removed his knife from its sheath. Granier pointed the tip of the knife to his Adam's apple, then handed the knife to Coyle. The VC said something else. Coyle grunted again. Unhappy with Coyle's response, the VC moved up further next to Coyle and looked over at Granier's face in the dark. The VC seemed to recognize his enemy and his eyes widened. Coyle could feel his hands sweating and wondered if the knife's handle would slip from his hand. There was no choice. He had to act. Coyle twisted around and slammed the knife's blade into the VC's throat. The VC tried to yell but only gurgled. Horrified by what he had just done, Coyle released the knife. Granier crawled over Coyle and put his hand over the VC's mouth. After a few seconds, the VC went limp. None of the other VC noticed what had happened and continued toward the village. Granier's face was less than a foot from Coyle's. Coyle looked Granier in the eyes and shrugged. Granier silently chuckled. Coyle had done his best. It was enough for the moment. He looked back at the rice field behind them for more VC. There were none.

Turning back toward the rice field in front of them, Granier raised his head slowly and looked over the top of the tree stump. The line of VC were already forty yards closer to the village. He was impressed by their silence and speed. He made a mental note to mention it in his report. The enemy was well-trained in stealth. Granier heard the thrum of airplane engines. He turned to Coyle. Coyle made a motion of a flare exploding. It was a flare ship approaching the village.

Spaced a hundred yards apart, two flares dropped from the backdoor of the C-47 flare ship, bursting into a blinding brilliance when their parachutes opened. The two flares illuminated the village and the surrounding rice fields. It also illuminated the plane that had launched it. The plane was turning in a circle at 2,000 feet and out of range from small arms fire. The flare ship would stay on station through the night dropping flares every few minutes until the battle was over.

The VC dropped to the ground hoping not to be seen. Too late. The machine gun guarding the main entrance to the hamlet opened fire. Tracer rounds streaked across the rice fields and over the heads of the VC hugging the mud.

Granier ducked back down just before two rounds hit the tree stump. One of the rounds was a tracer. The bullet's burning magnesium coating ignited a tiny fire around a hole in the stump. It drew attention to their position. Granier didn't like it.

The shrills of incoming arti rounds grabbed the VC's attention and struck fear into their hearts. ARVN artillery rained down on the VC's positions in the rice fields. Shells from 105s and 155s churned the fields and berms launching tons of mud and water mixed with steaming shrapnel into the air. Nowhere was safe. Waiting until the gunfire and cannon fire died down was not an option for the Viet Cong.

The VC commander knew all too well that the American warplanes would soon arrive. Only the Americans were trained in night flying. If the VC were caught in the open rice fields, the fighter-bombers would strafe them with rockets and gunfire. They would be massacred. They needed to grab the enemy by the belt to prevent the American pilots from unleashing hell. The VC needed to close in on the hamlet and that meant taking out the machine gun. On their commander's signal, all the VC rose and opened fire on the source of the tracer rounds. Just as the tracer rounds showed the gunner the path of his bullets and allowed him to correct his aim, the tracer rounds also revealed the exact position of the machine gun. The VC did not need to see the actual weapon, only where the tracer rounds originated. The sound of 100 rifles and submachine guns firing in unison was thunderous. By massing their fire, the VC overwhelmed the machine-gun crew. Bullets pelted their bodies with sickening thuds and the gun crew fell dead. Once the weapon was silenced, the VC didn't wait. They ceased fire, once again becoming invisible, and advanced in the darkness.

Granier and Coyle watched in silence. Another pair of parachute flares dropped from the C-47 flying above. The VC were illuminated on one side. That was enough. Alerted to the danger, the villagers fired their rifles through gaps in the wooden palisades. With little training, the gunfire from the villagers had a limited effect on the advancing VC. The farmers, closing their eyes when pulling their rifles' triggers, simply missed their enemy.

Four A-1E Skyraiders from the 602nd Air Commando Squadron approached the battlefield flying low over the surrounding rice fields. Because of their superior load capability, the Skyraiders had been flown in from Nha Trang Air Base in Khanh Hoa Province and were refueled at Tan Son Nhut Air Base before launching their air assault. In addition to its four 20 mm cannons, the Skyraider had fifteen hardpoints under its wings and fuselage. Each warplane carried a combination of rocket pods, napalm canisters, and bombs. It was the most lethal weapon system in South Vietnam for air-to-ground operations. With a maximum airspeed of 333 mph, the "Spad," as the Skyraider was nicknamed, was slower than its predecessor - the T-28 fighter-bomber. But the Skyraider carried a weapon load three times the size of the T-28.

Directed by the C-47 flare ship above the battlefield, the Skyraiders approached one at a time lining up their runs along the same axis at the VC's line of attack. They flew near their top speed to reduce damage from enemy ground fire. The speed gave them less than a couple of seconds over the target. If they weren't aligned correctly there was little opportunity for correction. While offering more time on target, dive-bombing had its own problems including additional enemy ground fire and the need to release their bombs 1,000 feet above the ground, so the pilots had room to pull out of their dives. The limitations of speed and altitude made air-to-ground support less effective than perceived. The pilots missed their targets far more than they hit them. This was dangerous for friendly forces on the ground, especially if the enemy was close.

The Skyraiders' first runs released bombs and napalm canisters. The bomb explosions were dramatic and shook the earth but did little damage to the enemy advancing on the village. The napalm was slightly more effective. When the canisters hit the ground, they burst open and ignited the fuel inside. The momentum of the fiery liquid carried it for as much as two thousand feet forming an impenetrable wall of flame as it spread engulfing the enemy in its path. Anyone not consumed by the inferno but stupid enough not to turn away had the skin on their faces blistered from the intense heat. It didn't kill 'em but it hurt like hell. Napalm's greatest advantage was the psychological effect. Seeing their comrades burned alive struck fear in the enemy's heart and often broke entire units. But the VC company assaulting the hamlet did not break and kept advancing.

Their veteran commander knew that closing on the enemy was their only hope of surviving. In his pre-mission briefing, the commander had warned the troops what they would be facing and told them point-blank what they must do to survive – attack, always attack.

The Skyraiders' second attack run was meant to strafe the enemy with rockets and 20 mm cannon fire. Only the lead Skyraider was able to fire its weapons at the enemy before they reached the wooden stake wall around the hamlet. The VC had finally grabbed the enemy by the belt. Unwilling to risk the lives of the villagers from collateral damage, the commander of the Skyraiders broke off the staffing attacks. Whatever assault on the enemy could be launched would need to be done from the ground. With nothing more they could do, the Skyraiders headed back to base.

The VC sappers were the first to attack the hamlet. Running up as far as they could without stepping on the punji sticks in the ground and slope, they threw smoking satchel charges against the wooden-stake barrier. Explosions ripped large holes in the fortifications allowing the VC to attack the hamlet from multiple entry points. The sappers continued to clear the way with long knifes hacking off the sharp tips of the punji sticks, then throwing down grass-woven mats in front of the breached palisades.

The farmers inside the hamlet fought back shooting through the breached holes in the wooden stakes trying to drive away the sappers before they could complete their mission. It was useless against the fearless VC sappers. Untrained and frightened, the villagers' repulse was timid.

The VC poured through the holes in the wooden stakes firing their weapons and hurling grenades. It was a one-sided contest with the VC's aggression overwhelming the villagers.

The ARVN ground forces arrived just as the VC claimed the hamlet. The ARVN commanders were not nearly as respectful of civilian casualties as the American commanders. If a hamlet was occupied by the Viet Cong, everyone inside the defenses was a target. There was no quick way to tell who was the enemy and who was not. The ARVN's heavy machine guns and recoilless rifles laid into the village's fortifications splintering the wooden stakes and breaking them into pieces. Villagers and VC alike were shredded by gunfire and pelted with shards of flying wood.

The hamlet was now a trap for the Viet Cong. The commander ordered his troops to gather their dead and wounded, then execute a fighting withdrawal. They took whatever supplies they could easily carry and recruited three village teenagers with the points of their bayonets. Mothers wept at seeing their sons taken.

The surviving sappers used their long knives to cut the ropes between the stakes on the far side of the village. The VC fought fiercely as they escaped through gaps in the broken wall. The last few VC that remained poured suppressing fire into the holes at the front of the village palisades as the ARVN tried to enter. The VC needed to buy time for their comrades racing for cover in the nearby jungle. Once they reached the jungle, they would take up firing positions and cover the retreat of those VC still inside the hamlet.

The VC commander knew that once the ARVN had recaptured the hamlet, the ARVN commanders would be reluctant to follow the VC into the surrounding jungle. The American aircraft could not attack what they could not see below the thick jungle canopy. Once all his men reached the jungle, they were safe and could slip away with their booty and new recruits.

The entire VC assault and retreat was over in less than an hour. Except for twelve VC, three ARVN, and seven villagers killed, neither side in the conflict had gained an advantage. It didn't matter. The commanders on each side would claim victory in hopes of promotion.

Granier and Coyle rejoined their team at the edge of the rice fields. "So, we won, right?" said one of the team members.

"It's a sad day if you call that winning," said Granier.

Saigon, South Vietnam

Back in their civilian clothes, Granier and Coyle sat in their favorite go-go bar outside of the airbase and sipped their bottles of cold beer. Both seemed lost in thought. Neither paid attention to the underage stage dancers wearing too much makeup and short dresses with go-go boots. It was Coyle that spoke first, "Did you notice the flight path of the flare ship?"

"You mean a big circle?" said Granier.

"Yeah. They just hung up there above the fray."

"That's kinda their job… launching flares. No need to get shot at."

"Yeah, but what if they were more than that?"

"What do you mean?"

Coyle motioned for the waitress to come over. Without asking Coyle took her ordering pencil from behind her ear and handed her a dollar as payment. She smiled and left in search of more pencils to sell to the stupid American. Coyle grabbed a cocktail napkin and drew a diagram of the outline of a cone shape with a circle on top and two lines descending into a point below. "What's that got to do with the price of eggs?" said Granier looking at Coyle's drawing.

"Imagine if the flare ship had a heavy machine gun mounted in the side like they do with bombers," said Coyle. "It could shoot down at the enemy while circling."

"I don't think one more machine gun is going to

make much of a difference."

"It might. Unlike the fighter-bombers that can only fire their machine guns and air cannons at the enemy in front of them at 300 mph, this thing could generate constant fire on the enemy below from any point in its flight path."

Granier thought about it for a moment, then examined the drawing closer. "What kind of altitude and airspeed are you talking about?"

"I don't know. Maybe 2,000 to 3,000 feet at 120 miles per hour."

"The gunner would have to be one hell of a shot. The engine vibration alone could turn his aim to shit."

"Maybe. We'd have to try it."

Granier could see that Coyle was excited about the idea and for the moment had forgotten about his dead girlfriend. He was starting to sound like his old self again. The way Granier saw anything was an improvement on Coyle's moping. "Do you have a C-47 we could use?" said Granier.

"I'm sure I could get one. We'd need a Ma Deuce," said Coyle

"I can get us a Ma Deuce."

"Let's try it and see what happens."

They paid their bills and left the bar. The young dancers stopped their prancing and sat down on the side of the stage with disappointed faces. Their only customers had left.

White House – Washington D.C., USA

Sitting behind his desk in the oval office, President Johnson was in a funk. It had been over a month since Kennedy had been assassinated in Dallas and Johnson had been sworn in as the 36th president of the United States of America. He hardly had time to absorb Kennedy's passing before being inundated with America's problems. He was the boss now. It was a job he had wanted but a couple of days of mourning and head-clearing would have been nice before being buried by the avalanche of decisions that only a president could make. There was a part of him that felt like he had stolen the office. He hadn't won an election to become president. It was handed to him without his consent… not that he would have turned it down.

Johnson already felt mired in Texan mud. He was an experienced politician and had big plans for America. He called it "The Great Society." With the goal of permanently eliminating poverty and racial injustice in America, The Great Society was made up of more than 1,000 pieces of legislation and was designed to forever alter the social and political landscape of America. It was similar in scope to Franklin D. Roosevelt's New Deal and Johnson wanted it to be his legacy. But it seemed that the only thing anyone wanted to talk about was the war in Vietnam. That damned war was fouling up his domestic agenda. There were health and education programs that Americans needed like the Job Corps, Medicaid, and Medicare. But even with a roaring economy, every spare dollar was being sent to South Vietnam to fight off the communist expansion. It was frustrating as hell for Johnson, and he let his advisors and cabinet know his feelings every chance he got.

Before entering politics, Johnson had been a teacher in a segregated school in Cotulla, Texas where all the children were Mexican American. He saw firsthand the effects of poverty and racism on children. He didn't like what he saw and swore to himself to change it. Those children were what caused him to enter politics.

A force to be reconned with, Johnson's favorite Bible verse was Isaiah 1:18. "Come now, and let us reason together..." While in Congress Johnson was known for the Johnson Treatment in which he imposed his large size and stature to get his way over his smaller fellow congressmen. While the treatment usually ended with a good laugh, it was surprisingly effective. The battle for The Great Society was a battle worth fighting and Johnson was up to the task… if he could only figure out how to end the war and redirect the money back into America's coffers.

Even without Vietnam, there were other initiatives that needed funding like the Space program. Johnson saw the benefits of NASA and pushed for further funding for the Apollo program. And there was the rest of the Cold War that needed attention… and money. The communists weren't going to stop and neither could the Americans. It seemed like in every direction he turned, something needed to be funded. Raising taxes was no way to get reelected in November 1964, but neither was sitting on his hands. He had to move and move quickly.

Johnson did not want a coup in South Vietnam, but he got one right before taking over the reins of the presidency. South Vietnam's President Diem had been a two-edged sword having firm control of his military, until he didn't, and constantly upsetting the people of South Vietnam. Diem did not have popular support and that made things difficult for his major ally – America. When Diem and his brother Nhu were killed during the coup, that obstacle went away making Johnson's life easier… sort of.

The new South Vietnamese president General Duong Van Minh would last a little less than three months before he was overthrown by General Nguyen Khanh. Khanh would last less than a month before General Minh overthrew him and came back into power as president. It was like musical chairs for generals which was a lousy way to fight a war and an even worse way to run a country. Fortunately for Johnson, both Minh and Khanh were pro-American and gave the American military advisors more power to control the South Vietnamese troops in the field. It helped, but not a lot. The Viet Cong were still kicking the ass of ARVN forces and taking territory during the chaos caused by the South Vietnamese generals. With their generals squabbling over political power, none of the soldiers in the South seemed to know who they were fighting for, only against, and that wasn't enough to inspire them to risk their lives any more than was necessary which was much. Some soldiers even refused to leave their barracks when ordered. Everything the American advisors had worked so hard to build was falling apart before their eyes and there wasn't anything they could do about it.

During his term as vice-president, Johnson had watched President Kenney waffle back and forth on important decisions concerning Vietnam. Johnson saw the back-and-forth as counterproductive and sending the wrong signal to the North Vietnamese and Viet Cong. He knew that the communists would never give up the territory they had taken without a fight. He wanted to get on with it and do what was needed to win the war. That was the fastest way to get back to advancing his domestic policies – to win the war in Vietnam. Pulling out wasn't a realistic option, not if he wanted to remain president. The Republicans would barbeque him for being soft on communism. Americans believed in democracy and capitalism. The idea of letting the communists take over Vietnam was not something the average American could stomach. At the beginning of Johnson's presidency, the vast majority of Americans supported the war in Vietnam. So, winning became the only real option. It just took commitment and that was something Johnson knew how to do.

Switching horses in mid-stream was never a good idea. Kennedy had been a popular president and Johnson wanted to keep riding that wave. Johnson had convinced most of Kennedy's cabinet and advisors to stay with him, at least until he was able to stabilize his administration and get reelected. During his new term as president, he could find suitable replacements for those that wanted to move on. Except for Ted Sorensen and Arthur Schlesinger Jr. who left shortly after Kennedy's death, nobody wanted to rock the boat and destroy the good work they had done under Kennedy. The most surprising holdover was Attorney General Robert Kennedy. More than any other cabinet member, the younger Kennedy had a particularly bad rapport with Johnson. And yet, Johnson asked him to stay. Johnson knew that continuity was the key to winning reelection. Kennedy left Johnson's administration after ten months when he decided to run for the U.S. senate.

When Johnson took office, there were 16,700 military personnel in South Vietnam, most of which were advisors and aircrews. He did not want to increase America's commitment on the ground, not yet. He sought other means of ending the war in victory. His biggest hope was that the newly formed South Vietnamese government would get its act together and go after the Viet Cong. Johnson was sorely disappointed.

The new South Vietnamese government was made up of the generals that had planned and participated in the coup that overthrew Diem and his family. It made sense that the generals would advance the war effort. General Minh who had led the coup to overthrow Diem, was elected Chairman of the Military Revolutionary Council (MRC), but each of the twelve generals in the council had veto power over any legislation or government programs. It was an impossible way to govern. In addition, Minh was criticized for being lethargic in his prosecution of the war. He seemed more interested in wining and dining with his military colleagues than leading the country. During his tenure, many of South Vietnam's domestic problems grew in intensity and the Viet Cong made gains taking over more territory.

The first coup occurred only three months into the new South Vietnamese administration when General Nguyen Khanh overthrew General Duong Van Minh. With the exception of Minh's bodyguard, Major Nguyen Van Nhung who was summarily executed, the coup was bloodless.

General Harkin, the commander of MACV, liked Khanh and thought he was a man of action. But the South Vietnamese generals distrusted Khanh and recognized his fondness for intrigue.

Khanh lasted a little more than a month before he was overthrown by his predecessor General Minh and the generals that supported him.

Minh lasted seven months before he was again

ousted by General Khanh.

And so, it went on for years, one government forming, then falling. In the three years that followed Diem's death, the South Vietnamese government would be reorganized twelve times, three of which were military coups.

Johnson was beyond frustrated. He had warned Kennedy that removing Diem, a strong but corrupt leader, would only create a power vacuum. But what was done, was done. Johnson would have to deal with it. The US military's solution was to prosecute the war as they saw fit. There was little the Saigon government could do if they wanted US aid which they desperately needed to continue funding the government and the military. The problem was that without their preoccupied generals to lead them, the ARVN stayed in their barracks and the Viet Cong ran amok. With no troops in the country, the US military was forced to depend on their Air Force and Navy assets.

At first, Johnson agreed with the Pentagon's plan of cutting off the Viet Cong supply lines to strangle the Viet Cong. He did not want to commit American troops. But without a declaration of war against the North, the US Air Force and Navy could not attack cargo ships in North Vietnamese waters. The only alternative was to bomb supply lines in Laos which proved ineffective. Even with the power of the free world behind him, Johnson felt he was hog-tied. Most of his cabinet and White House advisors were leaning toward expanding the war and some even wanted boots on the ground. Johnson was adamant that there would be no American combat troops committed to Vietnam until after his reelection, and even then, only if all other means failed.

Without a clear solution, the war would continue indefinitely, and his Great Society legislation would languish. Poverty-stricken Americans would continue to suffer, and his reelection would be thwarted. Johnson had to find another way to move forward.

NEUTRALIZATION

January 14, 1964 – White House - Washington DC, USA

In December, Senator Mike Mansfield had proposed the neutralization of South Vietnam in which America's ally would become neutral and reject all foreign influence in exchange for North Vietnam backing off of their aggressive expansion. After a period of time, elections would be held, and the Vietnamese people could decide their fate. Although he found little enthusiasm for his proposal in the United States, Mansfield found support from overseas government leaders.

While he wouldn't admit it publicly, the concept of neutralization was somewhat appealing to Johnson. It was a way out of the quagmire and could seem like the United States was being magnanimous, especially if the South Vietnamese generals came onboard. But the Pentagon recognized that it was just a more palatable form of surrender and wanted nothing to do with it.

Theodore Sorensen had been one of former President John F. Kennedy's most trusted aides. He left the White House shortly after Kennedy's assassination. Even though Johnson had asked him to stay on, it was too much emotionally for Sorenson to handle and be effective as an advisor. After hearing the reports that French President Charles de Gaulle had proposed the neutralization of South Vietnam, Sorensen sent a letter to President Johnson. Sorenson wrote that neutralization would most likely result in a communist takeover of South Vietnam. In addition, it would weaken the U.S. position in Asia, and cause political problems for the Democratic Party. As Johnson's principal advisers, Dean Rusk, Robert McNamara, McGeorge Bundy, and Walter Rostow echoed Sorensen's views.

After giving it more thought, Johnson concluded that neutralization was not a path he wanted to go down. There was too much risk that things would only become worse if it failed. Another dead-end in his quest to end the war.

January 20, 1964 - Hanoi, North Vietnam

After the death of Diem and the chaos brought about by the new government in Saigon, the leaders of the Communist Party of Vietnam met in Hanoi. Diem and his family were gone and with them the focus of the hatred from the people of South Vietnam. The communist leaders had hoped that the government of South Vietnam would have fallen on its own from all the infighting between its new political leaders. It hadn't. At least not yet. They believed that as long as the Americans continued to support South Vietnam, the government would meander along keeping the people beholden to their capitalist ideals and a false economy built on American aid. And why shouldn't they? The people of South Vietnam were doing far better financially than the North Vietnamese. By living off American aid which was plentiful and not worrying about the future, they had lulled themselves into complacency. For the North to win the war and reunite the country, South Vietnam needed a final push and that was the purpose of their meeting.

The moderate followers of Ho Chi Minh and General Giap believed that patience was required and that the South would fall eventually because it was corrupt and only benefitted the richest segment of the population. They wanted to keep up the pressure the Viet Cong forces were applying against the ARVN with their American advisors. The Americans would eventually tire of supporting the hopeless South Vietnamese government and abandon their efforts to save a nation that did not deserve to be saved. The Americans would go home. North and South could co-exist until the South was ready to fall into the communist fold. More bloodshed was not needed. Seeking to reduce tensions with the western nations, this was the path that the Soviets hoped North Vietnam would follow.

With China on their side, the more radical followers of Le Duan and Le Duc Tho were tired of waiting and wanted to advance the Maoist Global Revolution and liberate the South Vietnamese. They believed there would never be a better opportunity now that Diem and his family were gone. The South Vietnamese government was clearly in disarray and the Viet Cong had already made significant gains in territory. If the North fully committed to the revolution, the South would fall from the additional pressure and the country would be reunited under a communist-controlled government. Yes, there would be more bloodshed, but that was better than letting the people of the South languish under an incompetent government backed by an imperialist nation. The Band-Aid needed to be ripped off, so the wound could finally heal properly. It was time to expand the war and fully commit to helping the South win its freedom.

After days of impassioned speeches and arguments between members, a vote was taken on Resolution 9 which secretly declared all-out war on the South and would hopefully thwart the Americans from inserting US troops to protect South Vietnam from falling. The North would strike before the US could act. The radicals won the vote and the resolution was passed. The North would finally go to war with the South and finish what they had started.

Tan Son Nhut Airbase – Saigon, South Vietnam

A well-worn C-47 that had previously been used as a mail transport aircraft sat in the middle of a hangar. Using a case of Johnnie Walker scotch whisky as a "present," Coyle had convinced a South Vietnamese lieutenant to temporarily loan him the C-47 for an undisclosed CIA mission. Granier had used a similar tactic to secure an M2 machine gun and several boxes of ammunition from an armory supply sergeant.

They had already removed the back cargo door from the aircraft and tied down the machine guns tripod just inside the doorway. The machine gun had been placed on the tripod and locked down in a level position. Coyle and Granier sat on the aircraft's deck assembling the disintegrating ammunition belts with the .50 Cal bullets from the ammo cases. "I don't understand why we need a Ma Deuce. An M1 would do just as well for a test," said Coyle.

"The M2 tracer rounds will be easier to see," said Granier.

"Yeah, but the bullets are so damned heavy."

"Just be glad you'll be on the shooting end."

"Speaking of which, what are we gonna use as a target?"

"I was thinking partially filled gasoline drums. That way we'll know when we hit something without having to land."

"Good idea. There's an abandoned airfield about twelve miles south of Ben Cat. I figure we can use it as our test range. The South Vietnamese government pays the local villagers to keep squatters off the land, so there's nobody around that could get hurt during our test."

"That's good. But if a water buffalo or any other critter wanders onto the runway, they're an open target."

"Sure. Knock yourself out."

"I'm serious. You can bet the Viet Cong ain't gonna stand still when fired at. A moving practice target would be much more realistic."

"We should be so lucky. Besides, once that Ma Deuce opens fire, I would think that anything mulling around in the bushes is gonna hightail it outta there."

"You're probably right."

"Maybe we should buy a couple of Banh mi before we go just in case we get hungry."

"This is a weapon field test, not a picnic."

"Okay. Let me rephrase that… I am going to buy a Banh mi before we go just in case, I get hungry."

"Better get me one too… just in case…with a couple of bottles of orange Nehi."

"Anything else, Your Majesty?"

"I wouldn't shoot you if you bought a block of ice in banana leaves. I like my Nehi cold."

"I'll fetch lunch while you finish up."

"Deal."

Coyle moved off while Granier finished loading the ammo belts.

Ben Cat Airfield – South Vietnam

Sitting in the cockpit flying the aircraft without a co-pilot, Coyle put the C-47 into a pylon turn above the abandoned airfield 2,000 feet below. He spoke into his headset, "Alright. We're in a turn. I'll hold her steady."

Granier sat in the cargo area at the back of the machine gun just inside the back doorway. He chambered the first round and twisted the pintle lock release cam allowing the machine gun to move freely on the tripod. "Copy that," he said.

He sighted one of three fifty-five-gallon drums off to one side of the runway below. As a marine, Granier had been trained to shoot targets at 500 meters on a range. Over the years as a sniper, he had improved his distance to 1000 meters under ideal conditions. Shooting a machine gun from the back of a plane was far from being ideal conditions. The C-47 was not the smoothest flying aircraft. It bucked with the changes in wind velocity and direction. He was also using the M2's iron sight rather than a rifle scope.

On top of that, Granier could barely see the drums below. He glanced at the closed cockpit door, then reached into his shirt pocket and pulled out an eyeglass case. Few things embarrassed Granier, but his eyeglasses were one of them. He only used them when firing at extreme distances. He slipped them on and took another look at the target below. He could see the drums clearly. He aimed at the first drum and slowly pushed the trigger lever. The weapon fired. It was loud as hell inside the aircraft's hold. Even with the tripod, the gun bucked wildly. Granier immediately regretted not using the smaller M1 machine gun for the test.

On the airfield below, the bullet impacts kicked up dirt clods around the three drums. On the third burst of gunfire, a tracer round found its target, and the drum exploded sending a ball of flame into the air.

Inside the aircraft, Granier grinned. "About time," said Coyle over the intercom.

"Hey, if you think you can do better…" said Granier annoyed.

"Actually, I was thinking I might be able to. Can you lock down the machine gun?"

"Sure. Why?"

"I think I can aim using the plane."

"Bullshit."

"No, really. It's just like firing a fixed weapon from a fighter… but sideways. You'll still have to push the trigger."

"Well, it's worth a try. What angle do you want it locked down?"

"I don't. Let's try it level. We can always adjust it."

Granier leveled the machine gun and locked down the pintle lock release cam. "Okay. It's ready. Let me know when you want me to fire," said Granier.

"I'll need a spotting round first," said Coyle.

Granier flipped up the single-shot restrictor-plate below the machine gun's trigger.

Coyle placed the aircraft in a pylon turn tipping the plane at an angle so the machine gun would be aligned with the drums below. "Fire," said Coyle.

Granier pressed the trigger and fired one round.

Coyle couldn't see where it hit and said, "I didn't see it. Give me another round. Fire."

Granier fired another round. It was a tracer round.

Coyle followed the glowing round down to the ground and saw where it hit on the airfield. He was way off. He corrected the angle and course to where he thought it should be. He reached into his flight jacket and pulled out the pencil he used with his notepad. "One more," he said. "Fire."

The gun fired and he saw a puff of dirt ten feet to the West of one of the drums. He used the pencil to mark the placement of the round on his window. He used the pencil mark to align the plane with the drums below. "Give me a two-second burst," said Coyle.

Granier lowered the single-round restrictor and fired a two-second burst.

Coyle watched as the dirt around the drums kicked up and then one exploded. He realigned the plane to match the remaining drum and said, "Give me another burst."

Granier fired again.

The third drum blew up.

Coyle yipped. "Not bad shooting, Mr. Earp," said Granier.

"You're damned right," said Coyle.

Granier appeared in the cockpit doorway with two cold Nehis in his hands. He popped the tops off using the doorway frame as a bottle opener, then handed one to Coyle and they clinked the bottlenecks before swallowing the orange drink. "Any idea what you're gonna call this gadget?" said Granier.

"Not yet. But I'm sure we'll think of something," said Coyle with a grin.

The C-47 banked hard as they headed back to Saigon.

January 22, 1964 - White House – Washington D.C., USA

Sitting in his White House office, U.S. Secretary of Defense Robert McNamara poured over the classified memorandum that he had received from the U.S. Joint Chiefs of Staff. Like the computers he often used, McNamara loved data. The more the better. Knowing this, the Joint Chiefs had purposely packed their proposals and reports to the secretary with charts, graphs, and well-documented data points. Strangely, McNamara appreciated their obvious manipulation. They were speaking his language. What annoyed McNamara was that the generals had chosen to put their grievances in writing and entered them into the official record. He thought it cowardly. The generals didn't want to be left holding the bag if things didn't go well and South Vietnam was lost. McNamara understood that the Pentagon was an organization that had its own way of presenting its findings and suggestions. Memorandums and reports were the languages of the Pentagon. At least the charts and graphs were nice.

McNamara wasn't surprised by their conclusions. In fact, he agreed with many of them. After presenting a boatload of statistics and historical observations, the Joint Chiefs urged the administration to expand U.S. involvement in the war. They wanted heavy bombing of North Vietnam and the deployment of American troops in South Vietnam. They also suggested that the only real way of winning the war was to eventually invade the North and seize Hanoi.

While McNamara thought bombing the North into submission was questionable, he did like the idea because it was more disavowable than actual American boots on the ground. Who was to say the nationality of the pilots flying the bombers? They could be South Vietnamese pilots. After the Bay of Pigs fiasco, Kennedy was focused on deniability. Johnson was more concerned about getting re-elected by the American public than appeasing the international community. In both cases, being able to disavow questionable actions was key to their political strategies.

As far as the eventual invasion of North Vietnam, McNamara saw it as the generals' pipedream, and he doubted it would ever happen. There was too much risk of China entering the war to save North Vietnam which was on its border. It would be like Korea all over again with Chinese troops streaming across the border and the Americans fighting back the hordes. Nobody wanted that. If the bombing of the North came to fruition, McNamara believed that it may not win the war, but the South Vietnamese might use the bombing as a bargaining chip to negotiate a peace treaty with the North and end the war. It was better than doing nothing.

Getting President Johnson to agree on any strategy in Vietnam was another matter. Johnson was so focused on his Great Society that McNamara thought it doubtful that he would agree to expand the war. McNamara wondered if there was some way he could approach it that would allow Johnson to accept part of the Joint Chiefs' proposal. After consideration, McNamara's solution was to present the proposal as is but not before laying a little groundwork. McNamara did not consider himself Machiavellian by nature. He preferred to convince people with facts and logic, not manipulation. However, he was not opposed to tactics if they increased the odds of success. McNamara loved to win and to do so in Vietnam, he needed to control the administration's policies and military strategies.

Johnson knew very well that McNamara was the leader of Kennedy's whiz kids. Although he saw McNamara as a bit stiff and humorless, he wanted a highly intelligent secretary of defense that was capable of considering all the options, especially during a war. It's why Johnson convinced McNamara to stay after Kennedy's death.

Johnson did not want to keep the status quo when it came to Vietnam. He wanted more aggressive military action against the communists, but he also didn't want American boots on the ground. He knew that the majority of Americans supported the war. He also knew that nothing would dishearten the American public more than seeing its young men coming home in coffins. Johnson needed the people to get re-elected. He didn't need the Joint Chiefs going around saying he was weak on communism. He needed to keep the Pentagon somewhat happy and the people very happy. He sought other solutions to win the war.

McNamara started his meeting with Johnson by complaining that the ARVN generals in Saigon were less than worthless. As he had feared, by eliminating Diem South Vietnam had turned disorderly and mired down. With veto power for each of the twelve generals, the Military Revolutionary Council had brought legislation in South Vietnam to a standstill. They couldn't make a decision without debating it ad nauseam and even then, almost nothing passed into law. When they weren't arguing, the generals would use the new expense accounts they had given themselves at fancy restaurants and nightclubs. They had found that governing had its perks.

In the meantime, the Viet Cong were making progress and capturing territory. There was no telling what the leadership in the North was thinking. Johnson agreed with all of it. It was with that foundation that McNamara presented the Joint Chief's memorandum.

Johnson listened intently and asked a lot of questions as McNamara presented the findings. He let Johnson refuse the deployment of US troops into South Vietnam. And he let Johnson choose the stepped-up bombing of the North as the only acceptable course of action. He agreed with the president and said he would inform the generals of the president's decision.

Before adjourning the meeting, Johnson asked McNamara to make several visits to Vietnam before the election. He wanted McNamara to placate the critics of his administration including Ambassador Lodge. McNamara didn't like getting involved in politics because they didn't follow any logical or consistent pattern as far as he could tell. Nevertheless, he recognized Johnson's needs and agreed to the trips.

As soon as McNamara had left the oval office, Johnson asked to see John McCone, the director of the CIA. McCone's office was at the newly built CIA headquarters in Langley, Virginia. It was late in the day and McCone suggested they meet first thing in the morning. Johnson didn't want to wait and said he would meet McCone at his office. It was very unusual for the president to leave the White House to meet with a cabinet member, especially one with an office outside of D.C.

After Kennedy's assassination, the secret service was not wild about the idea of the president performing an unscheduled visit anywhere. It meant traveling without a protection plan or preparation. Technically, the Director of the Secret Service had the authority to overrule the president if it was in the interest of national security. But how could the director convince his agents to tackle the most powerful man in the world if he hailed a cab or used a civilian car? It was usually much easier to make a compromise with the president. In this case, it wasn't such a big deal. After all, the president had use of Marine One, a Sikorsky SH-3 Sea King helicopter. The president's helicopter was overkill for the nine-mile trip to CIA headquarters, but it was safer than traveling on an uninspected road or highway.

The use of helicopters started with President Eisenhower, who wanted a quick way to reach his summer house in Pennsylvania on the weekends. Those were the days when presidents had a life outside the White House, especially during holidays and weekends. The original helicopters used by the presidents were far from luxurious. They didn't even have air conditioning. But they were usually the fastest way to get from Point A to Point B if Air Force One could not be used. To save even more time, the president's helicopter started using the White House

South lawn as a landing pad. The 9-ton helicopter's wheel dents in the perfectly groomed grass drove the White House Garden Superintendent nuts.

When Johnson arrived with his entourage of secret service agents, the CIA guards were unsure what they should do. All outsiders were required to have a badge and an escort when inside the building. But this was the president and technically their boss. Fortunately, Director McCone showed up and greeted the president. He offered to give the president a tour of the new facility, but Johnson wanted to get straight to business. They went to McCone's office.

McCone had coffee served and said, "How may I be of service, Mr. President?"

"The Domino Theory. What do you know about it?" said Johnson.

"Everything, I think. What specifically did you want to know about?"

"If South Vietnam fell to the communists, what would happen?"

"It's tough to know for sure, but I think there is little doubt the communists would be encouraged to continue their revolution in the surrounding countries. Laos and Cambodia would both fall, then Burma because it shares a long border with China. Thailand would probably follow although I think the Thais would put up a good fight. Then it's a toss-up between The Philippines and Malaysia, maybe even Indonesia. Singapore would fall shortly after Malaysia, maybe even at the same time."

"Hold your horses, John. Are you telling me that all of those nations will fall if South Vietnam falls?"

"Well, that's the theory. But, of course, it depends

on what we do to protect those countries. Although, if South Vietnam falls, I doubt the leaders of other Southeast Asian countries will put much faith in America. They may try to make a deal with the communists just to keep some of their autonomy."

"Holy shit. All that cuz we chose the wrong ally?"

"I am afraid so. What makes you feel like we chose the wrong ally, Mr. President?"

"Don't be coy, John. You know what's going on."

"I do, but I see Diem's departure as a positive move in the right direction."

"It's a barn-sized mess if I have ever seen one. Generals were meant to run wars, not countries."

"I'm sure it'll work itself out in time."

"We ain't got time. The Viet Cong are kicking our asses all over that country."

"Are you thinking of pulling out?"

"That's not really an option. Not if I want to get re-elected. I got plans that will really make a difference to Americans. I can't get 'em done if I'm on the sidelines."

"I see. So, we win."

"Yep. The Big Win. Now we just gotta figure out how."

Johnson approved the Joint Chiefs' plan to expand bombing in the North. The generals felt it fell short of what was needed, but at least it was a start, and more than Kennedy was willing to do. They would need to prepare a list of targets and Johnson would have the final say. He didn't want things to get out of hand and he sure didn't want the images of dead North Vietnamese women and children on the front pages of newspapers. Johnson would confine the bombings to clear military targets away from civilian population centers. He made his restrictions clear to the Joint Chiefs and would ride roughshod on them if required. There was no need. They had their marching orders and would carry them out to the letter.

The other question was timing. Johnson did not want to start the bombing campaign until after his re-election. He did want to rile up the American public unnecessarily. His opponent in the election was Senator Barry Goldwater. Johnson saw Goldwater as a warmonger. He liked the contrast between them but didn't like to be accused of being soft on communism. Bombing North Vietnam would certainly silence those critics. But elections were tricky things as was bombing another country. If something went wrong and civilians were killed, there was no telling how the truth could be twisted by experienced politicians which Goldwater certainly was.

The American people were happy. Let 'em be was Johnson's thinking. Once he had the mandate of the American people, he could do what he wanted in Vietnam, and they would support him. Expanding the war could wait until he was re-elected. McNamara and the Joint Chiefs were not so sure. Things were getting worse by the day and the election was still ten months off. South Vietnam may not last that long.

January 30, 1964 – Saigon, South Vietnam

General Nguyen Khanh was angry. Long regarded by his fellow officers as ambitious and unscrupulous, Khanh was a French-trained officer that had fought for the French in the First Indochina War. He knew how to fight and few were reckless enough to question his bravery. He had supported Ngo Dinh Diem during his rise to power and even saved Diem's life during the 1960 coup. In the 1963 coup, Khanh changed sides and helped overthrow the president which led to Diem and his brother's deaths. He could not be trusted and once the generals came to power, they wanted little to do with him.

In a move to deny Khanh a seat on the twelve-man Military Revolutionary Council that controlled the new government, General Minh had reassigned Khanh to be the commander of I Corps near Hue and Da Nang. Khanh recognized Minh's intrigue but took the job anyway. Refusing Minh's orders would mean that Khanh was without an army and would be permanently relegated to the political and military sideline. Instead, he bided his time and garnered the loyalty of the officers in his new command. Khanh may have been untrustworthy, but he wasn't stupid.

US Commander of MACV, General Paul Harkins liked Khanh more than most of the generals on the council. He was a warrior. While the generals in Saigon were enjoying the expense accounts and playing politics, Khanh was fighting the Viet Cong. That's what the Pentagon and President Johnson wanted. Like Khanh, Harkins was not popular with the generals in Saigon. While publicly remaining neutral, Harkins had secretly sided with Diem during the 1963 coup and the generals knew it. The generals had purposely kept Harkins out of the loop on what they were planning, and Harkins resented it.

Harkins saw Khanh as an ally against the generals and their council. Harkin's approval gave Khanh confidence. Whomever the Americans backed would eventually end up in control of South Vietnam. Everyone recognized the need for American financial and military aid. Nobody wanted to kill the golden goose. Harkins misread Khanh's attitude toward being assigned to I Corps and thought the general was happy with his new post. Harkins thought Khanh was content to focus on military matters rather than politics and was unaware of Khanh's anger at being sidelined.

By the first of the year, the South Vietnamese government was plagued with infighting among the generals and administrators that controlled it. The military council was paralyzed because all of the generals had equal power which included the power to veto any matter before the council. A civilian government and cabinet were appointed by the military council to ease its workload and Nguyen Ngoc Tho became Prime Minister. It didn't work. Any general that didn't like what the civilian government was doing would simply veto their proposals and that was the end of it. The debate between the military and the civilian administration was endless. Anything that had even a hope of passing needed to be explained and debated with each general privately to garner their support before presenting it to the council as a whole. The generals did not see the administrators as their equals and therefore gave them little consideration when it came to their proposals. The generals vetoed almost everything brought before them. It was a useless and ineffective government bureaucracy.

General Minh, the head of the military council, was criticized for being lethargic and uninterested in running the country. Attacks from the Viet Cong were on the rise since the 1963 coup. Since the generals in the council wanted to keep their commands close by, most of the troops in the capital had not been redeployed after the coup to the countryside where the

Viet Cong were running amuck. When word came of a possible Viet Cong offensive against the capital, only then did Minh order his fellow generals to redeploy their troops.

One of the reasons Minh had misread Khanh's intentions was that US Ambassador Lodge had assured Minh that he had the complete support of the United States as the leader of South Vietnam. Who would possibly go against him when America was behind him? It gave him overconfidence that he was in complete control of the government and military. He was wrong.

During the previous month, Khanh had been approached by General Do Mau. The head of military security under the recently deposed President Diem, Mau was the puppet master when it came to generals. He was well-respected and feared by men that seemed far more powerful than he. Most generals had armies at their disposal, Mau had secrets…powerful secrets that he could use like an assassin's knife against those that opposed him. He was far more skilled at intrigue than most but gave the impression he was an honorable man.

Mau could see that the current government was failing and needed to be replaced. In addition to Khanh, Mau also contacted General Khiem who had formally been a fellow cadet of Khanh's at the Military Academy and had two divisions under his command. Mau, Khanh, and Khiem recruited other officers that felt threatened by Minh and the military council because of their past association with former President Diem and his family. Most of the officers behind the potential coup preferred Khiem as their new leader, but Khiem had changed his religion to Catholic to ingratiate Diem and feared the reaction of the Buddhists if he ever led the government. Instead, Khanh was chosen as the new leader if the coup was successful. Khanh grew a small goatee that he promised he would keep unshaven until the coup was successful.

Khanh had previously informed Lucien Conein of his plans and asked the CIA officer's opinion. Having helped plan the 1963 coup of Diem and his family, Conein made a few suggestions. When asked if the Americans would support him, Conein replied that it might be best to stage the coup and then ask permission of the Americans after the fact. He doubted they would object, especially if the coup was relatively bloodless and the troops used were put back into the field quickly. "We Americans are more about the war than who is running the government," said Conein.

Dutiful to his country, Conein wrote a report outlining the conversation with Khanh and that he believed Khanh would eventually attempt to seize power. Conein submitted the report to senior US officials in Washington. As with much of Conein's advice, they ignored it and filed it away.

Conein believed himself as the master of chaos and that mayhem could be a powerful weapon if wielded in the right hands. When something underhanded needed to be done, Conein was often the go-to guy and many sought his advice. He knew he would never get credit for most of the successful missions he had planned and executed. He was okay with that as long as they served his country… and him. Conein knew that the war in Vietnam would not last forever and he planned to retire rich. In a country like Vietnam, there was plenty of opportunity for a man with his connections and skill set. It was just a matter of picking and choosing the most beneficial business models and if necessary… eliminating the competition. Conein had a moral code. It was just more flexible than most depending on what the situation and opportunity required.

Toward the end of January, the coup plotters began to spread rumors that French President Charles de Gaulle's agents in Saigon were going to secretly install a pro-communist government that could implement plans for the neutralization of Vietnam and the removal of the Americans. Since General Minh was in support of neutralization, the rumors of a potential French takeover would give the coup plotters a reason to act against him.

Since the end of the First Indochina War, nobody liked the French, and many readily accepted the theory of a secret French conspiracy. When the French Foreign Office announced plans to establish diplomatic relations with the Chinese on January 28th, Khanh used the occasion to play up the American anti-neutralist sentiment. Even the American diplomats became suspect of French intentions in Vietnam. Unknowingly, De Gaulle made matters worse when he attempted to cultivate relations with communist China by publicly calling on the US troops to leave Vietnam.

US military advisor Colonel Jasper Wilson was used as a covert liaison between Khanh and the US Embassy. The day before the coup was planned, Wilson carried a message from Khanh to Ambassador Lodge which stated that Khanh had documents that proved that French agents and several South Vietnamese leaders were about to stage a coup and neutralize South Vietnam. Khanh felt that the concept of neutralization might strike a responsive chord among some of the junior South Vietnamese officers and therefore any coup by pro-neutralization forces must be crushed before it can be executed. At 3 PM Wilson called Khanh and used a predetermined codeword to confirm that MACV and the embassy did not object.

At 2 AM the next morning, Khanh, wearing his paratrooper uniform, arrived at Tan Son Nhut Air Base outside of Saigon where he was supposed to join General Khiem's forces to march on the capital. To Khanh's surprise, the base was empty except for a few guards. Khanh telephoned Khiem and found that he had failed to set his alarm clock and overslept.

Despite the debacle, by daybreak, Khanh and his forces had surrounded the houses of all the generals in the military council, including Minh's, and taken over key positions throughout the city. In less than four hours, Khanh had successfully overthrown the South Vietnamese government without a shot being fired.

Khanh used the coup to enact retribution against many of the generals on the council and leaders in the government that he considered enemies. To placate the remaining generals, Khanh made General Minh president while he retained the higher position of prime minister for himself.

As much as they disliked instability created by any coup, the Americans accepted Khanh and his new government. They hoped Khanh would be more active in fighting the Viet Cong than Minh had been. Conein had been right – the Americans were more focused on the war than the government. They didn't care who was in power as long as they prosecuted the war and defeated the communists.

TURNING UP THE HEAT

February 4, 1064 – Hau May, South Vietnam

Thirty-five miles to the west of Saigon, Hau May was not much of a city. Its only claim to fame was that it was an ARVN battalion headquarters. Security was tight around the perimeter of the headquarters. Like most South Vietnamese battalions, its headquarters had its own security force and did not rely on the companies within the battalion for manpower.

The headquarters consisted of operations, intelligence, communications, and field command offices within the command building structure which was usually an overly large tent or a quickly prepared wooden or metal structure surrounded and topped by sandbags. While it was not designed to withstand a heavy artillery direct hit, it was capable of enduring mortar rounds. The battalion commander's quarters, power generators, and an officers' latrine were within the barbed wire that surrounded the entire compound. There was only one way in and one way out which was guarded by a sentry. Since it was usually in the middle of the battalion, there was little need for extra security. The battalion protected its headquarters.

Attacks on smaller ARVN facilities and outposts by

Viet Cong were common, especially in the Mekong Delta and Central Highlands. But few Viet Cong commanders had the stones to attack an actual battalion. As usual, the battalion would go out on assignment during the day and retire to their protective compound during the night. Everyone knew that the Viet Cong owned the night. Nobody wanted to tangle with them after the sun went down. The opposite was also true — the Viet Cong did not attack the ARVN during daylight unless it was forced upon them. That day, however, was different.

The Viet Cong sappers had moved up into position under the cover of darkness and placed their satchel charges on the barbed wire that surrounded the battalion compound. Then they retreated and waited…

As usual, the companies within the battalion left for missions or training leaving the compound all but empty except for the guard units assigned to protect it while the troops were gone. It was late in the morning when the Viet Cong chose to attack.

The assault began with a VC mortar barrage. Well-placed mortar rounds took out the ARVN machine-gun emplacements killing the gunners and their assistants.

The VC sappers used long lengths of twine caked with a mud camouflage to pull the safety rings on the satchel charge detonators. The multiple explosions tore gaps in the outer perimeter. A VC company charged through the torn wire and into the compound. Without the covering fire from the battalion's machine guns, the remaining soldiers were quickly overwhelmed. Many ARVN threw down their weapons and surrendered.

The officers in the command compound usually did

not get directly involved in any fighting. Their job was to control the battle and they couldn't do that and fight at the same time. But it occurred to the commander that most of his battalion was gone. He could see the VC mowing down the troops that remained. He ordered every abled body to take up arms and defend the headquarters. The problem was that the officers didn't have a lot of ammunition with them. They rarely needed it and they could always call the armorer to send some ammo if they required it. At the beginning of the assault, a VC sapper had thrown a satchel charge into the ammunition dump and the resulting explosion rocked the entire compound. The officers took cover wherever they could and returned fire on the Viet Cong. They conserved ammunition when possible and made every shot count. The executive officer radioed the ARVN company commanders to return to base ASAP. It would take time and time was not something the command compound had.

The commander ordered an artillery strike within the outer perimeter but away from the command compound. There wasn't much room between the two as shells began raining down. It did give the Viet Cong pause. They could retreat or overwhelm the battalion command post. They chose the latter and the VC commander ordered an all-out push.

The VC charged the inner compound tossing grenades and using satchel charges to tear holes in the defenses.

The ARVN officers fought back rapidly firing their weapons and burning through their ammunition. The barrage sent many VC to their deaths and more to the ground. The fighting was fierce as ARVN artillery rounds continued to explode outside the command post while the VC mortar rounds exploded within the command post perimeter. The two sides were locked in a death grip with neither giving way.

It was a single American Skyraider returning from an air-to-ground support mission that tipped the balance. The pilot had heard the ARVN radio operator pleading for help in broken English. The warplane's rockets and bombs were already gone, but he still had a three-second burst left in two of his machine guns. He flew low as he approached the compound at top speed. He was going more for effect than substance. He fired his machine guns into the Viet Cong lines with little success. He gunned his engine as he flew over the heads of the Viet Cong. It was too much. The VC broke and ran. His armament spent, the pilot banked hard and flew over the fleeing VC once more to ensure they didn't reconsider their decision to retreat. They didn't.

When the rest of the battalion finally arrived, the battle was over. The Viet Cong had killed twelve ARVN soldiers, three of which were officers. Dozens more were wounded. The ARVN commander was grateful he and his men had survived. Two days later as his command was on its way to recovery, he turned in his papers resigning his commission. He had fought the Viet Cong for over eight years, and he had enough.

White House - Washington D.C., USA

General Taylor presented the president with target suggestions in North Vietnam for the upcoming bombing campaign. Although Johnson had no objections to the target suggestions, he said, "I don't want any bombing until after the election. There is no need to get our people all riled up before they enter the voting booth."

"No need?" said Taylor.

"I know what you're thinking, I honestly don't think it will make a difference in the long run if we wait a few extra months before the kickoff."

Taylor was visibly perturbed that Johnson's re-election took precedent over the war. It was however the reality of politics.

Saigon, South Vietnam

Wearing his newest uniform, Conein waited patiently in General Harkins's reception area within the US Embassy. He wondered why generals, who could have whatever they wished, still used officers as their receptionists. He made a mental note to himself that when he became a general, he would hire the most attractive female receptionists that money could buy. He didn't care if her appearance ruffled the feathers of his fellow generals. He figured he deserved her. The squawk-box on the receptionist's desk buzzed followed by some garbled words which he presumed were from Harkins. "You can go in now, Colonel," said the receptionist, an Army captain wearing a freshly pressed uniform. "Can I bring you some coffee?"

"Is the general having coffee?" said Conein.

"He lives off it."

"Then yeah, black," said Conein.

The captain opened the door to the Harkins's office and closed it once Conein was inside.

Conein saluted as was tradition. Harkins saluted back from his desk but did not rise. It was a bit of a slap in the face to Conein that the general could not show him the mutual respect he felt he deserved, but that was a general's prerogative. "Sit, Colonel," said Harkins also wearing a freshly pressed uniform. "You're becoming quite the legend."

"Really? How's that?" said Conein.

Harkins smiled, "I don't think you need me to repeat your resume."

"No, of course not, General. I just meant I don't consider anything I have done beyond my duty."

"Bullshit. There is nothing wrong with being proud of what you have accomplished. Just don't forget your place in the pecking order. Even the mighty can fall."

"I'll try to remember that, General."

The captain knocked and entered with two cups of coffee in china cups. Conein looked surprised as he was handed his cup. "This isn't the field, Colonel. We drink our coffee pinkies out in this office," said Harkins.

Conein smiled and lifted his pinky as he took his first sip. "I was actually thinking about how many sips you get out of a cup that size."

"Three. But refills are free."

"Good to know."

"You're probably curious as to why I asked to see you. So, I'll get right to it. Like most things discussed in this office, what we are about to discuss is highly confidential. I suppose that's why you were requested. You are known for keeping your mouth shut."

"Requested?"

"Yes… requested. You were not my first choice. It's not that I don't think you're capable. I just don't care for your attitude. At times, it's unprofessional."

"I see. So, whoever requested me has more power than you?"

"Yes. But that's all you need to know."

"That's all I wanted to know."

"I'm sure you are aware that there have been high-level discussions about expanding the war. Now that Diem is gone, which I personally think was a mistake, the Pentagon believes it is a good time to take the initiative. There have been several proposals and Secretary McNamara has chosen to bomb North Vietnam in hopes of bending the will of the communists."

"And you think that will work… bombing?"

"I think I have my orders and I will carry them out. The results of such a strategy remain to be seen. But that's not why you are here, Colonel. Secretary McNamara has President Johnson's approval to carry out the bombing of the North."

"But?"

"Yes… but the president wishes us to wait until an event occurs forcing us to take action against the North, preferably after his re-election."

"What kind of event?"

"That's up to the president's discretion. But it must be something that the international community sees as aggression by the North. That way, America will be forced to retaliate."

"That could take a while."

"It could. That's why you are here."

"You want me to pick a fight?"

"Something like that."

Conein chuckled, "Okay. I can do that."

"I'm sure you can. Everyone knows you are very capable of stirring the pot."

"Can I choose the target, or did you have an idea of what you want?"

"We were thinking something along the lines of Operation Vulcan."

Conein squirmed a bit at the name of the operation and said, "Not my best work. I lost a lot of men."

"Yes, you did and that is always regrettable. But you also succeeded at sinking half of North Vietnam's navy."

"It was three patrol boats. Hardly the Normandy invasion."

"Regardless, the mission was a success."

"Alright. How much time do I have?"

"Sooner is better than later."

"I'll get right on it."

"See that you do."

Conein rose and saluted. Harkins rose, saluted back, and said, "Good hunting, Colonel."

Conein left the office. He had imagined that he could coast after "landing the plane" on the coup of Diem and his family. Fate thought otherwise and handed him the biggest operation of his career. He was excited at the prospect of a legacy.

Back in his office, Conein surveyed his map of Vietnam. He knew from his participation in Operation Vulcan that American vessels were performing surveillance on the North Vietnamese communications. The Americans wanted to prove that the Soviets and Chinese were providing aid to North Vietnam and the Viet Cong. He thought it was a wasteful strategy. One only needed to look at a captured Viet Cong RPG to see that it was from the Soviet Union or China. The debate of who was supplying whom was stupid. Everyone was supplying everyone. However, just because the thinking behind it was stupid, didn't mean that American vessels couldn't be useful in his current strategy. They were performing their surveillance from international waters very close to North Vietnamese territory. In the heat of the moment, things could get confusing.

He looked closer at the North Vietnamese installations off the coast. The ones that caught his attention were radar installations on the islands of Hon Me and Hon Ngu. Radar facilities tended to be small affairs with few troops defending them. They were however very important to North Vietnamese that used them to track sea and air traffic. Before he got too far along in planning a mission, Conein wanted reconnaissance on the islands. Knowing the number of troops and their weapons would be essential to any successful mission. He would use Granier.

Conein hated Granier to the point where he had secretly tried to kill him several times, but that was before Conein had become the commander of the paramilitary operations. Although he hated to admit it, Granier was his most reliable team commander and scout. Plus, Granier was one hell of a shot. While he still hoped that Granier would lose a couple of toes or maybe a finger or two, he didn't want him dead. Maimed a bit was okay. It was an important and dangerous mission. Conein needed someone just as competent as himself. Conein knew that if he sent Granier to recon the islands, the information he brought back would be reliable. But if Granier died in the process, well… that would be a very nice shame.

February 9, 1964 – Saigon, South Vietnam

Located near Tan Son Nhut Airbase, Pershing Field

was a stadium used by American military and aid personnel. In addition to the baseball field with two dugouts, the complex had a pair of bleachers for friends and family to observe the games which were usually one service unit against another. It was all great fun and made for a nice afternoon if it didn't rain.

Security had been stepped up at the field when ARVN intelligence received word that the Viet Cong had sent terror specialists to Saigon with the mission of targeting Americans. An American serviceman had died earlier that week, and everyone was on edge and keeping an eye out for anything suspicious. But there was nothing to see out of the ordinary on the day of the game, except for the lack of Vietnamese children that usually mulled through the trash under the bleachers for half-eaten hotdogs and discarded boxes of popcorn.

During the previous night, two Viet Cong terrorists had planted two American-made aerial fragmentation bombs under the bleachers. The bombs' detonators were connected by buried wire to remote electric plungers fifty feet away behind an equipment shed.

The VC waited until halfway through the game when the bleachers were mostly full before setting off the bombs. Fortunately, the first bomb malfunctioned and failed to explode. The second exploded and sent shrapnel through wooden benches and into the spectators. Directly under the bomb, two American servicemen were launched into the air and their broken bodies landed on the field. Both were dead. Forty-one Americans were wounded, including four women and five children, many with shrapnel in their legs, bottoms, and genitals.

The terrorists escaped without detection. It was the

largest number of American casualties from a terrorist attack to date. One month later, another bomb at the Kinh Do movie theater in Saigon killed three Americans and wounded another thirty-two, most dependents of American servicemen. The bomb design was the same as the Pershing Field bombs – an aerial fragmentation bomb planted behind the movie screen and detonated remotely.

During Diem's tenure as president of South Vietnam, terrorist attacks against Americans in Saigon were almost unheard of. Now, major attacks on foreigners were occurring on a monthly basis.

February 15, 1964 – Laotian-North Vietnam Border

The border between North Vietnam and Laos was mostly a long mountain range covered with jungle. Getting lost in the bad bush was almost a guaranteed death sentence. A lush primordial landscape, it was dangerously beautiful.

A large shadow danced across the top of the green canopy of leaves as an American C-123 Provider flew over the dense mountain jungle. The aircrew had spent the night in Long Cheng, CIA headquarters in Laos, after unloading the cargo and laying out a fuel bladder in the empty cargo hold. The fuel bladder would allow them to fly to their next cargo pick-up in Saigon without refueling. With no stopovers, it was a twenty-seven-hour flight. The crew chief was already stretched out on the sleeping bag he always carried on board for just such occasions. He was reading Catch-22 by Joseph Heller and wondering how similar he was to the M&M character that traded black market merchandise to build his empire.

In the cockpit, the co-pilot had the controls while the pilot sipped the coffee from his thermos cup. "Hey, Cap. What is that?" said the co-pilot pointing to an approaching aircraft.

"Looks like a T-28. Could be an escort," said the pilot.

"So, why didn't we get a heads up?"

"It's Laos. You count yourself lucky if you can get a current weather report."

"He's heading straight at us."

"Don't get your panties in a bunch. I'll call him."

The pilot used the radio to call the approaching pilot but got no response. "That's weird," said the pilot.

The T-28 zoomed past the cargo aircraft with less than fifty feet of clearance. "What the hell?" said the co-pilot.

The pilot looked pale and said, "Did you get a look at the insignia?"

"No. Was it Laotian?"

"No. It was North Vietnamese."

"What are you talking about? The North Vietnamese don't have any fighter aircraft."

"Tell them that."

The previous year, Chert Saibory, a Thai pilot flying for the Royal Laotian Air Force had defected to North Vietnam in his North American Trojan T-28. When he landed at the North Vietnamese airfield at Dien Bien Phu, the local authorities didn't know what to do with him, so they threw him in jail and confiscated his plane. When word reached Hanoi of the confiscated aircraft, the Vietnam People's Air Force (VPAF) commander commandeered the warplane, slapped on a new insignia, and North Vietnam finally had its first fighter aircraft. Nguyen Van Ba, considered North Vietnam's best pilot, was given the honor of piloting the T-28 and sat behind the controls as he flew past the American aircraft.

"Where is he?" said the co-pilot looking out his side window.

"I don't know. I don't see him. I'm taking control of the aircraft."

"You've got control."

Just as the co-pilot released the controls, a stream of tracer rounds zipped over the cockpit. "Jesus. He's firing at us," said the co-pilot.

The American pilot put the plane in a dive. There wasn't much room between the aircraft and the jungle. He was forced to pull up after only a moment, but it was enough to put the aircraft out of the T-28's kill zone.

The T-28 overshot the C-123 and banked around a mountain ridge.

The pilot of the C-123 had no idea where the Trojan would emerge for its next attack. It didn't take long to find out.

The T-28 rose over the mountain range forming a perfect T-bone with the side of the Provider in its sights. Ba opened fire. The Provider flew into the barrage of bullets as they stitched across the cockpit and into the cargo hold. The pilot was torn to shreds by the .50-Cal shells spattering the co-pilot with blood and bits of flesh. After passing through the pilot, the enemy shells thrashed the aircraft's controls sending sparks flying. The co-pilot was in shock, unable to move from fear.

In the cargo hold, the crew chief watched as the

enemy shells punctured the aircraft's aluminum walls and punctured the fuel bladder. Fuel poured out from the holes flooding the deck and surrounding his boots. A late tracer round set the fuel a blaze and engulfed the crew chief.

Strangely, the burning aircraft did not explode. Instead, it tilted over on its side and crashed into the mountain range.

Watching with pride, Ba did a flyover to confirm his kill. The flaming wreckage was strewn across the mountain top. The North Vietnamese Air Force had its first victory over the Americans.

Even more strange was the survival of the badly burned American co-pilot when he was rescued by a SOG team that just happened to be in the area and witnessed the one-sided dogfight and crash. After several weeks of treatment and recovery, he was transported to Thailand, then back to the United States. His war was over.

February 26, 1964 – Long Dinh, South Vietnam

Forty-eight miles south of Saigon, Long Dinh was a rural township of slight strategic importance. Because it was relatively close to Saigon, US surveillance helicopters routinely patrolled the area but encountered little to report. It just wasn't a place anyone cared about except those that lived there.

Early one morning, an American pilot and co-pilot spotted a large group of Viet Cong running for cover under a jungle canopy at the edge of a series of flooded rice paddies. They often spotted what they thought might be Viet Cong, but never in this number. They reported it immediately.

When South Vietnamese General Nguyen Khanh received the Americans' surveillance report, he ordered his commanders to assemble their troops and prepare for an assault. Using the brigade's M113 armored personal carriers, Khanh's troops sped to Long Dinh in hopes of catching the Viet Cong before they escaped. Before midday, Khanh's forces of 3,000 infantry soldiers surrounded the Viet Cong 514th Battalion. The ARVN brigade had the VC battalion outnumbered three to one.

For the next eight hours, the two sides fought. The ARVN did not attack the VC positions. Instead, they kept the VC contained and used artillery and airpower to hammer the enemy. Interspersed with artillery and heavy mortar barrages, South Vietnamese T-28s and American Huey gunships pounded the VC positions with rockets and machine guns. While the VC took losses, they were not defeated outright. The ARVN commanders' reluctance to use their troops in an assault gave the VC commanders time to locate weak points in the ARVN defensive ring.

As the night descended, the VC used the darkness to break out of the encirclement and retreat to a nearby river. VC snipers cleared the way allowing the battalion to cross the river and escape into a jungle. By morning, an entire VC battalion had slipped through the grip of the ARVN soldiers. The unit commanders were dumbfounded. Even though they had won the battle by killing more men than they lost, forty to sixteen killed respectively, the ARVN commanders knew they were in deep shit for letting the bulk of the VC battalion escape, especially since they had overwhelming forces surrounding their enemy.

When Khanh received word of the debacle, he was

furious. He immediately demoted all of the commanders involved for incompetence. But as much as Khanh and the other ARVN generals hated to admit it, this was not an unusual event. More and more, the unit commanders who feared punishment for losing large amounts of troops, relied on artillery and air power to fight their battles for them while their men stayed in defensive positions. The Battle of Long Dinh was an embarrassment. Fortunately for Khanh, the generals in Saigon were too busy squabbling among themselves to give notice of the battle. It was just another in a long series of ARVN defeats since the generals in Saigon has ceased power from Diem and his family. More and more, superior artillery and airpower were no longer enough to defeat the well-disciplined Viet Cong fighters.

March 15, 1964 – Yale University - New Haven, Connecticut, USA

A college student with a handful of flyers, a staple gun, and a roll of Scotch tape walked down the sidewalk posting flyers on telephone poles and store windows. The flyers were an announcement of a three-day conference on the Yale University campus on socialism put on by Students for a Democratic Society.

Karen Dickson, Coyle's daughter, sat in a coffee shop finishing her breakfast. She was in New Haven on assignment from her newspaper covering the dedication of a controversial statue in front of city hall. She watched as the student with the flyers entered and spoke with the restaurant owner. She seemed harmless and polite. The owner nodded in agreement and the student taped a flyer to the window.

On leaving the restaurant Karen glanced at the flyer. Socialism was an interesting topic and she wondered if her editor might like some photos of the conference. It was after all Yale, one of America's top universities. She decided to attend the conference and take the photos without her editor's permission. Sometimes it was better just to take action and ask permission later after the photos had been developed. She figured he could always just say "No." No harm, no foul.

Karen entered the conference late and was given a press pass. She stood at the back of the lecture hall listening and snapping photos of the speakers and the students listening. They weren't talking about socialism. The subject of discussion was the War in Vietnam and America's involvement. Her twin brother Scott, a helicopter pilot, was part of the American mission in Vietnam. He had been shot down during the battle of Ap Bac and almost died. She couldn't help but think about him as she listened. Tears welled up in her eyes.

The speaker was talking about an anti-war demonstration that the organization was putting together for May 2nd in New York. It would be the first of its kind for the Vietnam War and was designed to let the Johnson Administration and the public know how the college students felt – the war was an unnecessary waste of human life. The students felt they could not sit idly by and watch American soldiers die in a far-off land that few could even find on a map. They had to do something.

Karen was moved by the speaker's passion and decided she would cover the demonstration in New York no matter what her editor said. It was important.

The world needed to know what was going on. The crusade to demonstrate in New York was named, "May 2nd Movement (M2M)."

March 17, 1964 - White House - Washington D.C., USA

McNamara laid the reasoning and groundwork for the expanded war in Vietnam when he created National Security Action Memorandum 288. In it, he stated, "We seek an independent non-communist South Vietnam. Unless we can achieve this objective... almost all of Southeast Asia will probably fall under Communist dominance, starting with South Vietnam, Laos, and Cambodia, followed by Burma and Malaysia. Thailand might hold for a period with our help but would be under grave pressure. Even the Philippines would become shaky and the threat to India to the west, Australia, New Zealand to the south, and Taiwan, Korea, and Japan to the north and east would be greatly increased."

President Johnson approved the memorandum that would be the official basis for "The Domino Theory" and the expansion of the war in Vietnam. The vast majority of Americans supported the war and Johnson's approval ratings went up when the memorandum was printed in the nation's newspapers and announced on television by the evening news broadcasts. Americans now had a clear reason to support the war. Whether the theory was true or not remained to be seen. For most Americans, it didn't matter. They trusted their president and the White House to do the right thing and protect them. That was enough to keep their support.

March 26, 1964 – Quang Tri Province, South Vietnam

Captain Floyd James Thompson was on a reconnaissance flight in Quang Tri Province where his Green Beret unit was stationed. Captain Richard Whiteside was the pilot of the 0-1 Bird Dog they were using. They had flown together before and enjoyed each other's company. Discussing their favorite fishing holes was the usual topic. There was a lot of time in the air for discussion. The mission was to search out possible enemy units in the jungle. It was almost impossible to see through the dense canopy, but occasionally Thompson got lucky and spotted something of interest. Whiteside brought along a couple of Pork Bahn Mis with bottled Cokes for lunch. He called them the U.S. Army's "In-flight" service.

The aircraft flew a couple of hundred feet above the treetops. Just enough so Thompson got a good view, but not so far that they could become an easy target. The Viet Cong in the area didn't have anti-aircraft guns, so Whiteside was not too worried. It was the random rifle shot that concerned him. A pilot just never knew when his aircraft could be hit and there wasn't much he could do about it until it happened.

In the jungle below, a VC platoon was making its way to a nearby village where they planned on raiding for supplies and if they got lucky a few fresh recruits. The villagers had not entered the Strategic Hamlet program and were unprotected except for their hunting bows, a handful of wooden spears, and three old muskets. It wouldn't be much of a fight which was fine with the VC commander. He wanted to get in and get out before the ARVN showed up. The commander heard the thrum of an airplane engine approaching. There was a clearing ahead. He ordered his troops to run to the clearing and point their weapons skyward. The odds were slim that they would see an aircraft, but he had his orders. Aircraft were considered high-priority targets, especially if they were American.

When the reconnaissance aircraft passed directly over the clearing, the Viet Cong opened fire.

Whiteside was surprised when he heard the thud of a bullet hitting the fuselage near the rear of the aircraft. A second hit beneath him and entered his leg just above the knee. "Oh, shit. I think they got me," he said in a lighthearted matter.

"Where?" said Thompson.

A spot of blood formed on Whiteside's trousers. "Right there," he said looking down.

"I'll get the first aid kit," said Thompson unbuckling and climbing over the seat. "Where is it?"

"Should be right behind your seat."

"Got it," said Thompson climbing back in his seat holding the box.

He opened the lid and searched inside the kit for a pressure dressing. He felt himself being pushed forward and looked up. The plane was starting to dive. He looked over at Whiteside his face was ghost-white, and his trousers were soaked with blood which was pooling on the floor below the control. The bullet had severed an artery in his leg. He was unconscious. "Dick, can you hear me?" said Thompson in a panic. "I can't fly this thing."

There was no response. Thompson knew that if he didn't stop the bleeding fast, Whiteside was sure to bleed out and die. But by the time he saved his friend, the plane would crash. Everything was happening at once and all of it meant life or death. He had watched plenty of pilots fly their aircraft over the years of working in intelligence, but he never paid much attention to the details. He ripped open the package holding the pressure dressing and tossed it in Whiteside's lap. He would help his friend once he had leveled out the plane. He placed his hands on the yoke and – it was already too late.

The plane slammed into the jungle canopy. The prop chewed through the leaves and small branches continuing to give the plane speed as it dove to the ground. When the plane smashed into the jungle floor, Thompson was not wearing his seatbelt. He was thrown forward. His belt buckle caught on the controls and prevented him from being launched through the windshield. His head slammed face-first on the top of the control panel knocking him unconscious. Everything went black.

He woke up to the sound of Vietnamese arguing loudly. At least he thought it was Vietnamese. He didn't speak the language. He had no idea how long he had been out. He looked over at Whiteside. He wasn't moving. He knew his friend was dead and felt ashamed that he couldn't save him. He heard the aircraft door beside him being pried open. Hands reached in and pulled him out of his seat. He was placed on the ground, and someone was tending to a large gash on his forehead from where he had hit the control panel. His eyes were blurry from the blood that had trickled down, but he could make the face of the man treating him. His face was Vietnamese, and he was wearing black pajamas. He was Viet Cong. Thompson realized that he was a prisoner of the VC. He knew very well that the Viet Cong hated American pilots. He imagined that they could not tell the difference between a pilot and a passenger and wondered if they were keeping him alive so they could hang him or worse.

Once the VC medic finished tending to his wounds, Thompson was helped to his feet, the escorted back to the VC camp. He found that he was the only western prisoner and was placed in a bamboo cage exposed to the elements. He wondered how long it would take be his Green Beret comrades would report him missing and another scout plane was sent to find him and Whiteside. He wondered if he would be found and rescued in time before the VC killed him. There was little he could do to improve his chances. He tried to keep a positive attitude, but it wasn't easy. He was starving and growing weaker. As the days, weeks, and months passed, he felt helpless and depressed. Did anyone know he was alive? Had his buddies forgotten him?

Thompson recovered from his wounds and remained with the Viet Cong in the jungle for three years before he was transferred to a North Vietnamese prison. During his captivity, Captain Thompson was tortured, starved, and held in solitary confinement for years on end. He suffered from a variety of infections and diseases including malaria and dysentery. Just ten days short of nine years in captivity he was finally released on March 16, 1973, as part of Operation Homecoming. He was the longest-serving American prisoner of the Vietnam War.

White House – Washington DC, USA

With sleepless bags under his eyes, President Johnson spoke with his National Security Advisor, McGeorge Bundy on the phone. Bundy and the other cabinet members and advisors did not know that Johnson was secretly recording all the phone calls in the oval office. Overwhelmed by the decisions that only the commander-in-chief can make, the exhausted president was almost incoherent at times, his train of thought trailing off, then stabbing at a new idea. Johnson said, "I will tell you the more I just stayed awake last night thinking of this thing, and the more that I think of it I don't know what in the hell, it looks like to me that we're getting into another Korea. It just worries the hell out of me. I don't see what we can ever hope to get out of there with once we're committed. I believe the Chinese Communists are coming into it. I don't think that we can fight them 10,000 miles away from home and ever get anywhere in that area. I don't think it's worth fighting for and I don't think we can get out. And it's just the biggest damned mess that I ever saw."

"It is an awful mess," said Bundy.

"And we just got to think about it. I'm looking at this sergeant of mine this morning and he's got six little old kids over there, and he's getting out my things, and bringing me in my night reading, and all that kind of stuff, and I just thought about ordering all those kids in there. And what in the hell am I ordering them out there for? What in the hell is Vietnam worth to me? What is Laos worth to me? What is it worth to this country? We've got a treaty but hell, everybody else has got a treaty out there, and they're not doing a thing about it."

"Yeah, yeah."

"Of course, if you start running from the Communists, they may just chase you right into your own kitchen."

"Yeah, that's the trouble. And that is what the rest of that half of the world is going to think if this thing comes apart on us. That's the dilemma, that's exactly the dilemma."

"But this is a terrible thing that we're getting ready to do."

"Mr. President, I just think it figures it is really the only big decision in one sense, this is the one that we have to either reach up and get it, or we let it go by. And I'm not telling you today what I'd do in your position. I just think that the most that we have to do with it is pray with it for another while."

"Anybody else that we got that can advise with, that might have any judgment on this question, that might be fresh, that might have some new approach. Would Bradley be any good? Would Clay be any good?"

"No, Bradley would be no good. I do not think Clay would add. I think you're constantly searching, if I understand you correctly, for some means of stiffening this thing that does not have this escalating aspect to it, and I've been up and down this with Bob McNamara, and I have up and down it again with Mike Forrestal. And I think that there are some marginal things that we can do . . . but I think, also, Mr. President, you can do, what I think Kennedy did at least once which is to make the threat without having made your own internal decision that you would actually carry it through. Now I think that the risk in that is that we have, at least, seemed to do it about once or twice before. And there's another dilemma in here, which is the difficulty your own people have. I'm not talking about Dean Rusk or Bob McNamara or me, but people who are at second removed, who just find it very hard to be firm, if they're not absolutely clear what your decision is."

"It's damned easy to get into a war, but if it's going to be awful hard to ever extricate yourself if you get in. What does Lippmann think that you ought to do?

"Well, I'm going to talk with him at greater length, but what he really thinks is that you should provide a diplomatic structure within which the thing can go under the control of Hanoi and walk away from it. I don't think that's an unfair statement, but I will ask him."

"You mean that he thinks that Hanoi ought to take South Vietnam?"

"Yes, sir, diplomatically. Maybe by calling it a neutralization and removing American force and letting it slip away the way that Laos did, would if we didn't do anything, and will if we don't do anything. We would guarantee the neutrality in some sort of a treaty that we would write. I think, I'm sorry, I'm not sure that I'm the best person to describe Lippmann's views, because I don't agree with them."

"I'd try to get his ideas a little more concrete before I leave here. And I'd like to have him talk to McNamara. I might, I might just have the three of you in this afternoon sometime. I'd like to hear Walter and McNamara debate it, then draw my own conclusions."

"I'll see to it, Mr. President."

RECON

Hon Me Island, North Vietnam

A fishing boat approached Hon Me Island bobbing in the waves of the Eastern Vietnam Sea. The barrel-stave-design boat had a high bow with an eye painted on each side to keep crocodiles away when traveling in rivers. Toward the stern, a small cabin where the crew of two could sleep or rest from the hot sun after their meals. A small inboard engine powered the dilapidated vessel that looked like it could sink at any minute and was badly in need of a paint job.

The pilot was a South Vietnamese marine disguised as a peasant fisherman. His passenger acting as a crew member was Granier wearing a ragged conical hat to hide his face and tattered clothes. Anyone with half a brain could see from a distance that he was a foreigner. He was too damned tall to be Vietnamese. He kept low, hunching over as he moved across the deck.

The boat had motored its way up the coast from the northern edge of South Vietnam. It took several days to reach the island of Hon Me.

In the late afternoon, the pilot stopped a good distance from the island and threw out his fishing nets.

Using the cabin's doorway, Granier sat in the shadows peering through his binoculars. There wasn't much to see. Only one vessel, a mail boat tied up at the island's pier. It was a short visit to drop off mail to the NVA soldiers and the villagers that inhabited the island. Returning from the coastal markets where they had dropped off their catch, the village fishing boats had already landed on the rocky beach surrounding the island. Fishing usually began before sunrise and only lasted until late morning before their boats were full. The waters off the coast were plentiful. The problem was there were a lot of boats and not enough customers. Vietnamese loved fish, but even they had their limits. In the spirit of compromise, the fishermen had agreed to limit their catches. They spent their afternoons mending their nets and drinking homemade rice wine stored in ten-gallon fuel cans. The key was to drink enough to get drunk but not so much to cause a hangover that would prevent them from going fishing the next morning. That strategy met with varying degrees of success.

The pilot did not like fishing in the afternoon. It was against the local rules and could create suspicion from the villagers. They didn't like interlopers in their traditional fishing grounds and would protect them if an unknown fishing boat was discovered. But Granier insisted. He needed to observe vessel traffic to and from the island as part of his recon mission. He was more concerned with the North Vietnamese patrol boats that were known to inspect any boats they encountered.

Two submachine guns and four grenades were hidden under the boat's fishing nets. They wouldn't help much against the North Vietnamese patrol boat armed with a .50 Cal deck machine gun. The large-caliber bullets would punch holes in the boat's wooden hull and sinking was a high probability. If stopped by a patrol boat their only hope was to draw the enemy vessel in close before a firefight began. It was a strategy, but not a good one. A firefight would also end their mission. Granier did not like failure and would go to great lengths and risk to complete his assignment. The pilot was a veteran fighter, but less gun-ho.

As the sun set, the pilot gathered his net and dumped his catch on the deck of the boat as was the tradition. Under the cover of darkness and without running lights, the boat drew closer to the island while Granier slipped into a sniper's ghillie suit. Not wanting to cause alarm with the locals, Granier slipped over the side of the boat while it was still moving and swam the last mile to shore. The boat would continue its journey to nowhere in particular then circle back and pick up Granier at the designated time.

The swim was uneventful. Even though he was getting older, Granier was in great shape and made good time. If there were sharks in the area, they elected to leave him alone. As he reached the pebble-strewn beach, he moved quickly into the tree line. His face and hands heavily camouflaged with grease paint, he disappeared.

He pulled his pistol from a rubber rucksack and chambered a round. It wasn't much in the way of protection considering he was behind enemy lines, but the idea was not to not be detected. He would only use the pistol as a last resort if he thought he might be captured or killed. He knew where he was going… a hilltop on one end of the island. He moved quietly through the trees. As planned, there was no moon. His eyes quickly adjusted to the darkness. He scanned the ground in front of him for boobytraps. He knew that the odds of seeing a tripwire were slim without moonlight or a flashlight, but that didn't stop him from trying. Sometimes, it was the little differences that kept him alive.

It took him an hour to reach the top of the hill. He slowed as he approached the North Vietnamese radar facility. There would be guards. His job was to find out how many and the type of weapons they were using. He would also examine the layout of any defenses.

Peering through the foliage, Granier could see that the azimuth and altitude antennas and the radar dish were of Soviet-design and well built. He made a mental note that extra heavy satchel charges might be needed. There was an anti-aircraft machine gun that doubled as a ground assault deterrent. The weapon was surrounded by three layers of sandbags making it resistant to enemy machine gun fire and mortar rounds. He observed a four-man guard, not counting the gunner and loader of the anti-aircraft gun. There were also two technicians operating the radar installation. There was a long hut that he imagined was a barracks. He moved closer to have a look.

The barracks had another six guards and two technicians inside playing cards and sacking out before their shift. He got a good look at their weapons stored on a rack. There were six newly issued AKM assault rifles that had replaced the AK-47. That meant that this unit was probably elite. They also had two RPK light machine guns with seventy-five-round drum magazines and an 82 mm mortar. He wondered why the mortar was not set up outside but figured they wanted to keep it out of the rain until it was needed.

Two dozen ammunition and shell cases were stacked against the wall along with two cases of grenades. They were armed for bear. The North Vietnamese were taking the threat of assault seriously.

Granier made his way around the entire hilltop facility to make sure he wasn't missing anything. He watched for another hour to observe the actions of the NVA soldiers. They seemed like veterans which made them all the more dangerous. Finished with his recon, he made his way back to the beach by a different route. If the NVA had discovered him, they would have hunted him down, not placed boobytraps along a trail. But old habits die hard.

He unloaded and slipped his pistol back into the rubber rucksack and entered the water. He swam out to the pickup spot and trod water until the boat showed up. The boat slowed but did not stop. Granier grabbed a tire hung on the side and let the boat drag him in the water. Tying off the steering wheel, the pilot reached over the side and help pull Granier into the boat.

Two days later, Granier reconned the second island of Hon Nhu and found a similar setup with the addition of a radio tower used to monitor inland communications. It too had an elite unit of soldiers protecting it from sabotage plus a total of six technicians that operated the radar and radio monitoring equipment.

Once back aboard the boat, Granier and the pilot headed back to South Vietnam. They were cautious taking their time to keep up the cover of being a fishing boat. They had been lucky and didn't want to press it.

Saigon, South Vietnam

Conein was anxious to hear his report when Granier showed up in his office, unshaven and smelling ripe. Conein didn't care. It was the intelligence he wanted. He asked a lot of questions and Granier seemed to have an answer for all of them. Conein had chosen the right man for the job. He gave himself kudos.

Conein liked the setup. It wasn't perfect, but it would do for what he had in mind – to tickle the dragon. After several more days to work out the details of his plan, Conein called Harkins's office at MACV and asked for a meeting.

Drinking two pots of hot coffee during the meeting, Conein spent an entire afternoon laying out his plan to Harkins including several options and alternatives should the plan need to be modified to adjust for changes on the ground. Harkins too asked a lot of questions. When he was satisfied, he could see that Conein had done his research and thought through everything that needed consideration. It was a creative and impressive operation that required absolute secrecy.

Harkins wondered how far up the ladder he would need to go to get the plan approved and moving forward. The more people that knew about the operation, the more chances word would leak to the press… or worse, the enemy. He realized that Conein's plan did not need to be fully exposed. Only the parts that needed approval. His superiors didn't need to know the particulars behind the plan. He knew that they would probably see its genius for themselves, but by not telling them every detail he was, in fact, protecting them. He was giving them deniability. He also decided that there was no need to tell them Conein was behind it. He would see that Conein was properly rewarded, but credit for the operation would be his alone. Everyone knew that generals had planning staffs, so it wasn't like he was lying. Generals were expected to take the credit when things went well.

April 19, 1964 – Vientiane, Laos

Without question, South Vietnam was facing major problems. It seemed the more the Americans tried to stabilize the government and focus on the war, the worse things became in Saigon. Every move was the wrong move. But South Vietnam was not alone in its quest for stability. Cambodia and Laos struggled with rogue political and military factions that wanted control of the government.

Laos had been living on a knife's edge since the signing of the International Agreement on the Neutrality of Laos in 1962. A coalition government had been formed with Prince Souvanna Phouma as prime minister. Souvanna's brother Prince Souphanouvong, nicknamed The Red Prince, was the leader of the Pathet Lao and part of the coalition government. Few were happy with the arrangement and even fewer respected the neutrality agreement. Although the fighting rarely reached the major cities, the Pathet Lao supported by the North Vietnamese continued to fight in the mountains near the border and on the Plain of Jars.

As a counterweight, American special forces, CIA, and SOG teams secretly supplied, trained, and led indigenous tribesmen against the communists. It was a secret war that everyone knew existed, but never admitted to being part of it. Air America played a major role in supplying the tribesmen, while American fighters and bombers flew out of Northeastern Thailand attempting to cut off the Ho Chi Minh Trail and to provide air-to-ground support missions for the Tribesmen when engaging the Pathet Lao or NVA.

On April 18th, the Laotian prime minister met with the Red Prince on the Plain of Jars. The Red Prince threatened to leave the coalition if his demand to demilitarize Luang Prabang and Vientiane was not satisfied. Whether the Red Prince would admit it or not, Souvanna knew that the demilitarization of the royal and administrative capitals would lead to the overthrow of the government. He could not comply with his brother's demands.

Discouraged, Souvanna returned to Vientiane and informed King Sisavang Vatthana, the head of the Laotian state, that he wished to resign. The king wanted his prime minister to think about his decision and refused to accept his resignation until the next day.

Unknowingly, at the same time, a coup was afoot. Laotian General Siho Lamphouthacoul had built two battalions of paramilitary police into a national power. Recruiting from local military police and National Police, Siho's highly trained police battalions reached a total strength of 6,500 men.

In secret talks held in Saigon, Siho persuaded Laotian Military General Kouprasith Abhay to join him in a military coup against Souvanna's government. Kouprasith commanded Military Region 5 which included a regiment of regulars, Mobile Group 17, four volunteer battalions, a GMS airborne-qualified regiment, and nine ADC militia companies. It was a sizeable force and well-located to participate in the coup. While most of Kouprasith's forces were stationed in and near Vientiane, Mobile Group 17 was temporarily posted to the Plain of Jars in Military Region 2 as a counterbalance to The Red Prince's Pathet Lao forces.

Siho and Kouprasith chose April 18th for their coup because US Ambassador for Laos, Leonard Unger was away in Saigon for meetings with McNamara and Bundy. The two generals planned on executing the coup, then forcing the Americans to accept their new government upon Unger's return.

After Kouprasith ordered Mobile Group 17 back to the capital to support the coup, everything went according to plan with the generals' forces seizing strategic national government buildings and arresting key government officials including Prime Minister Souvanna. Souvanna was placed under house arrest. "The Revolutionary Committee of the National Army" took over the government with Kouprasith as its head and Siho as his deputy.

Hearing reports of the coup, Ambassador Unger immediately flew back to Vientiane. He was seething with anger and demanded to meet with Siho and Kouprasith. Unger didn't mince words and informed the two generals that America would not be recognizing their new government and all financial and military aid would be cut off. He demanded that they release the prime minister and other officials immediately and restore the rightful government. Unwilling to meet his gaze, the two generals acted like embarrassed schoolboys and agreed to all of Unger's terms. They had lost face.

With Group Mobile 17 gone from the battlefield,

the Red Prince and the Pathet Lao took advantage of the situation and seized control of the Plain of Jars, a vital strategic point for Northern Laos. It was a huge blunder on the part of the Royal Laotian Army and shifted the balance of power in a major way for years to come.

When the prime minister was released from house arrest, he refused to return to work claiming that he had resigned. Ambassador Unger drove out to Souvanna's house and knocked on the front door. Opening the door, Souvanna's butler informed the American ambassador that the prime minister was not accepting visitors at the moment and closed the door. Unger was dumbfounded. He walked out onto the front lawn and called out to Souvanna like Romeo calling for Juliet. Souvanna appeared on the second-story patio and asked Unger to go away. Knowing that Souvanna was the only Laotian that could hold the government together, Unger pleaded with Souvanna to return to work and assured him that America would support him. After almost an hour, Souvanna finally agreed to return to his post as prime minister and asked the American ambassador in for tea. The crisis was averted and the secret war in Laos would continue.

April 30, 1964 – Boston, Massachusetts, USA

Just as his brother's opinions had evolved during his tenure in office, Robert Kennedy's opinions also evolved. Robert had reluctantly accepted Johnson's offer to continue as US Attorney General. He wanted to ensure that the work he had done on civil rights with his brother would remain intact and continue as the nation matured. It was a long-term process that he nurtured. He was also considering a run for congress in the upcoming elections and wanted to continue the national exposure that only a cabinet position could provide. He still felt he was living in the shadow of his brother. It was the nature of the beast. JFK had been larger than life, while Robert struggled with shyness and confidence. Journalists were more interested in discussing JFK's policies and opinions than his own. He was proud of his brother and knew that much of his own fame was due to his brother's popularity.

RFK's political leanings were similar to JFK's when he was alive, but they didn't always agree. Robert also needed to be careful not to contradict President Johnson's policies. Johnson and his attorney general were on the same page concerning most issues… but not all. While serving Johnson, Robert did not feel like he could speak his mind. During an interview for the Kennedy Library, Robert discussed his recollection of his brother's feelings on Vietnam and said, "President Kennedy has a strong overwhelming reason for being in Vietnam and that he should win the war. There has been a lot of talk that Jack wanted to withdraw American advisors. It's not true. He believed in their mission and wanted to see South Vietnam survive as an independent democracy. Of course, there were major challenges with President Diem and his family. To encourage Diem's cooperation, it became necessary for President Kennedy to rotate American advisors in and out of the country and even threaten to cut off aid. But all of that was an attempt to guide the South Vietnamese onto a path of victory. At times, a strong hand was needed but my brother never flinched when it came to America's deep commitment to South Vietnam and the end of communist expansionism into

Southeast Asia. As far as my brother's desire to increase America's military commitment to include American troops in Vietnam, I would say he had a wait-and-see attitude. There were other paths being explored to stop the communists. My brother was anxious not to expand the war if possible, but that doesn't mean that he would shirk his responsibility if necessary. I feel the same… we will do what is required, but not until it is absolutely necessary."

May 2, 1964 – Saigon, South Vietnam

The flagship of a Hunter-Killer task group, the USS Card was a Bogue-class escort carrier that served in the US Navy during World War II. She carried a variety of fighters and anti-submarine aircraft including Grumman Wildcats and Avengers. When World War II ended, the Card was decommissioned and tucked away as part of the reserve fleet.

When the Vietnam War started, the Card was reactivated and designated the USNS Card because it was operated by a civilian crew and used primarily as an aircraft transport. In December 1961, the Card left Quonset Point Naval Station in Rhode Island with a cargo of H-21 Shawnee helicopters along with their aircrews and maintenance crews.

The Card and her sister ship, the USNS Core, were used to transport heavy artillery, M113 armored personnel carriers, aircraft, helicopters, and ammunition along with other supplies to South Vietnam. The twin ships regularly docked at the Port of Saigon located between the Te and Ben Nghe Canals. The South Vietnamese Navy deployed vessels to patrol the river and shores around the port. In addition, an ARVN Airborne battalion was based just across the river from the port. Both the Americans and the South Vietnamese knew that the port and the vessels unloading their cargo and equipment were a prime target for the Viet Cong.

Tran Hai Phung, commander of the Viet Cong's Saigon-Gia Dinh Military District, ordered the 65th Special Operations Group to attack the USNS Card. Despite the Republic of Vietnam National Police and their undercover agents, the South Vietnamese could not control the Viet Cong agents from operating in and around the port. It was just too big and there were too many workers to keep tabs on everyone. Many slipped through the cracks and even obtained civilian jobs working at the port. Lam Son Nao, a VC commando of the 65th Special Operations Group, was also an electrician at the port facility.

Taking advantage of his position at the port, Nao was assigned the mission to reconnoiter the USNS Card and design a strategy to sink the vessel along with all the military cargo she had on board. Having previously worked at the port as a tradesman, Nao's father had memorized all the tunnels and sewage systems at the facility. When Nao went to him for advice, his father advised his son that the best way to enter the area where American ships normally anchored was through the sewer tunnel opposite Thu Theim.

To avoid suspension, Nao bathed in the Saigon River while inspecting the sewer tunnel accessing the American area of the port. Nao concluded that his father was correct, it was the best way to get to the American vessel, but it also had challenges that his father had not foreseen. Along with human waste, toxic oils were dumped into the sewage tunnel. To prevent blindness that could occur from exposure to the toxic sewage, Nao and his men would need to navigate the tunnel with their eyes closed. Each man would need to memorize the path on a map, then extrapolate it into real life to find his way. One wrong calculation would most likely lead to permanent blindness or even death from chemical exposure. Once the mission was completed, Nao and his men would need to clean themselves with powerful soaps to purge themselves from the deadly odors and to avoid detection by South Vietnamese police who were sure to search the immediate area for the perpetrators.

Nao decided to use high explosives detonated by a timer, so he and his men would have time to escape before the explosions. The problem was the amount of explosives required. The vessel's hull was made of thick steel plates that would not be easy to penetrate. After consulting with an engineer and an explosives expert, Nao calculated that he would need 180 pounds of high explosives to sink the ship.

Nao spent several days going over the plan and making changes. When he was satisfied that it would work, he presented the plan to Saigon-Gia Dinh Military District Headquarters. Nao's superiors' only real concern was civilian casualties from the massive explosions. They ordered Nao to launch the attack before sunrise to avoid killing local Vietnamese during work hours. Nao agreed.

Nao assembled the supplies he would need for the mission. His first choice of explosives was C4 plastic explosives because of their compact size and water resistance. But C4 was in short supply among the Viet Cong and Nao was forced to also use TNT to obtain enough explosive power. Nao recruited and trained two new commandos, Nguyen Phu Hung, an electrician, and Nguyen Van Cay, a mason, to support his operation.

As finishing touches on plans were being completed, Nao and his team received news that the USNS Card had arrived in Saigon and was due to dock at the port facility within a few hours. The vessel was loaded down with armored personnel carriers, artillery, and aircraft. Sinking the ship before it was unloaded by the dockworkers would be a great achievement. They had to move swiftly to be ready before morning.

The explosive packages were divided in two, one using C4 and the other waterproofed TNT. They carried them through the sewer tunnels. Swimming under the cover of darkness, the commando team attached the explosives to the vessel's hull just above the waterline, one near the bilge and the other next to the engine compartment. Connected to a battery with wires, the timers were synchronized and set. The team swam to the safety of the sewage tunnels and waited. Nothing happened.

Even with all their planning, the electrician had failed to check that the battery held a sufficient charge to operate the timers and ignite the explosives. It failed. Hung lost face. As the electrician, it was his responsibility to check all the electrical components of the explosive packages. But Nao did not give up. The bombs had not been discovered. He ordered his men to retrieve the explosive package and prevent the Americans and South Vietnamese from discovering their plot to sabotage the vessel.

With only minutes of darkness remaining, the team swam back out to the vessel and removed the explosive packages. They made it back to the sewage tunnel just as the sun cracked over the horizon. As long as their plans remained undiscovered, they could try another day. It was only when Nao reported the failure to his superiors that he discovered that they were going to sink the wrong ship. The vessel that had docked at the port was not the USNS Card, but her sister ship, the USNS Core. The intelligence had been wrong. Nao and his team felt like complete amateurs.

With a new battery in hand and checked multiple times each day by Hung, the team waited for another opportunity. It didn't take long. Viet Cong Intelligence teams reported that they had spotted the USNS Card as it sailed through Ganh Rai Bay and entered the Long Tau River on its way to unload. Its decks were filled with military helicopters and spare parts. The cargo of the USNS Card was considered to be more important than the cargo of the USNS Core. Nao and his crew were more determined than ever to sink the Card.

Nao knew better than to use the same path of entry into the American area of the port. There was too much of a chance that the team's ingress and egress had been discovered by South Vietnamese intelligence forces. Instead, he had decided to use two canoes to transport the explosive packages. Cay had become ill, probably from exposure to the toxic chemicals in the sewer tunnels. That meant that only Nao and Hung would be executing the mission. It made things more difficult because of the weight of the explosives and the time needed to place them on the hull. They would do their best to carry out the operation even with limited resources. Hung checked the battery one more time before leaving. For obvious reasons, Hung was paranoid that he forgot to do something. Nao tried to calm and reassure him. While diligence was good, too much stress could cause mistakes to be made and that was something they could not afford this time around.

Each piloting a canoe, Nao and Hung paddled out into the Saigon River toward the port. Fortunately, there were other small vessels on the river even at that time of the morning. Nao and Hung mixed in with the water traffic as they ventured closer to their objective. As they left the group of boats, a South Vietnamese patrol boat spotted them and gave chase. The patrol boat stopped sixty feet from Nao's canoe. The patrol boat commander questioned both Nao and Hung as to what they were doing so close to the port. Nao explained that they were heading to the other side of the river to buy clothes at the market. When the commander ordered them to turn around and go back the way they came, Nao offered him a 1000 Vietnamese Dong bribe to let them pass. The commander accepted the bribe but informed Nao he would expect a second bribe if they were to come back the same way on their return. Nao agreed and the commandos were allowed to pass.

Nao and Hung docked next to the sewer tunnels where they could assemble the explosive packages without being seen. As before, they swam with the packages toward the American vessel. With sunrise approaching, they attached the bombs to the ship's hull and set the timers attached to the battery. They swam back to the sewer tunnels and retrieved their canoes.

As expected, the patrol boat was waiting. The commander wanted his bribe. As the two canoes approached the patrol boat, a bright flash lit up the sky and was followed by the boom of a loud explosion. The patrol boat fired up its engines and raced toward the American vessel in the distance. The patrol boat's wake almost capsized Nao and Hung's canoes. Having avoided detection, the saboteurs continued their escape. Only one of the two bombs had detonated. Nao and Hung hoped it was enough to sink the ship. It was.

Its engine compartment completely flooded, the USNS Card was the largest military vessel in Saigon when it sunk in forty-eight feet of water and settled onto the muddy bottom of the Saigon River. Its valuable cargo of helicopters and parts sank with it destroying the aircraft. The explosion had torn a hole twelve feet long and three feet high, on the starboard side of the ship's hull. Five American crewmen either died in the explosion or shortly thereafter from their wounds.

Even though the USNS Card was refloated and returned to service before the end of the year, the North Vietnamese made strong use of the successful sabotage as propaganda. The event was memorialized when the North Vietnamese government issued a postage stamp that praised the commandos that had carried out the mission. Nao, Hung, and Cay were heroes and never had to buy their own beer again.

The USNS Card remained in service until 1970 when it was retired from service and placed in the Reserve Fleet.

May 2, 1964 – New York, USA

While the USNS Card sat on the bottom of the Saigon River, another major event was taking place in New York. A long line of buses pulled into Times Square. One thousand college students and teachers from twenty-five different universities across America exited the buses, opened the baggage doors, and removed the signs and placards they had made earlier that morning. Most were clean-cut young adults between the ages of eighteen and twenty-five. Although there were some Hippies, the counterculture movement had not yet gained momentum leaving the college students to protest and draw the public's attention to the war in Vietnam. There were similar protests in San Francisco, Seattle, Boston, Madison, and Wisconsin on the same day. The protests in New York and other major cities were organized by the Progressive Labor Party with help from the Young Socialist Alliance, many of which attended Yale University where the May 2nd Movement had begun.

Karen was there from the beginning snapping photos as the students disembarked the buses and gathered along the crowded sidewalk, some spilling out into the street and blocking traffic. The words written on the signs and shouted by the protestors were sharp and to the point. They rejected the social norms of the day and sought to chart a new path for America. Many were socialists, while others simply wanted to stop the war that they believed was unjust. Karen was unsure how she felt but recognized that the event had historical importance. It was the first major protest in America against the Vietnam War.

She sought to represent the protest fairly in her photos. She took photos of angry, almost militant protestors and photos of college kids just happy to be part of the group. She took photos of tourists, many of which had never seen a protest and were surprised by the liberal use of cursing among the demonstrators. She took photos of police, some on horseback, walking alongside the protestors, trying to keep them from spilling into the streets and blocking traffic. They seemed ill-prepared for such a large group of demonstrators and were hesitant to use force.

As the rally moved through Times Square, the demonstrators marched through Manhattan's Midtown East as they headed for the United Nations building a mile and a half away. They were loud but not violent. That would come later. Any protest of that size would draw the press like bees to flowers. That's what the organizers wanted, awareness of what was happening and what the American government was doing without the people's knowledge. They felt that once the people realized what was happening halfway across the world, the politicians would be held to account and the war would be stopped. But they were far from that goal. The majority of Americans supported the war and wanted communist expansionism stopped. They believed in the Domino Theory promoted by their leaders. America was still innocent and followed blindly.

Businessmen trying to get to work and shoppers heading to the department stores shouted at the protestors for making trouble and blocking the sidewalk. Most of the demonstrators ignored them, some did not. Shouting matches between the two sides broke out. The police moved to intervene before things got out of hand. The police did not take sides. The demonstrators had a right to free speech and the New Yorkers had the right to use their sidewalks unmolested. The police separated the hotheads from both sides and kept them apart as the demonstration moved on.

Karen struggled to capture the feelings of the

demonstrators and those who opposed them. She took photos of conflict wherever it occurred along the long line of demonstrators. She was surprised by the passion of both sides. The New Yorkers shouted at the students for being unpatriotic and not supporting the government. The protestors shouted back anti-war slogans and propaganda. The protestors were educated and knew their rights. They understood what was at stake and were determined to make a difference. It was the beginning of a movement that would change the world… a world that many did not want to be changed. People were uneasy when they heard that their government was lying to them. They still trusted the government to do what was best for America even if they didn't know what their leaders were doing. Karen was in the middle of it fighting to capture the moment the only way she knew how… with her camera. She was shoved and jostled. At times she struggled to keep her balance and kept shooting, roll after roll of film.

When the demonstration finally ended in front of the United Nations building, Karen headed for a photo lab she had arranged to rent for several hours. She didn't want to wait to see what she had captured on film. As a skilled photographer, she didn't trust anyone else with her film. She developed more than a dozen rolls and clipped the negative images to the drying wires. She didn't need to print the negatives to see what they showed. Experience told her what she was seeing as she looked down at her work on the light table. She was shocked by what she had done. It was all there. The emotion. The event. The history. The photos would make her famous. It was just the start. She now knew her mission in life. She would tell the story of the Vietnam War. She promised herself she would be unbiased and strive to always capture the truth of what was happening. Good or bad, the people would judge the war through her images. She thought about her twin brother Scott, a helicopter pilot in Vietnam. She wondered how her photographs would affect him… if they could save him and other soldiers like him. She thought about the Vietnamese and their struggle for freedom. She knew nothing of their lives but imagined they loved their country as she loved hers. If she stuck to the truth, she couldn't go wrong. She was naïve like so many Americans.

RANGERS

May 14, 1964 – Saigon, South Vietnam

During the night, the Viet Cong had seized a strategic hamlet twenty miles north of Saigon. It was too close for comfort. The ARVN generals wanted it back. Intelligence reported the enemy force was no bigger than one hundred Viet Cong. Under the Diem regime, the ARVN would fire an artillery barrage or send in their fighter/bombers with napalm until the Viet Cong left the village. But this was close to Saigon and there was a good chance the newspapers would report on the counterattack. Civilian casualties needed to be kept to a minimum, so the ARVN looked like heroes not uncaring oppressors.

A company of ARVN Rangers was sent to retake the village in the early morning. It was possible that the Viet Cong would have already left by the time the rangers would have arrived. The VC didn't like to fight in the daylight unless forced. American or South Vietnamese warplanes could easily spot them. If they chose to retreat, napalm strikes in open rice fields could devastate the VC by wiping out a large number of troops. A great victory would be turned into a tragic loss. The VC listened to Mau Zedong and only fought when they were sure to win. If they left the hamlet before sunrise, they were sure to be winners. Anything beyond that was a risk.

The rangers traveled by M113 armored personnel carriers and trucks. When they came within a couple of miles of the hamlet, they disembarked from the trucks and advanced on foot. The M113 led the way with the rangers on foot following close behind. If there was trouble, the foot soldiers would move up and protect the APCs from any anti-armor weapons the enemy might be using. The APCs would use their shielded machine guns to cover the foot soldiers. Even armor required teamwork to be effective.

Four South Vietnamese T-28s flew over the hamlet. There was nobody in sight. That was strange. If the Viet Cong had left, the villagers would be tending to their wounded and animals. If the Viet Cong were still in the hamlet, they would be in defensive positions behind the palisades made of tall wooden stakes.

The radio report of no activity in or around the hamlet concerned the Ranger captain and his American advisor. The only way to find out what had happened was to enter the hamlet and see for themselves. But they would be cautious as the scouts approached. The road to the hamlet was surrounded by fruit orchards, mostly durian with its overwhelming aroma. The American advisor hated the smell, but the Vietnamese rangers were enchanted by it. One of the rangers climbed one of the tall trees at the edge of the orchard. He thumped the thick-skinned husks with the butt end of his bayonet to determine which were ripe, then cut several of the basketball-sized durians, each weighing up to eighteen pounds, from their thick tree branches. They dropped to the ground below where two more rangers loaded the fruit into the M113s as a reward for the rangers when the battle was won.

The American advisor had learned through experience not to criticize the ARVN soldiers when they stopped right in the middle of an operation to gather food. He didn't want them losing face right before a battle. He needed the company of men to be confident. Still, it was annoying as hell and exposed the Rangers unnecessarily to the enemy.

When finished cutting the durians from the tree, the ranger cleaned his bayonet on his pants and sheathed his weapon. It was at that moment that something caught his eye deeper in the orchard. Something moved in the branches of another tree. It was hard to see clearly what it was, maybe a monkey or a large bird or maybe something else. He squinted in an attempt to get a better look. When his eyes focused, he saw a sniper scope pointed straight at him. A moment later, his life ended with the sound of a rifle crack and the thump of a bullet hitting his face just below his left eye. He fell from the tree and landed on the ground. There was nothing to be done. He was gone.

Realizing that the company of rangers had walked into an ambush, the American advisor turned to the ARVN captain and said nothing as he too was hit in the face with a sniper bullet from another tree deep in the orchard. He fell dead. The captain froze for a moment, unsure of what was happening. He didn't have the experience of his advisor who was now dead. He knelt to check the American for life. There was none. A third sniper bullet ricocheted off the M113 he was kneeling next to. He was now the target. The M113 gunner opened fire spraying bullets wildly into the trees. Durians still on their branches burst open when hit by the machine gun shells. The petrified ranger captain shouted at the M113 driver to let him inside.

The ramp lowered and the captain scrambled inside to safety leaving his men leaderless for the moment. It was a selfish, but good move. Once safe, he was able to think clearly and barked out orders.

The rangers didn't need much in the way of commands. They were elite and their platoon commanders were veterans. They dispersed and took cover wherever they could while laying down suppressing fire into the orchard. Pre-targeted VC mortar rounds rained down on the road exploding. Shrapnel soared in all directions ripping into anyone exposed. A half dozen rangers were killed or wounded in the first minute of the mortar barrage. VC light machine guns opened fire from protected positions within the orchard. The rangers instinctively repositioned themselves to protect against the new threats.

A Chinese-made Type 52 recoilless rifle shell slammed into the side of one of the M113s and exploded. The soldiers inside the armored vehicle were lucky. The 75 mm shell had hit a toolbox anchored to the armored plating on the side of the vehicle. The metal box was torn to shreds but none of the red-hot shrapnel entered the crew compartment. A second shell hit the gun turret on top of the compartment instantly decapitating the gunner and rendering the machine gun useless. Realizing they were sitting ducks without their machine gun, the driver gunned the engine and the M113 took off down the road toward the hamlet. Moments later, it hit a mine that pierced the lightly shielded bottom of the vehicle and killed everyone inside. The vehicle ground to a halt blocking the road with thick trees on both sides.

The rangers were undeterred and fought back

valiantly. Their extensive training kicked in and kept them from panicking. Their unit commanders focused their troops like a spear, directing fire whenever an enemy position was spotted. It was effective and surprised the Viet Cong who watched their comrades die around them. Suffering from extensive casualties, the Rangers held their ground.

The South Vietnamese T-28s assigned to provide air-to-ground support for the rangers dropped their napalm canisters into the orchard setting it ablaze. The Viet Cong burned. Seeing that many of his men were already fleeing the battlefield, the VC commander ordered his men to retreat. The ambush had been a success. The VC had done enough damage to the rangers to call it a clear victory. The hamlet was also abandoned leaving what remained for the rangers to clean up.

When the wounded and dead were counted, the rangers had forty-three dead and twenty-one missing, presumed captured or deserted. The VC had carried off their wounded and dead preventing the rangers from claiming any kind of obscure victory. It was a clear win for the Viet Cong against an elite South Vietnamese company. The propaganda was enormous and used to recruit hundreds of new troops for the ranks of the Viet Cong.

May 16, 1964 – New York, New York, USA

Below the bronze statue of George Washington on his horse, a group of fifty protestors gathered in New York's Union Square with signs and placards displaying anti-war slogans. The demonstration was organized by the War Resisters League, an anti-war organization that began in the First World War and had protested against every war since then. There was no middle ground with the leaders of the organization. War was evil and must be stopped at all costs.

Having been notified of the protest, Karen stood nearby snapping photos of the demonstration, capturing the history of the Vietnam anti-war movement as it unfolded. Twelve men in their early twenties moved to the center of the group. One of the men took out his draft card and a Zippo lighter. Using the lighter, he lit one end of his card and watched it burn. The other eleven men pulled out their draft cards and used the first man's burning card to ignite their own cards. They let them burn halfway then dropped them to the ground to continue burning. When only ash remained, the card owners stomped on the ashes as a sign of disrespect for the US government's authority. Karen captured each moment and the faces of the protestors, the police keeping the peace, and the curious bystanders watching.

It wasn't the first time a draft card had been burned in public. That moment belonged to a twenty-two-year-old conscientious objector, Eugene Keyes, when he set fire to his card on Christmas Day in 1963. Each draft card-burning event that followed was bigger than the last. It was good theatre. Symbolic. The photos that Karen took of the events were popular in newspapers. They were stories told in a single or series of photos. Not much explanation was needed. The photos said it all. Everyone knew what they meant, and everyone had an opinion. The editors couldn't ask for much more than that.

It was not yet against the law to burn a draft card. The police stood by and watched. The most they could do was issue a ticket for littering if the protestors failed to pick up the ashes from the burned cards. That would change as the demonstration grew in size and the protestors became more outspoken against the war and their government that supported the slaughter of innocent Vietnamese civilians. It was a very one-sided argument.

May 21, 1964 – Eastern Mountains, Laos

The crews on the aircraft carrier USS Kitty Hawk nicknamed the Vought F-8 Crusader, "The Gator" because its nozzle and air intake were so low to the flight deck it looked like it would scoop up and swallow anyone in its path. With the landing gear mounted in the fuselage and not the overhead wings, the Crusader was not an easy aircraft to land. It suffered from yaw instability and the poorly designed nose undercarriage made steering on the deck a challenge. During its service, the aircraft had a high number of mishaps and the US Navy was not happy with Vought, the Crusader's manufacturer. But even with its problems, the Crusader was a beast and could fly at Mach 1.8. It also carried a large variety of armaments including four 20 mm Colt Mk 12 cannons mounted in the lower fuselage. It was the last US fight jet to use machine guns as a primary weapon.

With the Laotian mountains sweeping below him, US Navy Lieutenant Charles Klusmann was flying the reconnaissance variant of the aircraft, the RF-8A Crusader. The Pathet Lao had a few Russian-built anti-aircraft guns that protected their camps and supply depots. Klusmann was flying fast as he took photos of what he thought was the Ho Chi Minh Trail. Shrouded by the thick jungle canopy carpeting the mountains, he couldn't tell where the trail was except for the coordinates that he had been given. He took a photo whenever he saw a clearing which meant that he didn't take very many photos. It was not a hard mission and the mountains were beautiful with a vivid carpet of green foliage.

He was almost bored when he felt a hard thump and his aircraft shuttered. He couldn't see the damage but his training told him his aircraft had been hit. In fact, it was on fire. As luck would have it, Klusmann had flown directly over a Pathet Lao supply depot armed with a Soviet-made 61-K anti-aircraft gun. The single-barreled weapon mounted on a four-wheeled chassis fired 37 mm shells with a velocity of 2,887 ft/sec. To get the gun that high into the mountains, the Pathet Lao engineers had completely disassembled the weapon, carried the individual parts on foot, then reassembled it at its assigned location. For over a year, the reassembled weapon had sat, its gun crew bored out of their minds. Until that morning, heard the growing roar of Klusmann's Crusader. Having never before heard or seen an aircraft close enough to shoot, the gun crew was excited.

When an intelligence radio message reported the presence of an American aircraft near their location, the gun crew cranked up their weapon and pointed the gun barrel skyward. They were way beyond enthusiastic as they waited. When they heard the aircraft approaching overhead, the commander ordered them to start firing. The 61-K used five-shell magazines loaded by hand to feed the weapon. The loaders worked frantically to keep the gun fed and firing. Beyond firing the weapon, the gunner had little to do. There was nothing to aim at but a cloudy sky.

Klusmann did not see the muzzle blasts beneath the jungle canopy or the stream of shells flying into the sky. Unknowingly, he flew his aircraft straight into the path of the gun's barrel and was hit in the fuselage by one of the shells which had exploded on impact. The warning lights in his cockpit told him that his engine was on fire. Crashing into the jungle and surviving was not an option. Even with its engine on fire, the Crusader was still traveling at a high speed and would be torn to pieces, and Klusmann with it, on impact with the trees below. He considered ejecting. He looked down at the thick jungle and decided that was a bad idea. There was no way he could navigate himself out of the mountains without being caught and he had heard the stories of how the Pathet Lao treated US aircraft pilots when captured. It was not a pleasant thought. He decided to attempt to make it back into South Vietnam, then eject. Hopefully, the ARVN would find him before the Viet Cong.

He fought for altitude risking an explosion that would destroy his aircraft and most likely kill him. For the moment, the rushing air was holding the flames at bay. He needed to clear the mountain range to enter South Vietnamese air space. He didn't stress the engine or increase the fuel consumption but kept the power constant. He would trade speed for altitude by edging the aircraft skyward very slowly as he flew along the mountain ridge. He knew that if he slowed the aircraft's speed too much, the fire would propagate and most likely cause a catastrophic explosion. But slamming into the mountainside as he tried to clear the range was not a good option either. With warning lights flashing across his dashboard, he struggled to remain calm and patient. He believed his plan would work as long as he didn't rush it.

He flew for twenty minutes along the mountains knowing that somewhere below another anti-aircraft gun emplacement could knock him out of the sky with little effort. Suddenly, the fire warning light stopped flashing. He wondered what had happened. Could the fire have gone out on its own? He decided to ignore it for the moment. He had almost enough altitude to make it over the mountains. He didn't want to change his strategy even though it required great patience.

A few minutes later, he banked his aircraft and cleared the mountain ridge. Once over, he dipped the nose of his aircraft down and picked up speed. Still no fire warning light. So far, so good… or the warning light could have broken. He looked down at the foothills leading to the rice fields beyond. He thought about the best place to ditch his aircraft. The hills provided some cover, but he would be harder to find. The rice fields were just the opposite. Landing near a city was his best hope. The ARVN controlled the cities, even at night. He looked at his map. Da Nang airbase was not that far away. As long as nothing dramatic happened, the lieutenant thought he could make it. But then again… the Kitty Hawk was not that much farther. He wondered if he was being stupid and pushing his luck. It would be good to make it back to his squadron. He would complete his mission by returning with the reconnaissance film. He decided to go for it. It might cost him his life, but he took that risk every day he flew.

He radioed ahead to let the Kitty Hawk know what was happening. The fire crews would be ready. The fire warning lights behavior concerned him. Maybe the fire was out or maybe not… Fire was like that sometimes. It could hide like a predator and then start up again without warning.

He thought about opening the canopy once his wheels touched down. At landing speed, it would most likely be caught by the wind and torn away. He decided against it. Too much risk of something unexpected happening. The Crusader did not maneuver well on the ground. No sense in making it hard to control the aircraft even if it did save him a few precious seconds where the fire could get him. He thought about how to climb out of the aircraft once he had landed if the fire restarted while he was on the deck. It would only take seconds for the fire crew to reach the aircraft and put out any fire. He would move toward them and away from the burning aircraft. Would they reach him in time if he was on fire? If it was bad, would he want them to? He wanted to live, but he had seen pictures of fire victims. Would he want to live like that?

He looked down as he approached the coastline. The sea. He had made it that far. Only a dozen miles to go before reaching home. The tower was already calling him and giving him landing instructions. He tried to focus, listening to the air controller's voice as he had done so many times before. Images of fire rolled through his mind. Uncontrollable. He closed his eyes for a moment and cleared his head.

He opened his eyes. The Kitty Hawk was down there. It's long flight deck stretching out. A postage stamp from where he was, but he knew it would be bigger as he descended. He could see the sailors running around, getting into position. He spotted the fire crews. He wanted them as close as possible but that was not something he could control. Now things were happening fast, he let his training take over and fly the aircraft. Hundreds of landings. This was just another. He lowered his arresting hook. Oh, God… what if he missed. He forced the thought from his mind. Too many other things to focus on.

The Crusader slammed down on the deck. The hook caught on the cable. The aircraft jerked to a halt. He was home. He was safe. And then he saw it. Down around his feet. Flames licking at his boots. Was he imagining it? Or was it real? He didn't wait to find out. He opened the canopy, unbuckled his harness, and lifted himself. The flames climbed up toward the oxygen. He could feel the heat. The fire was real. It was awake and it wanted him.

He leaned over the edge of the cockpit and let himself fall onto the wing. He looked at his ankles. His flight suit was on fire. His boots were on fire. He was burning. He pushed himself onto his side and rolled down the wing until he fell on the deck. He was burning. He felt no pain and wondered where it was hiding like the fire. Waiting to hit him with its full force. He looked over and saw men in silver running toward him. White clouds burst from a black nozzle. The fire crew. They were there just like they were supposed to be. They would save him. He was sure of it. The white cloud enveloped him. He couldn't see anything. He didn't want to see. He just let them do their job. They would save him. The clouds cleared. He saw the conning tower above him. The flags waving. Men stared out over the railing, looking down on him. Was he burned? Was that what they were looking at? Medics swarmed around him, lifting him onto a wire stretcher, and carrying him away through a doorway into the darkness.

He panicked. He didn't know what was happening. Then the pain. His legs. The fire had gotten him. It felt like a razor cutting away the skin on his ankles and calves. He wanted to scream. He wanted to see the damage but was afraid. Him afraid? He was a fighter pilot. He was in the ship's medical bay. Doctors in white masks. His eyes were wide. Someone gave him a shot. Everything went blurry and he was out. The pain was gone.

Lieutenant Klusmann woke a few hours later. His lower legs were wrapped in gauze. A sickening yellow goop was seeping through the bandages. A corpsman came in and said, "You're awake. That's good."

"My legs?" Klusmann said, afraid of the answer.

"You're alright. Third-degree burns, but you'll survive. The docs here are real good at that kinda stuff."

"I'll walk?"

"Walk? Sure. Hell, you can run if you want to. Just give your wounds a couple of weeks to heal… and avoid any beauty pageants."

The corpsman was making jokes. Klusmann felt better. The panic was gone. He had survived. He would fly again.

May 27, 1964 – White House, Washington DC, USA

President Johnson sat down for lunch with Senator Richard Russell at the White House. It was considered an honor to be invited to the President's official home, especially to dine. The White House chef and his staff were more than capable of putting together an official dinner for 500 guests. The sandwiches that Johnson and Russel had requested were hardly a challenge but were delicious nonetheless.

Russel could see that Johnson seemed distracted and said, "Got a lot on your mind?"

"Goes with the territory, I guess," said Johnson.

"Anything I can help you with?"

"Nah. It's nothing I can't handle. I just gotta think through it."

"The war in Vietnam?"

"What else? My advisors are telling me to show some power and more force. Thing is… I don't think the American people are behind an expansion of the war."

"I agree with them. We don't have any business fighting a war that is not ours to fight and I doubt bombing the North is going to have much of an effect."

"Yeah. There ain't nothing to bomb up there. Industry is almost non-existent. The Soviets and the Chinese are providing them all the weapons they need, plus tractors and trains."

"So, what are you going to do?"

"I don't know. I can't seem to get anything important done while we're fighting in southeast Asia. It's not what I wanted. It's not why I wanted to be president. I wanna help Americans, not Vietnamese. But I don't know how to get out of the war. Congress would impeach me if I pull out."

"You really believe that?"

"Yeah, I do.

"I don't know how in the hell I'm gonna get out unless the Senate Republicans tell me to get out. I don't think South Vietnam is worth fighting for and I don't think I can get out. It's just the biggest damn mess I ever saw."

Johnson lost his appetite and pushed half a sandwich away in frustration, then said, "Can't even enjoy a damn roast beef sandwich without Vietnam fucking it up."

"You gonna eat that?" said Russell finishing his sandwich.

Johnson laughed, grateful for Russell's sense of humor.

Saigon, South Vietnam

Coyle and Granier watched a South Vietnamese mechanic assemble a remote firing switch for the machine gun in the C-47 gunship prototype. It was a mechanical device made of wires and pulleys allowing the pilot in the cockpit to fire the machine gun out the cargo door by pulling a ring on the end of a wire. It was crude, but it worked. That was all that was needed at the moment.

Coyle had already rigged up a gun sight out the pilot's side window. It was a piece of glass with crosshairs painted on it. The glass could be adjusted to align the crosshairs with the tracers hitting the target below. Again, it was crude but did the job.

By the time the mechanic finished up, it was too late in the day for a test flight. Coyle and Granier decided to try out their new gadgets early the next morning. Coyle paid the mechanic and they buttoned up the aircraft. Granier loaded up a wide-mouth shovel and an empty drum with the top cut off. "What are they for?" said Coyle.

"Expended shell casings. It can get a bit perilous

near the open doorway with brass rolling around on the deck," said Granier.

"I never saw you as a soldier that worried about that kind of stuff."

"I ain't normally. But I'd like to see this to the end. I can't do that if I fall out of the aircraft."

"Good thinking."

The next morning, they flew out to their makeshift test range with new gasoline drums. They placed the drums ten feet apart in a staggered formation, then checked to ensure that there was enough leftover gasoline in each of the drums to make an explosion. Any drum that was a bit too dry got a quick refill. It wasn't really about the gasoline as much as the fumes it produced. They left the cap off each of the drums open so some air could get in and mix with the fumes.

They climbed into the aircraft. Coyle taxied to the end of the runway, turned around, then took off.

They reached the right altitude in a couple of minutes and Coyle put the aircraft into a pylon turn. They were both anxious to see if their inventions worked. Using the wire attached to a ring, Coyle lined up the crosshairs with the drums below and fired a couple of bursts. He watched the path of the tracer rounds, then realigned his homemade sight. "Remote trigger works pretty good, don't it?" shouted Granier from the back of the plane.

"It's a little hinky but nothing we can't adjust back in the hangar," Coyle shouted back.

"Damned perfectionist," said Granier to himself.

Coyle lined up the crosshairs again and fired a long burst.

On the ground, all three drums were pierced with multiple tracers rounds and blew up.

Happy with the results, Coyle and Granier both shouted with joy mixed with a few expletives to put an exclamation point on it. Granier cleaned up the brass with his shovel and dumped the casings into the open drum. Coyle lined up the aircraft and fired into the drums already burning and on their sides. It wasn't nearly as dramatic, but he could see that the weapon system was working just fine. They headed back to the airbase.

Forty minutes later, they were sitting in a go-go bar, sipping beer. Beer loosened them up after work and allowed them to brainstorm more easily as long as they didn't drink too much. "I've been thinking," said Granier.

"That's dangerous," said Coyle.

"Why only one machine gun?"

"Cause that's all we got."

"I could get more."

"To what end?"

"A single machine gun will keep the enemy's head down but probably won't do much damage, especially if they're hidden in the jungle. It feels like we need more punch to make a real difference."

"You mean like a B-26 Invader?"

"Yeah. You know, lay down more lead on the target."

"Eight machine guns firing in unison seems like a bit of overkill for our purposes. We're firing sideways, not in front of the aircraft."

"Okay, so… not eight. How about two or three?"

"Three sounds good, but it's gonna get a bit

crowded in the doorway."

"So, let's not mount them in the doorway. How about the side portals? We could remove the windows."

"That might work. It would be one hell of sight at night. Tracer rounds from three machine guns firing in unison."

"That would strike fear into them… if they survived."

"It would break them up, that's for sure."

"That's what we want to do. Break them up when they attack in force."

"Yeah. I like it. Three's good. Maybe a smaller caliber."

"Yeah. M1s. I'll see what I can scrounge up."

"I'll work on some sort of mounting device. A tripod won't work for the portals. It's too low. Maybe some sort of pedestal."

They clicked their bottles. They had a plan.

It only took a few days to come up with a new working prototype using three machine guns all firing in unison off the left side of the aircraft. It wasn't pretty. Everything was jerry-rigged. But that wasn't the point. Killing Viet Cong and saving hamlets was the point.

This time, they brought nine empty gasoline drums and placed them more randomly along the side of the runway similar to how a squad of troops might be positioned.

High above the runway, Coyle put the aircraft in a pylon turn. He fired each machine gun to align the tracer rounds. It was Granier's job to readjust the machine guns so they aligned with Coyle's crosshairs. It took a lot longer to align them and the three weapons were not nearly as accurate as one. But as they had hoped, the pattern was wider and that meant more enemies killed.

After multiple test runs, Coyle was ready for the final test. He lined up his sight and let loose a long barrage. The noise from three machine guns firing in unison was deafening. In pain, Granier dropped his shovel and covered his ears. Brass landed on the deck and rolled around wildly.

Below, the bullets produced a wide path of divots along the runway, chewing up the asphalt. All nine drums were hit with tracer rounds and blew up.

When finished, they landed and examined the results. The drums were punctured in multiple places and burned. Coyle and Granier were both surprised by the destructive power of the weapon they had created. They smiled widely and their eyes lit up. The dragon was born.

June 4, 1964 – White House - Washington DC, USA

Ambassador Lodge knew that his time in Vietnam was coming to an end. Kennedy had talked Lodge into accepting the ambassadorship of South Vietnam. It was a difficult post. He was unpopular with his embassy staff which made his job all the more difficult.

Vice-President Johnson and Lodge had disagreed about supporting the coup that would eventually lead to South Vietnamese President Diem's assassination. Johnson did not want to change horses in mid-stream without knowing who would replace Diem. He thought the American military should just get on with fighting the war and not worry so much about South

Vietnamese politics. Lodge saw Diem and his family as a detriment to winning the war. Diem was very unpopular with the South Vietnamese population, especially after he punished and attacked the Buddhists. Lodge had wanted Diem and his family gone.

Now that Johnson was president, Lodge had lost interest in Vietnam. He was planning a run against Johnson for the presidency. But Lodge felt it was his duty to offer his opinion on the expansion of the war. He sent a cable to Johnson recommending that he not send more ground troops to South Vietnam. He cautioned that such a step could become a "venture of unlimited possibilities which could put us onto a slope along which we slide into a bottomless pit."

Johnson agreed with Lodge's assessment but didn't see any other path to ending the war except for expansion. The Viet Cong were not just going to give up and neither were the North Vietnamese and their Chinese allies. Johnson was concerned that bombing Hanoi directly or putting more American soldiers into South Vietnam could trigger the Chinese into entering the war as they had done in Korea. Johnson did not want another Korea, but he wasn't willing to let the communists continue their expansion without resistance. America was in until the war was won, or a satisfactory peace treaty could be negotiated. It seemed like both the Americans and the Chinese were stepping on eggshells trying to prevent the other side from entering the war but unwilling to end the war through capitulation.

Johnson realized that Lodge would most likely seek the Republican nomination and run against him for the presidency. He didn't want to give Lodge any more political ammunition than he already had. It was time for Lodge to go.

Johnson needed a strong replacement for Lodge. He needed someone that understood the situation and commanded respect. He chose the military's chief of staff, General Maxwell Taylor. Taylor knew what Johnson wanted – to expand the war without committing ground troops. Like Johnson, Taylor questioned how much of an effect bombing in the North would have on the communist, but he saw it as a good first step. The problem Taylor had was that Johnson didn't want to change the overall strategy until after the presidential election. Johnson didn't feel he had a mandate from the people since he had inherited the presidency on Kennedy's death and was not elected. Once he won the election, he would be free to do what he thought proper in Vietnam and the people would be behind him.

But the election was still a long way off and with the South Vietnamese generals fighting for political power, the military was in shambles. Leaderless, ARVN morale had been decimated and the Viet Cong were taking advantage of the chaos. The ARVN forces were losing the equivalent of one battalion per week from Viet Cong assaults. The Viet Cong were attacking the South Vietnamese hundreds of times each month. More than forty percent of the countryside and fifty percent of the people were under the control of the Viet Cong. Taylor didn't feel there would even be a South Vietnam after the American presidential election if things continued the way they were going. The American military needed to act now if it was going to save South Vietnam. On July 1, 1964, Taylor took over the South Vietnamese ambassadorship and Lodge soon left Vietnam returning to the United States. It was Taylor's turn in the cauldron. "It's going to be hell in a handbasket out there," said Taylor.

"I want the South Vietnamese to get off their butts and get out into those jungles and whip the hell out of some communists," said Johnson. "And then I want them to leave me alone because I've got bigger things to do right here at home."

Even though Johnson did not feel he could expand the war until after the election, he asked Bundy, his national security advisor, to draft a resolution to Congress that would give him authority to take further action when the time was right. Depending on events, Johnson wanted the ability to move quickly if required. He told Bundy, "I want it like Grandma's nightshirt, it needs to cover everything."

June 18, 1964 – Hanoi, North Vietnam

At the request of US Ambassador Taylor, Canadian diplomat Blair Seaborn arrived in Hanoi. Taylor wanted to reach out one last time to attempt to end the war without further carnage. Seaborn carried a message from the American Ambassador to the North Vietnamese prime minister Pham Van Dong - The US was determined to win the war against the communists, and it would expand the conflict rather than withdraw unless the North Vietnamese removed their support of the Viet Cong. But Seaborn's mission was more than just an errand boy. The Americans wanted to know the North Vietnamese state of mind concerning the war. They wanted to size up their opponent and were using the Canadian diplomat for reconnaissance. It didn't take long.

Prime Minister Dong responded that any peaceful settlement of the conflict had to result in the United States withdrawing its forces, the neutralization of South Vietnam, and the eventual reunification of North and South Vietnam. Seaborn was convinced that the leaders in North Vietnam had concluded that military action at any level was not going to bring success to the American and South Vietnamese forces. The Prime Minister emphasized the quiet determination of the North Vietnamese to carry on the struggle as long as necessary to achieve complete victory. North Vietnam was a vicious and resolute enemy that could never be defeated as long as one North Vietnamese remained alive.

Returning to Saigon before going back to Canada, Seaborn spent an entire day being debriefed by the American Ambassador, the CIA station chief, and the generals of MACV. He was bombarded with questions about what he saw and heard, but most importantly what he felt about North Vietnam and the prime minister. In the last couple of years, the CIA and South Vietnam intelligence had been unable to successfully place spies in Hanoi even though they had attempted it multiple times. This indicated a mole in the intelligence service that had not yet been discovered. Seaborn was a fresh set of eyes and relatively unbiased. Even though his diplomatic mission was a failure, the information he brought was invaluable. Canada was an American ally but did not want to get involved in the Vietnam War. The Canadians would help where they could, but they had limits. The information that Seaborn offered was meant to help end the war without further bloodshed. He too was naïve.

New York, New York, USA

The New York Times published the remarks of US military advisor Colonel Wilbur Wilson stationed in South Vietnam. Wilson didn't pull any punches when he stated that the Viet Cong were stronger and better armed than they had been three years earlier during his last assignment in the Central Highlands. He further stated that ninety percent of the Viet Cong's weapons were made by the United States, captured from ARVN forces. Wilson advocated that the only way to win the war was a massive expansion of the US military commitment in South Vietnam.

As much as the White House and the US Embassy in Saigon hated reading the colonel's comments in a prominent American newspaper, nobody denied that he was telling the truth. They just didn't want to admit it. Something needed to change before it was too late.

More and more politicians were concluding that something drastic needed to happen before it was too late but there was no way America could withdraw without losing face internationally and putting its relationship with its southeast Asian allies at risk. Republican Congressman Gerald Ford said that the US military should take command of all the military forces in Vietnam and not simply remain advisors. He failed to recognize that the generals in charge of the South Vietnamese government and military might have something to say about that. Ford's comments which were posted in multiple media outlets did not help the strained relationship between the US and their most important ally in southeast Asia. At times, it seemed that America's worst enemy was itself along with its headline-seeking politicians.

As always, the French were quick to criticize and offer up their opinions on the correct way to run the war. French Foreign Minister Maurice Couve de Murville appeared on the NBC news show *Meet the Press* and cautioned that America could not win the war even if it increased its involvement. "This is not an ordinary war," he said. "That means a war you can just settle by victory or defeat. It's not that simple… the problem cannot be settled by military means but should be settled by political means."

WESTY

June 20, 1964 – Saigon, South Vietnam

William Childs Westmoreland wanted to go to Vietnam even though he knew it was a military and political quagmire. Like most generals, he longed to command a large number of troops in the field. At that moment, Vietnam was the biggest battlefield in the world. After a distinguished military career, it seemed like an appropriate challenge for a man of his reputation and experience. He knew how to command troops and win wars. He felt it was his duty to go and do his best for his country.

An Eagle Boy Scout, West Point graduate as First Captain, and a recipient of the Pershing Sword for highest military proficiency, Westmoreland excelled at everything he did. After West Point, he became an artillery officer in the US Army and was given command of his own battery. In World War II, he fought in Tunisia, Sicily, France, and Germany. His career path was meteoric. Within eight years of graduation from West Point, he was promoted to colonel and became Chief of Staff of the 9th Infantry Division. When World War II ended, Westmoreland became a paratrooper and was given command of a regiment in the 82nd Airborne Division. During the Korean War, he commanded a combat regiment in the 101st Airborne Division. At the age of thirty-eight, he was promoted to brigadier general making him one of the youngest generals in the U.S. Army. And he was just getting warmed up…

In 1954, Westmoreland completed a management program at Harvard Business School. Not only an accomplished warrior, "Westy was a corporate executive in uniform," noted the historian, Stanley Karnow. After serving as the US Army Secretary of the General Staff under Maxwell Taylor, Westmoreland was given command of the 101st Airborne Division, then made the superintendent of West Point. Three years later, he was promoted to lieutenant general and given command of the XVIII Airborne Corps.

In 1964 at the age of forty-nine, Westmoreland was sent to Vietnam and made the deputy commander of MACV under General Harkins. Knowing Westmoreland's reputation, Harkins could already see the writing on the wall. He was to be replaced by the young general. It only took six months. Just enough time for Westmoreland to get the lay of the land and meet the right people. Harkins liked Westmoreland and he didn't envy his assignment since the South Vietnamese generals had taken over the government and were battling for power amongst themselves. Westmoreland was being dropped into a cauldron of chaos and Harkins knew it.

Harkins had fallen out of favor near the end of the Kennedy administration. It was his rosy assessment of the battle of Ap Bac that finally did him in. Because the enemy left the battlefield, Harkins had called it a victory for South Vietnam, but the world knew otherwise. The Viet Cong had kicked the ARVN and the Americans in the ass. Having supported Harkins's assessment, JFK was embarrassed. It didn't take more than that before rumors began about the search for Harkins's replacement.

When word of Westmoreland being assigned as his deputy reached Harkins, he knew it was over. A general with Westmoreland's experience and resume was not meant to be a deputy. Harkins knew it was time to leave and accepted his fate. Vietnam had not been an easy assignment and it certainly had not produced the glory he had obtained during World War II. When Harkins finally left Vietnam, he retired and took up a hobby – painting. Pouring himself into it, he became quite accomplished at it.

It was Chief of Staff General Taylor that had handpicked Westmoreland for Harkins's job. Many in the Pentagon did not agree with Taylor's choice. They thought Westmoreland was too concerned about what the government wanted and did not show enough concern for what the military needed to win the war. Westmoreland was similar to Harkins in many ways. They both had a tendency of spinning facts to support their assessments. But Taylor knew that President Johnson was going to expand the war and he wanted an experienced, well-organized commander in charge of Vietnam. He wanted a commander that would fight with aggression and determination. Westmoreland was Airborne and Airborne knew how to lean into a battle.

Westmoreland would be given an enormous amount of power when he became the leader of MACV. The field commander of US forces in Vietnam, the most powerful military in the world. Having worked with Westmoreland, Taylor trusted him with such a responsibility and had faith that the young general would find a way to win where others had failed.

If there was one thing that concerned Taylor about his new commander, it was that Westy seemed a little too confident and unbending. Once he made his mind up on the correct path, Westy was like an intercontinental missile, fixed on its target until its mission was completed. But that wouldn't matter as long as Westmoreland chose the correct path. Taylor knew he was throwing Westmoreland into the arena, but that was where Westmoreland did his best work… under fire.

Most of the officers that had previously worked for Westmoreland saw him as a Southern gentleman and a team player. Johnson had liked that about him. Johnson wanted a commander that stuck to the plan and didn't veer off to promote his own interests. Harkins had veered off from time to time to promote his career interests. He had caused problems for Kennedy. Johnson learned from the former president's mistakes. The new president was far more scrupulous about the commander of the Vietnam War. Adamant about avoiding conflict of interest, Westmoreland did not vote during his military career. Johnson liked that too. No political competition.

When asked by Johnson, Secretary of Defense McNamara said Westmoreland was "the best we have, without question." The fact that Johnson and McNamara had no experience commanding large numbers of troops in the field didn't seem to make much difference. They believed they could judge Westmoreland by his character and that was enough.

Before leaving for Vietnam, Westmoreland had told

Johnson that he didn't believe they needed troops on the ground to win the war. It was more a matter of motivating the South Vietnamese military into doing its job and fighting to save its homeland. He needed the ARVN generals to stop playing politics and focus on the war. Westmoreland felt he could give them the needed kick in the ass. But he did believe that America needed to expand its efforts through the bombing of the North and more military advisors. He wanted to create pressure to make the North give up its assistance to the Viet Cong, but he didn't want to risk more American lives if it could be helped. Westy's strategy aligned with the president. If Johnson had any qualms about Westmoreland, he chose not to reveal them and gave him his full support.

When Westmoreland arrived in Vietnam, he wasted no time in beginning his assessment of the military situation. He spent much of his time in planes and helicopters touring the areas where the enemy was most active and talking with the American advisors about the situation and what they thought was needed.

He also talked with the South Vietnamese field commanders and was impressed by some, but not all of them. He could see that some of the commanders were more interested in preserving the lives of their men than winning the war. To Westmoreland, that was not a good attitude for a field commander, and it concerned him. He needed commanders that wanted to get at the enemy. Strangely, some of the ARVN commanders saw the Viet Cong as rebels that had chosen the wrong path and needed to be convinced to change their direction, not killed outright. It was a nice thought but not the way to win a war. Westmoreland could see that the Vietnamese culture was different than American culture which was far more aggressive when it came to war. The Vietnamese believed in second chances, even for their enemies. It was not a good sign.

When backed into a corner or pressured to perform, the Vietnamese would often lash out in cruel ways and think little of the moral implications of their actions. They were far from barbarians, but they could be barbaric at times. That too was troubling, but for different reasons. The Americans wanted the ARVN to be professional soldiers, not renegades. The Vietnamese had been fighting for survival for over a thousand years and were set in their ways. It would be difficult to change them… maybe impossible.

Lastly, Westmoreland realized that the ARVN field commanders were still being promoted for their loyalty to those generals above them and not for the victories in battle that they had attained. This was sending them the wrong signal and heavily affecting their decisions in the field. Being an aggressive warrior was less important than being loyal and conserving the lives of those under your command. To Westmoreland, the attitude felt soft. A good commander needed to put his troops in harm's way at times. That was the job and why he had been chosen to lead in the first place.

As he began to understand the Vietnamese culture and what was happening in the field, Westmoreland changed his strategy to win the war. It would require more than he had originally thought.

To Westmoreland, the ARVN forces still seemed poorly trained when in the field fighting. The ARVN forces could fight the Viet Cong in and around the big cities, but once they moved into the mountains and jungles they were easily ambushed. The solution was that the ARVN commanders kept their forces away from the Viet Cong strongholds. Much like the North Vietnamese and Viet Cong strategy, the ARVN would only fight when they were sure they could win, and even then, they demanded artillery and the air force do most of the heavy lifting before their ground forces engaged the enemy. It was not a good strategy to win a war, but it did save the lives of South Vietnamese soldiers.

After months of watching the ARVN forces shirk from battle, Westmoreland decided on a new strategy – victory thru attrition. The ARVN would continue to fight the Viet Cong in and around cities. They would continue to use their artillery and airpower to inflict heavy casualties on the enemy and reduce their resources. The ARVN would also be responsible for protecting military installations such as airbases, supply depots, and command posts. Once the Viet Cong were driven from the heavily populated areas, the ARVN could focus their forces on retaking the countryside and reestablishing the government throughout South Vietnam. It was an important role and one that the ARVN could handle.

It was the Americans that would spearhead the fight against the enemy with large search and destroy missions in the jungles and mountains. They would force the enemy to fight and when they did, the Americans would use their superior airpower and artillery to pound the enemy and inflict the heavy losses they sought. When the enemy ran, they would pursue them forcing them to engage, again and again, each time forcing them to take more and more losses.

The Americans would build a series of fire bases through the Central Highlands and near the border.

Each fire base supported its neighboring fire bases and the troops in the field. Most of the fire bases were built on hilltops with the use of helicopters to bring in weapons, equipment, and supplies. The bases were well-protected with layers of wire, mines, interconnecting trenches, and blockhouses. The American engineers built heavily reinforced structures for command posts, artillery and mortar pits, hospitals, and three layers of sandbags around machine gun positions. An unmovable wall of firepower stretching across the country from west to east. If the enemy chose to attack the fire bases, the Americans would use the same strategy and pound them with artillery and airpower inflicting heavy casualties. Forcing the Viet Cong into battle, the Americans planned on punishing the enemy into submission. Eventually, the communists would reach the point where they would no longer be able to replace their losses on the battlefield and they would agree to a reasonable peace settlement. The war would finally end and America could focus its resources on Johnson's Great Society.

To pull it off, Westmoreland would need a lot more resources, such as artillery, aircraft, helicopters, armor, and most importantly... boots on the ground. It was a big ask.

Johnson's initial response was "No," but he knew deep down the only way to win was to take the fight to the enemy. It's why he had agreed to Westmoreland. He wanted an aggressive commander to end the war. But boots on the ground seemed like a point of no return once he crossed the line. It felt like there would be no way to stop it. At that moment, most Americans supported the war effort to stop communist expansion. But how would the American public feel once coffins filled with the bodies of dead soldiers started arriving by aircraft? Front pages of newspapers and magazines would be dominated by photos of military funerals with crying wives being handed folded flags and twenty-one-gun salutes. It had happened during World War II and in Korea, but this seemed different. Americans knew nothing of Vietnam and the battlefields with names they couldn't pronounce. They would soon learn.

Most of the battles during the Vietnam War involved units with less than 200 soldiers. The battles were sharp and produced a large number of casualties in just a few minutes. Most battles only last an hour or two before one of the combatants broke off… usually the Viet Cong as American artillery and airpower came into use. Bigger and longer conflicts were more publicized by the media but were fewer and far between. The Americans and South Vietnamese tended to do better in the larger battles and therefore gave the public a lopsided view of what was really happening during the war. The Viet Cong knew the terrain far better and were masters at setting bobby traps and ambushes. And most important of all, the Viet Cong owned the night and during the day they mixed with the civilians. How do you fight when you can't tell who is the enemy?

June 29, 1964 – Tan Son Nhut Air Base, South Vietnam

As it had done with Australia which had already committed military advisors to South Vietnam, the

United States put pressure on New Zealand to meet their obligations under the ANZUS Treaty. New Zealand responded by sending a twenty-five-man engineering unit to Tan Son Nhut Air Base where they would join an American advisory team. The two teams were to be based in Thu Dau Mot, the capital of Binh Duong Province.

While the American advisors worked with local forces and the ARVN units in the area, the New Zealand engineers were tasked with rebuilding roads and bridges that had been sabotaged by the Viet Cong. It was not particularly hard duty or even dangerous since they were well-protected by the local militias, but it did show a commitment to preventing communist expansion which is what the American military wanted. It was a symbolic assignment, but the New Zealanders did their duty and rebuilt infrastructure whenever required. Every bit helped in a country constantly devastated by war.

As part of the US "Many Flags" program, Australia had committed military advisors in 1962 and played an active role in fighting the Viet Cong. With the arrival of the Australians, the Chinese and North Vietnamese could no longer claim that the government of South Vietnam was a puppet regime of the US. Because of their experience gained during the Malayan Emergency, the Australians were good fighters, especially in the jungles and mountains. The Australians also had success at recruiting and training a force of Montagnard in the Central Highlands. Unfortunately, this made the ARVN commander in the area angry. He did not like foreigners undermining his battalion's own efforts to recruit the tribesmen.

Known for their stubbornness, the Australians ignored him.

Both the Australians and New Zealanders ended up fighting in Vietnam and lost a substantial number of soldiers. Like the US, anti-war moments were active in both countries and protested throughout the war. The Australian and New Zealand military stuck with the US until the Americans finally left. The Australians and New Zealanders returned home about the same time.

Hanoi, North Vietnam

Le Duan faced a similar problem to his American counterpart. Like Johnson, Duan wanted to expand the war in order to end it. He could see that the Americans would soon arrive in Vietnam in force. Duan wanted a quick and decisive victory before they arrived. But just as Johnson had political enemies that want to keep the US out of the war, Duan had members of the politburo that wanted to be patient and let South Vietnam collapse from its own incompetence. Ho Chi Minh and General Giap did not believe that expanding the war was a good idea. They believed it could cause America to join the fight sooner and with more resources. Like an unknowing frog, they proposed placing the Americans into a pot of cold water and slowly increasing the temperature until it reached a boiling point at which time it would be too late and South Vietnam would already be lost. "Never interrupt your enemy when he is making a mistake," warned Giap.

But Le Duan did not have the patience to wait. He saw the opportunity to win the war right now. The two sides debated back in forth for weeks. Duan finally convinced enough of his fellow members to follow him. A vote was taken and Le Duan won. North Vietnam would go to war and invade the South in hopes of toppling the government and preventing heavier US involvement. Ho Chi Minh was disappointed, but he also understood it was time to pass the baton to the younger generation of leaders that Le Duan represented. It would be their war and their country once it was won. As long as the two nations were reunited under one government, Ho Chi Minh was happy.

With a new, stronger mandate, Le Duan ordered that large numbers of North Vietnamese troops immediately begin their journey south on the Ho Chi Minh Trail through Laos.

Vietnam/Laotian Border

White mist rolled over the highest peak of a mountain range near the Vietnam/Laotian border. Since the successful raid on the truck park and weapons depot, Blackjack and his team were tasked with finding more targets to attack with a focus on curtailing convoys on the Ho Chi Minh Trail. The easiest way to do that was to find a pass into South Vietnam used by the North Vietnamese, then backtrack until they encountered a distribution area and supply depot.

The North Vietnamese were constantly shifting loads depending on the needs of the Viet Cong in different regions of South Vietnam. They also broke up larger shipments into small shipments, like a box of grenades or mortar shells split into two or three. It seemed to the North Vietnamese that there were never enough supplies to fulfill the Viet Cong's requests.

When the SOG team found what it was looking for, they would call in their Montagnard warriors. Together they would assault the North Vietnamese camp, destroy the weapons and supplies, then seal off the pass leading into South Vietnam. It would slow the North Vietnamese but not stop them. They would simply replace the weapons and supplies, then find another path through the mountains. That was the most Blackjack and his men could hope for… slowing down the river of supplies and weapons pouring into South Vietnam.

As they were backtracking from a pass, Blackjack and his team encountered a larger number of North Vietnamese soldiers than usual guarding a caravan of supplies and weapons. It seemed overkill by two to three times. The North Vietnamese were known for throwing manpower at problems but this seemed ridiculous even for them. And the North Vietnamese soldiers didn't seem to be the same quality of troops that usually guarded the convoys. These new troops were far more disciplined and better armed. They were elite. After several days of watching the convoy and its guards, one of the SOG team members said, "So, Boss. What do you think they're guarding? It must be pretty important cargo."

"They're not guarding any cargo," said Blackjack. "They are the cargo."

"I don't understand. They're NVA, aren't they?"

"The game's changed. The NVA are entering South Vietnam. Hanoi has chosen to expand the war."

"So, what do we do?"

"We start counting. We've got to figure out how many and how fast before we report in. But I can guarantee you one thing…"

"What's that?"

"All hell is about to break loose and we're gonna be right in the middle of it."

The SOG team broke into two teams to cover more territory. Their job was simply to count soldiers and analyze intervals of soldiers entering the pass. They needed to get a handle on the size of the new problem. When the results were correlated, Blackjack and his men were surprised. The number of troops on the trail had increased five-fold from the normal string of replacements. This was a major shift in strategy from Hanoi.

Blackjack and the SOG team hauled ass back to their camp and radioed in what they had found. The news shook up some of the commanders. Some questioned the accuracy of the SOG team's intel. It had to be an exaggeration… it just had to be. Through the embassy in Vientiane, the Joint Chiefs at the Pentagon ordered Blackjack and his men to go back out and confirm the intel. Blackjack knew better than to argue. He would play the game and confirm intel that he already knew was correct. He would take his Montagnard warriors with him. If a firefight broke out in the mountains, he and his team would need the extra firepower the Montagnard brought to the battlefield. Whatever was happening was not business as usual and Blackjack wanted to be prepared.

As always, the Montagnard warriors said their goodbyes to their lovers, children, and parents. A small ten-man contingent, mostly warriors still recovering from their wounds, was left behind to protect the village with the weapons the SOG had given them including a 60 mm mortar and a light machine gun located near the main entrance to the village.

Blackjack knew that by agreeing to fight for the Americans, the Montagnard were risking their own lives, but also those of their families. He made sure they were protected, especially when the warriors were out on missions with his team. He left a radio and trained a few of the wives of the warriors to use the gadget and call for help if needed. The SOG communication center in Vientiane continually monitored the emergency channels designated for the Montagnard and could respond with militia from neighboring villages and air support if needed.

The agreement between the Montagnard and the Americans was not one-sided. To make up for the absence of so many men, the Americans supplied food to the village. They also built a school for the children, many of which had never had any education. The Americans also paid the salary of the schoolteacher and supplies including books, paper, and pencils. The Montagnard were grateful that their children could receive an education that was normally reserved for rich people. In turn, the children taught their parents how to read, write, and perform arithmetic. Education lifted the entire village. Medics made regular visits to the village and inoculated the Montagnard to protect them from diseases like polio, chicken pox, and measles. Health aid workers were also flown in to help improve the sanitation in the village and dig wells for cleaner water.

The longer he stayed with the Montagnard, the more Blackjack felt like the Americans were taking advantage of the tribesmen. The Americans were buying off the Montagnard with trinkets of aid. The villagers just didn't know any better. Blackjack felt guilty. He tried to reassure himself that the Montagnard were better off if communism stayed out of Southeast Asia. But he wasn't sure. When you've got nothing, who cares about politics and government? He told himself that it wasn't up to him to tell the Montagnard what they should or shouldn't do. He was their advisor, not their leader.

The Hatchet team which included the SOG team and the Montagnard warriors set out early the next morning on a mission that Blackjack saw as a waste of time and resources. Despite their feelings, the SOG were elite soldiers and would obey the commands they were given. The sooner they could confirm the intel and get on with operations meant to stop the North Vietnamese infiltration, the better. With the help of the Montagnard, Blackjack was able to carry his cumbersome long-range radio set up into the mountains. This would allow him to convey his findings to SOG command without returning to the village. They could stay in the field longer.

Returning to the mountain pass where the North Vietnamese soldiers were crossing over into Vietnam, Blackjack split his force into eight-man reconnaissance units each with a SOG team member as the leader, and sent them in different directions to confirm what he already knew.

When the recon units returned after several days, Blackjack correlated the intel and was surprised by his findings. Not only were the North Vietnamese soldiers heading into South Vietnam, but their numbers had vastly increased since the first count a week ago. What was once a stream from a garden hose was now a blast from a firehose. The Montagnard had found parallel trails used by the North Vietnamese. They even found a second pass on the opposite side of the mountain peak. The North Vietnamese were pouring into South Vietnam. It was a serious enemy invasion.

The SOG team members and the Montagnard wanted to ambush the North Vietnamese columns. Blackjack wanted that too, but those weren't their orders. Their mission was recon only. They needed to get the new intel to SOG command as soon as possible. They were too close to the enemy to set up the radio's antenna. It would lead the North Vietnamese right to his team and they would be vastly outnumbered. Blackjack decided to set up the radio's antenna on the opposite slope of the next mountain range. It would be a tough trek, but Blackjack thought it would be worth it. He didn't want the North Vietnamese to know they were being watched. They could switch trails or passes and the team would lose track of them.

As the Hatchet team reached the valley below the mountain ridge and started up the opposite ridge, the clouds grew dark. That didn't mean much. The sky would often darken in a promise to cool the sun, only to open back up again to blue skies. Nature was unreliable in that part of the world.

Blackjack had been right… it was a hard trek, the slope steeper than its neighboring mountain ridge. The soil was looser and the vegetation thicker. Using their machetes, the Montagnard hacked their way up the mountain and the Americans followed. The SOG team had learned not to play tough guy. The Montagnard had lived in the mountains for centuries. They knew the terrain and how to deal with it. An American could spend an entire day and only travel a mile in the heavy bush. The Montagnard didn't fight the jungle like the Americans with their heavy backpacks. They were smaller and could slip under tree branches and tangles of vines with a few quick hacks from the machetes. It was much faster and less exhausting to simply follow the Montagnard when the jungle got thick and seemed impassable.

Halfway up the mountain, it began to rain. A sprinkle at first, it was welcomed. It cooled off the Americans and Montagnard. There was no such thing as reliable weather reports in Laos. Either it rained, or it didn't. The only way to see how heavy the rain would be was to wait and see. The size of the drops increased, and the spread between the drops grew tighter. The loose soil turned to mud. The foliage across the slope grew slippery. As the water flowing downward increased, the mountainside became more dangerous than the enemy. Slight waterfalls and streams turned to torrents pulling mud, vines, and rocks with them, making them impassable.

A Montagnard scout lost his footing and slid down the mountain grabbing at vines and branches. His feet found no traction. He crashed into others below him, knocking them from their feet, to join him on the slide downward. It was like a bad movie, a rolling rock turning into an avalanche. Broken rocks with sharp edges sliced at their arms, legs, and torsos. There was nothing they could do to protect themselves. It was all happening too fast, sliding uncontrollably. They were at the mercy of the slope. Before long, the slide of bodies reached the Americans and they too were knocked to the ground. In all, twenty-two soldiers slid down the mountain unable to stop. As the slope grew less steep, the soldiers slowed, some catching a branch or vine, grabbing their comrades as they slid past. The slide slowed to a stop. One of the Montagnard broke his back when he hit a boulder half-buried on the ground. He was in severe pain and unable to walk. Many of the warriors and SOG members were bleeding from gashes and compound fractures. The team was a mess. Non-operational.

With a deep cut on the side of his head, Blackjack was angry. Why risk his men to confirm intel that he already knew was correct? He took some solace that the increased troop count was new intel and would be useful. The SOG had worked hard to train and supply the Montagnard. But it all seemed like such a waste of talent and manpower. He wondered if the generals at the Pentagon understood the sacrifices that were being made. He wondered if generals even gave a damn.

Blackjack and his SOG team tended to their wounds and those of the Montagnard. One of the Montagnard scouts found a cave nearby. They moved the wounded into the cave. It smelled like mildew, but at least it was dry. After he was sure the Montagnard were being taken care of, Blackjack picked four warriors that had survived the slide unharmed and two of his SOG to head back up the mountain with the radio. He wasn't sure if the equipment had been damaged. He would find out when he attempted to radio his report.

Blackjack and his team climbed up the mountain. The rain was still coming down but it had slackened. It was still a tough climb up a slippery slope. He often felt it was three steps forward and two back. But it was progress and that is what he needed at the moment. As with most intel, the longer it was not reported, the less useful it became. When they finally reached the top of the ridge, Blackjack had the team continue another five hundred feet down the backside of the mountain before finding a place to set up the radio. The equipment seemed undamaged, but it was hard to tell with electronics. He switched the radio on and began broadcasting to the SOG communication center in Vientiane. He was relieved when he heard the operator on the other end respond. It worked.

He reported his intel including the higher troops count. He requested permission to attack the columns traveling over the two passes in hopes of slowing them down. His request was denied. SOG Command needed to report the intel to the Pentagon and devise a game plan before revealing the surveillance to the North Vietnamese forces. It didn't want to tip the enemy off until necessary and a SOG assault would tip them off.

Although he wouldn't reveal it to his team or command, Blackjack was relieved. The hatchet team was in no shape to attack the North Vietnamese. They needed to get their seriously wounded back to the village. It would take days. The wounded that were unable to walk and needed to be carried would slow them down and sap them of their energy. He ordered the team to pack up the gear. They would return with the others and help the wounded.

When they returned, they found that the Montagnard that had broken his back had taken his life with a knife. Blackjack wondered how that was possible since the warrior was paralyzed from the neck down, but he didn't voice his concerns. The Montagnard had done what was necessary for the good of the group. Blackjack believed the correct choice had been made. The jungle of Laos was harsh and required sacrifice from time to time for the village to survive. They would carry his body back with them so his family could pay their respects before he was buried. The village would mourn the hero as it should.

It was slow going back to the village. The hatchet team dared not take a straight route back to their home territory. They never knew who was watching or why. Instead, they twisted and turned. They took well-worn trails for a time then went off-path deep into the jungle and watched to make sure they weren't being followed. It wasn't a sure-fire method, but it helped keep the location of the village hidden.

On the final morning in the jungle, Blackjack set up his radio and called the communication center. He wanted to know if the intel had reached the Pentagon and if a decision had been made as to how to deal with the new influx of North Vietnamese soldiers. What he heard over the radio shook him to the core. A few hours after he had signed off from his last communiqué, the communication center had received a request for help from the Montagnard village. It was a woman shouting frantically in her native language. The operator didn't understand the words, but he knew the tone. She was terrified. Before he could find the Montagnard translator, the signal was lost. The operator had no clear idea what had happened or what type of help was needed. He reported the message to his commander, who immediately sent a reconnaissance plane to check on the village. It saw no activity in the village as it did its flyover, except for smoke from the smoldering huts. Blackjack signed off. He was alone and speechless. Tears welled up in his eyes. He was not the type of soldier who panicked or showed his fear. But he couldn't help himself. His hands were shaking.

Blackjack took a few moments to think through what needed to happen. If he told the Montagnard what he had just heard, many of the warriors would leave the group and run to the village. Those that remained would need to deal with the wounded. If the village had been attacked, it might have been to set up an enemy ambush. The warriors running to the village could be wiped out. That would also put those carrying the wounded at risk of being hunted down in the jungle. The entire Hatchet team could be wiped out.

But if he said nothing, he was betraying the warriors that had been so loyal to him and the other team members. They had protected him and fought beside him even when the odds were against them. They shared a common enemy, but this went way beyond that. They trusted each other with their lives. They were brothers in arms. Only a fellow warrior could know the meaning of such love.

Blackjack struggled to breathe as he made his decision. He would say nothing. He ordered the team to break camp and to send out extra scouts. He knew that an ambush was likely. As much as it pained him, he ordered his men to take a longer route, encircling the village from a distance while still under the cover of the jungle. It would take longer and that seemed a crime. There could be badly wounded survivors. Villagers could die if they didn't reach them in time. But Blackjack had to keep his warriors safe. He would accept whatever punishment the Montagnard sought if they discovered his deception. It was the way of the jungle.

As the Montagnard scouts approached the village,

they knew immediately something was wrong. There were no villagers keeping watch from the platforms the Americans had built in the trees at the edge of the jungle. They moved into the village. There were no villagers in sight. Everyone was gone. The animals had been slaughtered and the huts burned. But there were no bodies. Not knowing the fate of their families, the Montagnard warriors wept. Blackjack knew that until their families were found, the warriors would not leave the village. They would wait for their loved ones to return. Blackjack knew otherwise. They weren't coming back.

It was late in the afternoon when Blackjack saw a pair of eyes peering out of the jungle. His first reaction was that it was the enemy. But they were not the eyes of a soldier. They were the eyes of a child. Blackjack rose and moved with caution toward the jungle. The eyes disappeared. Blackjack ran to the position he had last seen the eyes. There was nothing. He wondered if he had imagined the eyes. A slight sound of leaves rustling behind him caught his attention. He turned slowly so as not to frighten the child. He did not move toward the child. He pulled a stick of gum from his pocket, carefully peeled off the wrapper, and held it out as an offering. The child cautiously stepped forward from the thick foliage and took the gum. Tears welled up in his eyes. He knew the child. It was the daughter of one of his warriors. He folded her up in his arms and smiled. She smiled back. She knew him.

Blackjack brought the girl to her father, who was overwhelmed with joy. When she was feeling secure, Blackjack asked the father to ask his daughter what had happened and where the villagers had gone. After a few moments, she replied that soldiers had come to the village and taken the people. She told them that she and several other children had run into the jungle to hide. The father asked where the other children were hiding. She pointed to the jungle. Blackjack ordered his men to spread out and search the jungle where the girl pointed.

It didn't take long. They found six more children hiding in the jungle. They were reunited with their fathers and told more of the story of what happened. The warriors that had been left behind, fought fiercely to defend the tribe. They were overwhelmed by the enemy soldiers and killed. Their bodies were dragged into the jungle. The rest of the villagers were taken prisoner and escorted away from the village to the Northwest. It had been two days since the villagers had disappeared. The children were too afraid to go into the village to hunt for food. Instead, they ate bugs and found fruit on trees and bushes in the jungle. Their parents had taught them well how to survive.

One of the warriors had found a paper written in Laotian. It was from the Pathet Lao commander. It said that the Montagnard could trade the American soldiers for their families. The Pathet Lao were watching them. The Montagnard would be allowed twenty-four hours to turn over the Americans or the families would be executed. Blackjack discussed the situation with his SOG team and said, "I don't think the Pathet Lao will kill us if we exchange ourselves for the Montagnard prisoners. We are too valuable. But even so, they will most likely torture us for information, then trade us for weapons and supplies with the North Vietnamese. There is no way to know for sure. But I do believe they will kill the prisoners if no exchange is made."

The SOG team members were not thrilled with the idea of surrendering themselves, but they agreed to turn themselves over to the Pathet Lao in exchange for the Montagnard families if necessary. Blackjack went to the Montagnard warriors and said, "We have agreed to exchange ourselves for your people. But before we do, I want you to know that I don't think the Pathet Lao will allow you to live. The Pathet Lao hate the Montagnard. Once the exchange is made, I believe they will ambush you and your families when you head back to your village. Some of you may make it, but most will not. That is what I believe. We leave the decision to you."

The Montagnard discussed the SOG team's offer among themselves. It took over an hour and not everyone agreed. Blackjack and his men waited to hear their fate.

The Montagnard escorted the SOG team through the jungle toward the village where the swap would happen. The Montagnard had already sent word to the Pathet Lao commander that they would trade the Americans for their people. Just before the village, the SOG team stopped and turned over their weapons to the Montagnard. The Montagnard tied their hands to bamboo poles so the Pathet Lao could see that they were unarmed prisoners.

The eldest Montagnard walked out of the jungle alone and unarmed. The Pathet Lao were waiting for him. They searched him roughly and spit on him. They escorted him into the village and brought him to a large animal pen where the captured Montagnard were being held under guard. He could see that most of the younger women and girls' faces were badly bruised and their lips bleeding from being hit. They were unwilling to meet his eyes and he knew they had been raped. There was no shame in it. He just wanted to get them out of there alive.

The Pathet Lao soldiers took him back through the village and let him go back into the jungle. He returned with the Americans and more of the warriors. The Pathet Lao soldiers moved up leaving their assigned posts to have a look at the American soldiers. Many had never seen their foreign enemy and were curious. The Pathet Lao commander said nothing. It was good for morale to see that the Americans were just men like them and not unbeatable monsters as was sometimes the rumor. All eyes were on the Americans that they hated.

What they did not see was a second group of Montagnard emerging from the jungle behind the village. They moved silently, many armed with traditional weapons including crossbows. They moved up behind the distracted soldiers and killed them quietly, slitting their throats or covering their mouths and stabbing them in the chest and abdomen. The dying were prevented from crying out to their comrades. The Montagnard warriors had learned how to kill effectively from the SOG and were taking their revenge. Bodies slumped to the ground. Blood flowed in tiny rivulets, pooling across the village. Dozens were killed.

The Pathet Lao took the Americans captive, spitting, hitting them with the butts of their rifles, and kicking them. It was what the Americans wanted… a distraction. The SOG objected loudly, cursing the Pathet Lao. After a kick in the crotch, Blackjack wailed trying to cover up the noise of the Montagnard already in the village killing the Pathet Lao. Blackjack was struck from behind and fell to his knees where the shorter Laotians could hit him more easily. He looked deep into the village and saw the Montagnard sneaking up and killing the guards surrounding a pen full of people. His people. To Blackjack, the continued beatings from the Pathet Lao were not so bad. Not if the Montagnard got their revenge and freed their people. "No more, please," he cried.

It only prompted more beatings by more soldiers. It was what he wanted. The more soldiers the better. One soldier pulled out his bayonet, pulled open the American's shirt, and sliced Blackjack across the chest. Mixed with his sweat, it stung like fire and Blackjack screamed in pain. He looked deep into the village and saw the last of the prisoners exiting the pen and running to the jungle behind the village. Blackjack called out, "Freedom."

A code word. He fell flat on the ground along with the other SOG team members. A light machine gun hidden in the jungle opened fire, mowing down the Pathet Lao around the Americans. They too fell to the ground… dead and wounded. The Pathet Lao took cover in the village and fought back. The Montagnard already in the village attacked them from behind. They fought hand to hand with bayonets and machetes. Each slicing and hacking at their enemy. Old warfare.

His hands still tied to the pole, Blackjack struggled to reach one of the Pathet Lao's bayonets stuck in the ground. He used the edge to cut the rope tying him to the pole. The soldier that had kicked him in the groin saw him escaping and ran to stop him. With one of his hands finally free, Blackjack grabbed the bayonet and plunged the blade into the crotch of the soldier trying to stop him. It only seemed fair. The soldier dropped to the ground in pain and horror, his trousers filling with blood. Blackjack retrieved the bayonet and cut his other hand loose. He threw the bayonet into the ground next to the closest SOG member allowing him to free himself.

Blackjack picked up a rifle from a fallen Pathet Lao soldier. Before firing, he looked around for his target – the Pathet Lao commander. He found him firing his pistol through the doorway of a hut. Blackjack aimed and fired. The bullet entered the left temple of the commander. The men around watched him fall to the ground, motionless, dead.

Under attack from front and rear, the leaderless Pathet Lao broke. Some tried to run and were gunned down by the Montagnard and Americans, now armed. Those that remained threw down their arms and surrendered. The Montagnard rounded up their prisoners and herded them into the animal pens where the Montagnard prisoners had been held.

Blackjack knew what was next. It wasn't what he wanted, but he wasn't going to try and stop it either. It was one thing to fight a Montagnard warrior on the battlefield. It was another thing to go after his family and the elders of the village. The warriors took one prisoner at a time out of the pen, made him kneel, then dismembered him in front of the other prisoners still in the animal pen. It was a horrifying scene as the arms, legs, heads, and torsos of the Pathet Lao were stacked up in a pile. Surprisingly, the prisoners wept but did not try to escape which would have been futile. They just watched their comrades get hacked into pieces and waited their turn. The Montagnard took their time giving each warrior his turn at retribution. The eldest warrior offered Blackjack a machete. Blackjack shook his head. He knew it would seem like a negative judgment from the Montagnard, but he didn't care. Although he understood their need for revenge, he wasn't a barbarian… not yet.

When they were through, the Montagnard burned the village to the ground leaving the pile of body parts untouched. They left the heads of their enemies on spears stuck in the ground throughout the burning village. They would be a symbol to anyone who saw them… don't fuck with the Montagnard.

When they returned to their village, the warriors cared for their wives and daughters. There was no shame in what had happened to the women. The village would raise any child born from rape as if it were their own. The child was innocent and the Pathet Lao had paid for their sins with their lives. As terrifying and cruel as the Montagnard could be, they were also loving and just people. It was the way of the jungle and they followed it like their gods' commandments.

It took several weeks before the Montagnard felt safe and returned to join the SOG in their raids on the Ho Chi Minh Trail. Blackjack didn't try to rush them. He knew they'd be back when they were ready. The North Vietnamese were their enemy and they would not stop fighting them until they were dead or gone from their lands.

NEW BOSS

Saigon, South Vietnam

Coyle and Granier walked toward the hangar where they were working on their gunship prototype. "I've been thinking about a movable reticle to replace the grease pencil markings on the side window. Maybe a piece of glass on some kinda slider mechanism using nobs for vertical and horizontal positioning of the sight," said Coyle.

"Sounds complicated. What's wrong with the grease pencil?" said Granier.

"Nothing. I mean… it works. It's just so ordinary."

"It's best if we keep things simple. Fewer things to go wrong."

"Yeah, but… a grease pencil. People are gonna laugh at us."

"Not after they see what our beast can do."

"I suppose that's true."

Granier stopped dead in his tracks and pointed to the door on the hangar. The lock had been broken off and the door was ajar. Coyle was unarmed except for a pocketknife which he pulled out. Granier removed a small revolver from an ankle holster. They charged through the doorway hoping to surprise the intruders.

The hangar looked empty. They moved toward the aircraft. Captain Ron Terry, Air Force Systems Command, peeked out the window in the cockpit and said, "Which one of you is Tom Coyle?"

"I am. Who the hell are you and why are you in my aircraft?" said Coyle.

"Your aircraft? Last time I checked this aircraft belonged to the United States Air Force."

"Well, you checked with the wrong people. This aircraft has been assigned to me."

"Are you saying it's a CIA aircraft?"

"I ain't saying and this conversation is over until you identify yourself."

"Captain Ron Terry. I'm with Air Force Systems Command."

"What the hell is Air Force Systems Command?" said Granier.

"You must be Rene Granier," said Terry. "UFSC is a unit that develops advanced weapon systems. How did you align all three machine guns?"

"That's a secret," said Granier. "We ain't telling you jackshit."

"You still haven't explained why you're poking around our aircraft," said Coyle.

"Because you got a problem."

"What's that?"

"You can't be developing this kinda stuff on your own. It's counterproductive. The Air Force has rules about this kinda thing. I am impressed with what you have done. You've got some good ideas… which I am going to use."

"Use on what?"

"My authorized project."

"What's that?"

"A gunship like this one… but authorized."

"You keep saying that like it's important. Authorized."

"Like I said, the Air Force frowns on unauthorized development of weapons. I'm gonna have to shut you guys down and confiscate your aircraft."

"Like hell, you will," said Granier. "This is our project."

"Look, you can fight me on this, but in the end, you will lose. Or you can cooperate and continue the development of your ideas as part of my team."

"We ain't joining no damned development team."

"Do you have Pentagon funding?" said Coyle.

"Of course," said Terry.

"Excuse us for a moment."

"Sure. Take your time."

Coyle pulled Granier aside and said, "We should take his offer. He's got funding and we don't."

"We're doing just fine with what we got," said Granier.

"No, we're not. We've begged and borrowed all we can to get this far and we still ain't done. Besides, we'd eventually need to show it to someone if it's ever going to be used in the field. This guy's already connected to the right people in charge… and he's got money."

"I don't like it. We did all the work and he's gonna take all the credit."

"We're covert ops. We can't take credit anyway."

"I didn't really think about that."

"I don't see what harm it can do to exchange ideas."

"Alright, but we ain't joining no team."

"Fine."

Coyle and Granier walked over to Terry as he was climbing out of the aircraft. "You've seen ours. Now, we wanna see yours," said Coyle.

"Alright. I've already checked up on both of you. You've got clearance," said Terry.

"Damned right we do," said Granier.

On the far side of the airbase Coyle, Granier, and Terry entered another hangar. Terry had been a fighter pilot flying F-86s and F-100s. The more Coyle and Granier talked with the captain, the more they realized that he knew his stuff when it came to flying air-to-ground support. Inside the hangar was a Convair C-131B twin-engine aircraft painted with standard Air Force insignia. The back door had been taken off and a 7.62 mm General Electric GAU-2/M134 minigun was mounted on the deck. "What the hell is that?" said Coyle.

"It's a Gatling gun," said Granier, intrigued.

"It's called a minigun," said Terry. "It's made by General Electric."

"You only have one," said Coyle.

"I only need one. That little beast has more firepower than ten machine guns."

"I heard about 'em, but I've never seen one," said Granier.

"There's only a few in-country. As you can imagine, they're in high demand."

"What's the rate of fire?"

"Six thousand rounds a minute max, but we usually run between 3,000 and 4,000."

"Nice. How does it work?"

"It has an electric motor that rotates the barrels. Let's take her up and I'll show you."

The Corsair gunship flew in a pylon turn over a patch

of jungle below. Twenty mannequins wearing black pajamas were randomly dispersed throughout the heavy foliage. They were much harder to see than the drums Coyle and Granier had used. It was a more accurate test of the weapon and pilot's capabilities.

Terry piloted the plane with a co-pilot sitting next to him and a flight engineer sitting nearby at his station. He lined up the target area in the grease pencil crosshair on the side window and flipped a switch on a small metal box to "Armed."

Coyle and Granier stood in the cargo area next to the minigun looking out through the windows and open doorway. A gunner and two assistants with shovels stood next to them. "You guys might want to cover your ears," shouted the gunner over the sound of the engines.

"I've fired a machine gun before. I know what they sound like," shouted Granier.

"Suit yourself."

As the barrels began to spin with an increasing whirr, Coyle erred on the side of caution and covered his ears with his hands. A moment later, the weapon fired. The echo inside the hull was deafening. Hundreds of hot shells bounced off the deck. "Holy shit!" said Granier covering his ears. The assistant gunners went to work clearing the casings with their shovels and throwing them into trashcans tied to the deck.

The jungle below turned into green confetti as the leaves were torn to shreds and launched into the air. The pattern of fire was tight… too tight. It decimated a forty-foot circle leaving many of the mannequins still standing while others were blown to smithereens.

Coyle and Granier grinned like children as they watched the minigun's performance. It was over in seconds as the 1,000-round belt was expended. "Now, that's a machine gun," said Coyle.

"Yeah, we gotta get us some of those," said Granier.

As the plane leveled out, the gunner reloaded the minigun with another belt and the assistant gunners finished chasing down the last casings rolling around on the deck. Terry stepped through the cockpit doorway and said, "Coyle, you wanna give her a try?"

"Is the Pope Catholic?" said Coyle moving toward the cockpit.

Coyle slid into the empty pilot's chair. Terry went over the procedure to fire the weapon. Coyle banked the aircraft and returned to the position over the gun range in the jungle. He looked through the side window and could see that there were still plenty of enemy mannequins waiting to be obliterated. He aimed using the grease pencil marks and flipped the switch on the box to armed. "Here we go," said Coyle as he pushed the weapon button Gerry-rigged on the steering wheel.

The weapon fired. Coyle maneuvered the aircraft, so the field of fire pivoted around the area already laid to waste. Terry was impressed as Coyle destroyed the remaining mannequins like a surgeon cutting out a tumor. "Nice shooting," said Terry as the gunfire ceased.

"That's one hell of weapon you got back there," said Coyle.

After the plane landed back at the airfield, Coyle, Granier, and Terry sat around an empty oil drum and strategized over coffee. "Can you get another two miniguns?" said Granier.

"Maybe. There's a long waiting list," said Terry. "I could call in some favors. If I can get them, do you think you can align them after they're mounted?"

"Sure, but you're gonna need to set a standard distance and define the field of fire."

"We can do that."

"Coyle, you're a hell of a shot. How would you like to be our test pilot?" said Terry.

"Hell, yeah," said Coyle.

"Welcome to the team, gentlemen."

"We can't join your team officially," said Granier.

"That's a shame," said Terry.

"We're under contract with MACV. But we can help you in-between our missions," said Coyle.

"I don't know… We're on a pretty tight development schedule," said Terry.

"We get a lot of free time. It won't be a problem," said Granier.

"Let's give it try and see how it goes," said Terry.

"One more thing," said Coyle.

"What's that?"

"I think you should consider using the C-47 as your aircraft."

"Why? The Corsair is faster and can fly longer without refueling."

"I agree it's a better aircraft. But there are not a lot of pilots in Vietnam that are trained on the Corsair. The C-47 has a ton of pilots that have been flying them for years. If it goes into production as a weapon system, you're gonna need good pilots. There are also a lot of them sitting around on airfields waiting to be scrapped. Spare parts aren't going to be a problem."

"Good points. Let me think about it," said Terry.

July 5, 1964 – Nam Dong, South Vietnam

Thirty-two miles west of Da Nang near the Laotian border, the CIDG (Civilian Irregular Defense Group) camp in the valley of Nam Dong was built to train local militias on how to fend off the Viet Cong assaults on their villages. It was staffed by both South Vietnamese, Australian, and American advisors, mostly Green Berets. At that moment, there were 300 South Vietnamese and sixty Montagnard being trained. In addition to protecting the camp, a strike force protected nine villages in the surrounding area. Once an assault began, the strike force could usually reach one of the nine villages before the VC could overrun it.

The Viet Cong saw the camp as a major thorn in their side and had assaulted it several times with little luck. The camp had multiple look-out towers and its defenses were well-built. The jungle had been bull-dozed back several hundred yards and layers of barbed wire and mines protected the outer and inner perimeters. Trenches and blockhouses with light and heavy machine guns protected the defenders. There were also several heavy mortar pits in the center of the camp that could reach out and touch the enemy beyond the outer perimeter. Warplanes and gunships from Da Nang's Air Base could reach the camp in thirty minutes and throw down a startling amount of air-to-ground firepower, including napalm canisters and rockets.

It was 2:26 AM when the first VC mortar shell hit the

mess hall and set it ablaze lighting up the early morning sky. More mortar rounds followed exploding all around the camp. In the previous days, the enemy's spies had mapped out the camp's key positions allowing its mortars to pre-target the command bunker, heavy mortar pits, and the ammunition depot.

In the communications bunker, Staff Sgt. Keith Daniels, shirtless with his sidearm around his waist, radioed Da Nang Air Base for a flare plane and an air strike. While on the radio, Daniels could hear and feel the enemy's mortar shells walking closer to the communications bunker. When the supply depot next door was hit, Daniels knew he was next. He ended his call, grabbed his rifle and a belt of ammunition, then raced out the door. Moments later, the communications bunker blew up. The explosion threw Daniels to the ground and scorched his shirtless back. He didn't stay there. He hopped up and headed for the closest trench within the inner perimeter.

Once in the trench, the South Vietnamese soldiers gave him a report on what they had seen so far. A volley of grenades exploded on the outer perimeter in an attempt to cut holes in the barbed wire and set off any mines that had been buried. Small arms fire erupted, followed by the war cries of attacking Viet Cong. The flare ship had not yet arrived, and the camp's mortars were busy hammering the enemy to hold them back. With only an occasional mortar flare, it was difficult for the South Vietnamese troops to see where the enemy was attacking. Only the muzzle flashes from their rifle fire gave away their positions. From their trenches and blockhouses, the South Vietnamese soldiers poured machine gun and rifle fire on the charging enemy driving them to the ground.

A few minutes later, a C-47 flare ship approached the camp from overhead. Two flares spaced a hundred yards apart, were thrown from the open cargo door, and were ignited when their parachutes popped open. Instead of circling the battlefield as it would normally do after launching its initial flares, the plane was called away to another nearby battlefield. The aircrew would serve double duty that night. The twin flares drifted slowly to the ground illuminating the area in an eerie yellow light. Dropped from 2,000 feet, the air-launched flares were more powerful and lasted much longer than the mortar flares launched from within the camp.

With the enemy visible, the South Vietnamese aim improved dramatically and assaulting Viet Cong began dropping like hail. The site of the enemy being killed encouraged the frightened militia trainees and their gunfire intensified. They no longer ducked down after firing each shot. Instead, they stood their ground in the well-protected trenches and kept the rate of fire constant.

But the Viet Cong did not pull back. They knew that the American warplanes and helicopter gunships would arrive shortly and the only way to survive the air attack was to get close to the enemy within the base. The Americans would not risk killing their allies. The VC pressed their assault.

VC sappers belly crawled through the minefield. One was blown into the air by an exploding mine and landed in a lump of torn flesh. The rest survived and used wire cutters to open holes in the barbed wire allowing the VC to breach the outer perimeter. The flicker of flames from the camp's burning bunkers danced across the faces of the attacking Viet Cong as they drew closer.

Two VC sappers had made it through the inner perimeter and climbed up to the roof of a concrete bunker. The sappers used grenades to silence one of the camp's heavy mortars. More sappers attacked the other mortar pits until all the heavy mortars had been destroyed. With the camp's heavy artillery gone, hundreds of Viet Cong emerged from the surrounding jungle and advanced on the camp firing their weapons and tossing grenades as they advanced on the camp's outer perimeter. Everything up to that point had been a VC probing assault to test the camp's defenses and create a pathway for a much larger force. The main force of over 800 VC ringed the camp attacking from all sides at the same time.

In a 60 MM mortar pit on one side of the camp, Australian Warrant Officer Kevin Conway was hit by a VC bullet right between his eyes. He fell to the ground, unconscious but alive. There was little anyone could do except make him comfortable. One of the Americans pulled off his shirt and made a pillow for Conway's head. Conway survived for another half hour before dying quietly. Conway was the first Australian soldier to die in Vietnam. There would be others.

As the Viet Cong were closing in on the camp, everything went dark. The two air-dropped flares had finally reached the ground and the C-47 had not yet returned to drop more flares. The surviving mortar crews scrambled to launch parachute flares from their 60MM tubes in all directions. They didn't create much light, once again making it difficult for the South Vietnamese to see their targets.

In the dim light, the VC took advantage and pushed their attack. VC within the wire popped up and ran toward the inner perimeter holding their fire so as not to give away their position. The battlefield turned into a grenade free-for-all with both sides tossing grenades wherever they thought the enemy might be.

Already badly burned from saving necessary supplies from a burning depot, Master Sgt. Gabriel Ralph Alamo was running toward a mortar pit under attack when he saw three VC running in the same direction a few yards away. Alamo stopped, aimed, and killed all three with his rifle. As he turned back toward the mortar pit, a grenade landed in front of him and exploded. He was blown backward and landed in a lump. He took shrapnel in his left shoulder and in the head just below his eye. He was stunned but managed to make it to his feet and entered the mortar pit. He seemed confused by what was happening and sat on the stairs. An enemy mortar shell targeting the 60 MM mortar pit landed directly behind Alamo and tossed him like a ragdoll onto the ground next to the mortar. His flesh was torn and bleeding badly from a large hole in his back. Seeing that the American sergeant was mortally wounded, the tribesman mortar crew did not stop to help him. The American advisor had trained them well and they continued to fire shells as fast as possible. Watching his former students perform as trained, Alamo let out his last breath and died.

The distant drone of aircraft engines froze the advancing VC in their tracks. Two parachute flares popped illuminating the battlefield once again. Trying to decide whether to advance or retreat, a platoon of VC was standing just thirty yards in front of a blockhouse. A heavy machine gun opened fire mowing them down. More than a dozen VC were ripped to shreds by the overly large bullets, and the rest hit the dirt. An American advisor ordered his trainees to use grenades. Eight grenades arced across the sky and landed between the inner and outer perimeters. Shrapnel raked across the VC on the ground killing four more. The survivors crawled away keeping as low as they could as more grenades exploded around them.

Sergeant John Houston was one of the camp's radio operators. The day before the battle, he received a letter from his wife saying she was going into labor, and he would soon have his first child. The young sergeant was thrilled and told everyone he knew at the camp that he would soon be a father.

After his radio was destroyed by an enemy mortar shell, Houston picked up his rifle and joined the fight to defend the camp. Running toward the perimeter, he saw one of his fellow sergeants knock unconscious and laying on the ground as mortar shells rained down. Houston pulled the wounded sergeant to safety and make sure a medic tended to his wounds. Houston continued toward the perimeter and was hit by a piece of shrapnel from a mortar round. It wasn't serious and he continued toward the perimeter where he discovered a large mound of dirt that had been created during the digging of a bunker. Standing on top of the mound, Houston had an excellent field of fire on the advancing enemy in his sector. With little regard for his own safety, he opened fire and single-handedly shattered a vicious enemy assault killing a half-dozen enemy troops. With bullets zinging around him and mortar shells exploding just a few yards away, Houston continued to stand on his mound for two hours fighting off the enemy assault. When he ran low on ammunition, he called to other soldiers to toss him additional rounds. He reloaded his rifle's magazine time and time again. An enemy bullet finally found

Houston giving him a mortal wound in the heart. His rifle was silenced, and he died on his dirt mound.

A few minutes later, the sound of helicopter blades cut through the air as 18 UH-34Ds filled with reinforcements and supplies approached the camp. The eighteen Choctaws were escorted by four UH-1B gunships and two A-1 Skyraiders. As the transport helicopters landed and emptied their reinforcements, the gunships and warplanes unleashed their rockets, machine guns, and napalm canisters on the enemy positions.

Seeking cover, the Viet Cong recoiled and pulled back from the perimeters around the camp. They were in no man's land between the camp and the jungle with nowhere to hide. The gunships and warplanes seemed everywhere at once. As much as the VC commander wanted to overrun the camp, he knew his men would be torn to shreds by the American aircraft if they continued their assault. He also knew that it was only a matter of time before a larger group of infantry reinforcements reached the camp from surrounding fire bases. As his men's beating continued, the commander realized that there was nothing they could do except die or retreat. He ordered his men to withdraw. The Viet Cong picked up their dead and wounded and retreated into the jungle where they were protected by the thick canopy. The Battle of Nam Dong was over.

Both sides had been badly mauled in the five-hour battle. The South Vietnamese lost fifty-seven ARVN and CIDG soldiers. Two American advisors and one Australian had been killed. The Viet Cong and their NVA advisors had sixty-two killed and several hundred wounded. Although the South Vietnamese could claim victory since the camp did not fall into enemy hands, it was hardly a time of celebration as the survivors tended to their wounded and began the long process of rebuilding their camp. Sergeants Alamo and Houston were posthumously awarded Distinguished Service Crosses, the nation's second-highest honor.

July 11, 1964 - New York, New York, USA

The editor of the New Times received and published a petition signed by more than 5,000 American academics urging the federal government to work toward neutralizing South Vietnam. Hans Morgenthau, a well-known political scientist and the spokesman of the group, said that escalating the war was not the answer. A leftover from the Kennedy administration, President Johnson dismissed Morgenthau as an advisor for his strong views against the Vietnam War. Over the course of his presidency, Johnson became less tolerant of the voices of opposition in the White House.

July 19, 1964 – Saigon, South Vietnam

During a rally, Prime Minister Khanh spoke before 100,000 South Vietnamese in a Saigon park. As the crowd cheered, he called on volunteers to not only defend the South but to liberate North Vietnam, then led the cry "Bac thien!" which translated to "To the North!" He went on to say that without an attack on the North, neutralism for South Vietnam would become a reality. Tired of a defensive-only posture, Khanh was determined to take the fight to the enemy and expand the war even further with or without the Americans. He would end the war through total victory.

TONKIN

July 29, 1964 – Da Nang, South Vietnam

Lucien Conein had created a masterpiece of deception and chaos. General Harkins had ordered him to "pick a fight" and that was exactly what he was planning. The fact that Harkins was no longer in command of MACV and Westmoreland had taken his place, didn't matter to Conein. He had his orders and until he was told otherwise, he would carry them out.

He planned to create a series of unrelated altercations that would trick the North Vietnamese into believing they were under a coordinated attack from the United States and overreact. Because the altercations were unrelated, the Americans would be able to plausibly deny the accusations and claim that it was American forces that had been attacked by North Vietnamese forces.

Conein began the execution of his engagement operations on July 29th. He had arraigned for MACV to launch a team of long-term South Vietnamese intelligence agents across the border into North Vietnam.

As a separate operation under Conein's orders,

Coyle flew a Caribou with North Vietnamese insignia across the border and the pair of South Vietnamese agents parachuted into the countryside. Staying low to the ground and using the hills for cover, Coyle made it back across the border without being detected.

As with most South Vietnamese agents inserted into the North, they were quickly captured by a North Vietnamese patrol. Hanoi linked the two operations and assumed that the Americans and South Vietnamese were escalating their assault on the North.

Earlier, Conein had arranged for MACV-SOG to covertly purchase a set of Nasty Class fast patrol boats from Norway and hire three young Norwegian skippers through a Norwegian intelligence officer, Alf Martens Meyer who operated in conjunction with US intelligence. The skippers and their patrol boats were sent to South Vietnam. Once they arrived, the patrol boats were crewed by South Vietnamese sailors.

Conein requested that Admiral U.S. Grant Sharp Jr., CINCPAC in Honolulu, who received his orders directly from the White House, sent two South Vietnamese commando teams by the covert patrol boats to take out the radar installation Granier had reconnoitered a few months earlier. The admiral complied.

On July 30th, South Vietnamese commandos were transported by four Norwegian patrol boats to just a few miles off the North Vietnamese coast. As the commandos prepared to go ashore, the sailors on the patrol boats fired mortars and recoilless rifles on Hon Me and Hon Ngu islands as preparative barrages. Once the shelling ceased, the commandos landed on shore and attacked the radar installations destroying the facilities and driving off the guards and radar operators. The commandos returned to their boats unmolested.

In addition to the commando raids and covert agent insertions, Conein requested MACV-SOG use one of its newly outfitted intelligence destroyers from Operation Plan 34-Alpha, in conjunction with the DESOTO operations, to intercept North Vietnamese radio communications in the Gulf of Tonkin. Conein was very specific in his request. He asked that the destroyer approach no closer than eight miles from North Vietnam's coast and four miles from Hon Nieu Island which kept the vessel in international waters. He also requested that all other DESOTO ships stay away from the area during the covert operations. Conein only wanted confusion that he had fabricated and didn't want a US ship to accidentally fire on the North Vietnamese before he had planned. He would control the fight to ensure the outcome he desired.

MACV-SOG complied and ordered Captain John J. Herrick, the commander of the USS Maddox, into the area for electronic surveillance operations. Believing it was just another covert intelligence mission, Herrick and his crew had not been informed of the commando operations or their expected role in Conein's plan. The Maddox began its new mission on July 31st as it unknowingly sailed toward its objective. An American aircraft carrier, the USS Ticonderoga, was stationed nearby Maddox's area of operations. To create plausible deniability, Conein ensured that the Maddox and the Ticonderoga did not participate in the South Vietnamese commando raids. The Maddox was 120 miles away when the South Vietnamese commandos attacked the North Vietnamese Island installations.

Another piece of Conein's plan was launched on August 1st from Laos. Thai mercenaries flew Laotian fighter-bombers across the border into Northwest North Vietnam. They bombed and strafed NVA outposts killing soldiers and heavily damaging the outposts. If any of the aircraft were shot down, the Laotians would claim that Thai civilians had stolen the fighter-bombers. None of the aircraft were damaged and the Thai flew back to Laos.

The North Vietnamese responded diplomatically, complaining to the International Control Commission that the Americans were behind the attacks and had violated the Geneva Accords. The Americans denied any involvement and Hanoi's complaints fell on deaf ears. The NVA sent more troops and anti-aircraft weapons to the Laotian border. It was too little, too late.

Hanoi was in panic mode. The North was under attack, and they had to respond to keep their enemies at bay. Border patrols and anti-aircraft units were put on heightened alert.

On August 1st, a squadron of North Vietnamese P-4 class torpedo boats was sent into the Bay of Tonkin and began tracking the USS Maddox as it approached its area of operation near the two islands that had been attacked. The North Vietnamese had little doubt that the Americans were behind the attacks on the radar installations and the USS Maddox was the most likely culprit from which the assaults had been launched.

The Maddox intercepted several communications that indicated that the North Vietnamese planned to attack the American destroyer. Deciding that caution was the better part of valor, Captain Herrick retreated to a safe distance from the torpedo boats.

The next day, the Maddox returned and continued its mission of gathering electronic intelligence. Once again, the torpedo boats returned and tracked the Maddox. And again, the Maddox intercepted radio communications that indicated that the torpedo boats planned to attack. Herrick once again, ordered the Maddox back out to sea to avoid a confrontation. At 10:45 AM, a secret radio communication was received by the Maddox. Reading the message Herrick altered his previous order and laid in a course back toward the coast just north of Hon Me Island. Herrick ordered his crew to prepare for an impending attack from the North Vietnamese torpedo boats.

The three Chinese-built torpedo boats had aluminum hulls and were from North Vietnamese Squadron 135. The commander of the squadron was Captain Le Duy Khoai. The boats were commanded by Khoai's brothers Van Bot, Van Tu, and Van Gian. With a complement of twelve seamen, the boats were powered by two Soviet M50 diesel engines giving the vessels a top speed of fifty-five knots. They were armed with two 450 mm torpedoes and two 14.5 mm KPV heavy machine guns. If they could get close enough, they had the potential of sinking the Maddox with their torpedoes.

The USS Maddox had been christened in 1944 and

participated in World War II and the Korean War. She was a Sumner-class destroyer weighing in at 3,515 tons fully loaded and had a top speed of thirty-four knots. The vessel was armed with six five-inch guns, twelve 40 mm Bofors anti-aircraft guns, eleven 20 mm Oerlikon cannons, two depth charge racks, six K-gun depth charge throwers, two triple Mark 2 torpedo tubes, and two twenty-one-inch torpedo tubes for Mark 37 torpedoes. She had a complement of 350 highly trained sailors looking for a fight and Herrick was confident in their abilities. There was little doubt of the winner if the North Vietnamese torpedo boats attacked. Each firing twelve rounds a minute by the skilled gun crews and using targeting radar, the six main guns on the Maddox could effectively hit a target at twelve miles.

In Hanoi, Le Duan secretly gave the order to attack the American destroyer. He wanted an escalation of the war, but he did not want to directly contradict Ho Chi Minh who advised patience and caution. Ho did not want the United States to enter the war any further than it already had. He had lived in America and observed firsthand the incredible power of its industries. Duan saw the attacks on the islands in North Vietnamese territory as a perfect opportunity to push the Americans. Like Conein, Duan wanted to pick a fight. Duan wrongly surmised that the USS Maddox must have been involved in the commando raids because it was so close to the islands. He had fallen into Conein's trap.

Following his commander's orders, Khoai ordered the squadron to hunt down the American destroyer. The torpedo boats increased their speed and headed to incept the USS Maddox. The weather conditions were fair and the seas were calm.

At 2:40 PM on August 2nd, radar operators, then lookouts on the Maddox spotted the three torpedo boats speeding toward the destroyer from the west. Herrick ordered his gun crews to fire warning shots at the three boats if they came within 10,000 yards of the Maddox. As a precautionary measure, he radioed the aircraft carrier USS Ticonderoga and asked for air support.

Within ten minutes, four Vought F-8 Crusaders took off from the Ticonderoga. Once airborne, the pilots formed up their aircraft and headed toward the Maddox at top speed. The jets were armed with two LAU-10 pods holding eight 127 mm Zuni rockets. In addition, each aircraft had four 20 mm Colt Mk 12 cannons with 125 rounds per gun. The Crusaders were the last American fighters with guns as a primary weapon and were known as "The Last of the Gunfighters."

As the torpedo boats approached the Maddox, they crossed the imaginary 10,000-yard line that Herrick had set. The US vessel was almost thirty miles from the North Vietnamese coast and clearly in international waters. At 3:08 AM, the Maddox five-inch gun crews fired three warning shots.

The three shells crossed over the bow of the lead North Vietnamese torpedo boat. Continuing the attack, Captain Khoai responded by ordering the boats in his squadron to fire their machine guns and torpedoes at the American ship. The Maddox was still five miles away and out of range. Maxing out their engines at fifty knots per hour, the torpedo boats closed the distance and opened fire. They were far from the effective range of their weapons. The lead boat launched one of its two torpedoes. As the lead boat veered off in hopes of launching a second torpedo at a different angle, the second boat launched one of its torpedoes and also veered off.

Discovering the torpedoes in the water with its sonar, the Maddox performed evasive maneuvers as it fired on the third North Vietnamese vessel still approaching at high speed.

While most of the shells from Maddox main guns missed their targets, the third North Vietnamese boat took a direct hit from a five-inch shell. It went dead in the water and smoke shrouded the heavily damaged vessel.

The gun crews on the Maddox cheered at the rising smoke. Herrick was less than impressed with their performance. The North Vietnamese torpedoes passed by the Maddox and were never closer than 200 yards from the ship's hull. A clear miss. One 14.5 mm bullet from the torpedo boats' machine guns was found lodged in Maddox's tower. It was the only physical evidence the United States had that proved the attack occurred. The surface engagement lasted twenty-two minutes before Captain Herrick broke off and the Maddox headed back out to see in the direction of the destroyer Turner Joy.

The four Crusaders flew over the Maddox at 3:30 PM and saw no damage. With orders to attack and destroy the torpedo boats, the Crusaders pursued the two functioning vessels as they turned back toward the shoreline. The crusader pilots made multiple passes strafing and rocketing the boats which were maneuvering evasively. The boats suffered heavy damage and causalities but did not sink. Each of the two remaining boats still had operational twin machine guns that were used as anti-aircraft weapons each time the American jets attacked. With North Vietnamese boats no longer a threat, the Crusaders broke off their attack and turned to escort the Maddox to the Turner Joy. The Americans wanted a clear victory in their first battle with the north. They got it.

White House – Washington D.C., USA

It was mid-morning until McNamara had enough information on the Gulf of Tonkin events that he felt comfortable reporting to the president. Johnson appreciated McNamara's thoroughness and felt like he was always getting the best information available at that time. Johnson was aware that the North Vietnamese torpedo boats had been tracking the Maddox and that an event had taken place but he didn't know the details. McNamara carefully went over the events that had occurred during the early morning while Johnson was still asleep. He described the attack in detail and made sure Johnson understood that some of the facts were still preliminary and might change as more after-action reports came in from the sailors and pilots involved. "I understand that, but I want it clear that the North Vietnamese fired first and that the Maddox was in international waters when the conflict took place."

"There is no doubt the Maddox was in international

waters when it was attacked by the North Vietnamese torpedo boats. Of that I am sure," said McNamara

"And what about who fired first? It was the North Vietnamese, right?"

"Apparently, the Maddox fired some warning shots at the torpedo boats to scare them off, but none of those shots were meant to hit the boats. But the first offensive fire came from the North Vietnamese. They launched two to seven torpedoes at the Maddox with the intent of sinking her."

"Two to seven is a pretty wide range. You should make it clear what happened, especially when it comes to clarifying who fired first. If the Maddox fired warning shots, I'm not sure that needs to be mentioned. Keep the story simple, Bob. The American people understand simple. We don't need to bog them down with too many details."

"Yes, Mr. President. I'll do that."

"We need to be on the same page when we talk with the press. Everyone needs to be on the same page with this thing. You need to make that clear."

"I will."

"So, what kind of response are you thinking?"

"Well, it's clear we need to do something. You don't fire torpedoes at an American warship and not suffer consequences."

"I agree. We need a measured response. You know, to let the North Vietnamese and Chinese know that we will not be provoked."

"A measured response?"

"Yeah. We don't want to go overboard."

"So, what are you thinking is overboard?"

"I'm not sure. But I'll know it when I hear it."

"Of course. You might want to gather the entire

cabinet, so you have a variety of options to choose from."

"That's a good idea. Let's do that right away. I don't want too much time to pass before we respond. It'll make us look indecisive and weak. We should ask a few important members of Congress to attend. We don't want a congressional investigation on this thing right now. If we include them in the debriefing and the decision-making process moving forward, they have no right to complain later."

"I agree."

Within the hour, Johnson met with his cabinet and some members of congress. McNamara, once again, went over the details of what had happened but left out the three warning shots fired by the Maddox as Johnson had suggested. Some of the cabinet members knew otherwise but said nothing. Everyone knew that Johnson did not want confusion and hated to be corrected by anyone, especially congress and the press. "The North Vietnamese have attacked an American vessel in international waters. It's clearly an act of war," said General Wheeler, the new Chairman of the Joint Chiefs. "Our response needs to be rigorous in no uncertain terms. It's time to bring in American ground forces and show the enemy what a real fighting force can do."

"While I agree we need a strong response, I'm not sure a couple of torpedoes that missed require an invasion of American troops," said McGeorge Bundy, National Security Advisor.

"I think a bombing campaign in the North would send a clear signal as to our intent concerning any further aggression toward US forces," said General

LeMay, Vice Chief of Staff of the Air Force.

"I agree," said Admiral Anderson, Chief of Naval Operations. "We could also shell their shore facilities."

The Chiefs of Staff and cabinet members continued to toss around methods of retaliation measuring the pros and cons of each and Hanoi's expected reaction to each. "Look, I like a lot of these ideas, but I think we need to do this thing in steps and not get ahead of ourselves. It's gonna take time to get US troops in place and I just don't think we are at the point where we want our boys tossed into the morass. As much as they support the war, Americans aren't ready to see coffins come home with their sons inside, especially right before an election. I wanna hold off on the whole boots on the ground thing," said Johnson. "On the other hand, I think a limited number of bombing missions would be something we do right away and could have the response we are looking for if we destroy the right targets. Our pilots will be at risk but that's a whole hell of a lot better than our soldiers fighting in the hills and jungles. In addition, I want the Maddox to return to its area of operation as soon as possible along with a second destroyer. I wanna show Hanoi, that we ain't running scared from their puny torpedo boats and we will navigate in international waters where we damn well, please."

The president had spoken and, although many had been hoping for more of a response, the cabinet and military fell in line. McNamara would prepare a list of bombing targets in conjunction with the Joint Chiefs. Johnson would have the final say on what should be bombed and what was off-limits.

Hanoi, North Vietnam

Receiving a report on the torpedo boats' assault on the American destroyer, Ho Chi Minh was furious. This was exactly what he didn't want, an excuse for the Americans to escalate the war against the North. He demanded that those that authorized the attack be punished. But only the captains of the boats were reprimanded and would later be treated as heroes of the revolution. Le Duan was never accused for his role in the Gulf of Tonkin event. Even with his reputation, Ho Chi Minh was not all-powerful and needed to accept that Le Duan was the new leader of the North. Because it was Duan's will, the war would escalate whether Ho approved or not. In the meantime, Le Duan prepared for his next move.

August 4th, 1964 - Gulf of Tonkin, North Vietnam

The sea was heavy with waves and the weather was rough as the USS Maddox and USS Turner Joy sailed back toward the North Vietnamese coastline. The aircraft on the Ticonderoga were grounded because of the harsh weather. They wouldn't be available to spot the enemy boats.

Once again, the crew on both destroyers intercepted radio communication that indicated the North Vietnamese planned to attack the two destroyers. The crews went to battle stations. Everyone was on edge. Even though the North Vietnamese boats were small, their torpedoes were deadly. A direct hit in the right place could heavily damage or even sink a destroyer. The American sailors knew they needed to keep the enemy boats away from their destroyers. With the heavy seas and weather, visual sightings were unlikely until it was too late, and the enemy boats were within striking distance. Everything fell to the radar and sonar operators.

At 9:40 PM, the radar operators picked up multiple surface contacts heading toward the American destroyers. Unlike the previous day, the North Vietnamese torpedo boats were attacking from all angles as they closed on the American ships. The destroyers took evasive maneuvers struggling to stay close to one another while not running into each other.

The gun crews fired their five-inch guns at the incoming boats' locations identified by radar. Radar crews reported two enemy vessels sunk when their images disappeared from their screens. But there were more enemy boats out there.

Sonar operators picked up the propellor sounds of torpedoes in the water coming from different angles of attack. Lookouts struggled to spot the incoming enemy weapons. The anti-aircraft 40 mm Bofors guns fired into the sea in hopes of stopping the torpedoes. It was a game of illusion as waves crashed down and shadows beneath the surface disappeared. Radio operators sent out messages saying both American destroyers were under attack from multiple enemy vessels.

For over two hours, the Americans shifted course one way and then another to avoid the torpedoes. In total, twenty-two torpedoes were identified. None found their target.

Finally, the weather calmed somewhat, and the enemy broke off its attack. There was an eerie silence. Everyone remained at battle stations and all eyes focused on the seas looking for the enemy boats to reappear and the battle to begin anew. It didn't happen.

The crews on both destroyers were relieved and exhausted. The stress had been unbearable for some as they broke down in tears, their bodies quivering.

It was Captain Herrick that first began to question what had happened. Why would the enemy break off its attack the moment the weather and seas calmed? He had a sinking feeling in the pit of his stomach. As a precaution, he sent a radio message discounting the reliability of his previous reports of the attack. He suspected that something had happened, but he wasn't sure what it was. He even questioned the attack two days before. Had he got it right? He studied his logs, reviewing every entry from both attacks. He was far from confident that the second set of attacks had even occurred at all. He was embarrassed. Professional commanders don't make those kinds of mistakes. But he wanted the truth. Too much was at stake. He dug deeper and had his officers interview his crew. Everyone onboard claimed that the enemy boats and the torpedoes were real and that the attack had occurred. But still, Herrick wondered.

White House – Washington DC, USA

When Johnson received reports of the second attack torpedo boat on the American destroyers he was surprised by the tenacity of the North Vietnamese. Surely, Ho Chi Minh must understand the futility of attacking American warships. He asked McNamara for the list of bombing targets. He asked Rusk for the document he had prepared for Congress giving him the authority to defend US forces in Vietnam. Finally, he asked for television time that evening so he could inform the American people about what had happened and what he planned to do about it. Whatever had happened in southeast Asia up to that point, he was about to become a war president and he wanted to ensure that the American people were behind him, especially this close to the election.

As Johnson prepared to pull the trigger on escalating the war, McNamara informed him that there had been contradictory reports on what had occurred during the second attack. Johnson was furious. He hated when people, especially the military waffled. He needed the facts. McNamara promised to find them… but said it may take time. That pissed off Johnson even more. There was no time. America needed to respond with resolve. There was no room for guesswork. As time passed America and its president would look weak and undecided. He told McNamara to get his people in line and come up with a solid story of what happened before he went on television that evening. McNamara agreed with the Commander-in-Chief. What else could he do?

McNamara left the oval office and immediately sent cables to the Pentagon and American Embassy in Saigon asking for clarification on what had happened. The return cables were vague and said they were working on getting to the bottom of what had really happened. McNamara feared that America was about to go to war on a lie and like all lies, there was a good chance it would eventually be discovered. But Johnson had made clear that waffling was not to be allowed. McNamara decided to piece together what he thought was the real story and stick to it as if it was the absolute truth. And it probably would have worked, except for a cog in the wheel called the Pentagon…

August 4, 1964 - Pentagon, Washington DC, USA

The cog was Daniel Ellsberg. Having completed his Ph.D. at Harvard, Ellsberg went to work for the Rand Corporation. It was during his time at Rand that Ellsberg first became aware of a secret study commissioned by Secretary of Defense McNamara. The study which would later be revealed as The Pentagon Papers was an ongoing record of the methods and data used to develop decisions made by the White House and Pentagon in the lead-up to and execution of the Vietnam War. It was designed to help future government and military leaders in making better evaluations and decisions before going to war. McNamara had been appalled at the lack of official historical information and statistical data concerning major military decisions and was determined not to continue the practice.

At the time, Ellsberg didn't think much of it beyond the good intentions behind the study. It would be several years later before the study would reveal the truth behind the war and change Ellsberg and America forever.

In August 1964, he went to work at the Defense Department at the Pentagon under Secretary of Defense Robert McNamara as a special assistant to Assistant Secretary of Defense for International Security Affairs John McNaughton.

All hell broke loose on Ellsberg's first day at the Pentagon - August 4, 1964. When he arrived at his new job, he found everyone in a panic. Several cables had been received describing multiple attacks on American warships by North Vietnamese torpedo boats. At least three torpedoes were confirmed to have been launched against the USS Maddox and USS Turner Joy. Ellsberg's new boss, McNaughton was already in his office selecting targets for retaliation. It seemed America was going to war.

Ellsberg was reading through the cables trying to get up to speed when another cable came in from the Commodore of the task force in the Gulf of Tonkin saying that all previous reports should be put on hold until he could gain more clarity as to what actually had happened. All reports of North Vietnamese torpedoes being fired at US warships were in question. Ellsberg realized that decisions were being made that could have been based on false information. He informed McNaughton of the new cable and was told to ignore it. Navy commanders were often overly cautious when it came to after-action reports.

Sidelined as the new guy that didn't know his place at the DOD, Ellsberg watched as the mechanisms of the Pentagon did what they did best – the planning and execution of warfare. It was like a train speeding down the track with everyone on board heading in the same direction. Thousands of people at the Pentagon, including Ellsberg, had read the new cable questioning the conclusions of the attack on the Maddox and Turner Joy. Nobody said anything. Everyone knew that President Johnson wanted clarity of the events before his speech to the American people scheduled for later that evening. No one was willing to rock the boat even if it meant going to war.

August 4, 1964 - White House – Washington DC, USA

At a little before midnight Eastern Standard Time,

President Johnson stood before a television camera broadcasting to millions of Americans. His tone was serious as he said, "My fellow Americans: As President and Commander-in-Chief, it is my duty to the American people to report that renewed hostile actions against United States ships on the high seas in the Gulf of Tonkin have today required me to order the military forces of the United States to take action in reply.

The initial attack on the destroyer Maddox, on August 2, was repeated today by a number of hostile vessels attacking two U.S. destroyers with torpedoes. The destroyers and supporting aircraft acted at once on the orders I gave after the initial act of aggression. We believe at least two of the attacking boats were sunk. There were no U.S. losses. The performance of commanders and crews in this engagement was in the highest tradition of the United States Navy. But repeated acts of violence against the Armed Forces of the United States must be met not only with alert defense but with a positive reply. That reply is being given as I speak to you tonight. Air action is now in execution against gunboats and certain supporting facilities in North Vietnam which have been used in these hostile operations. In the larger sense this new act of aggression aimed directly at our own forces, again brings home to all of us in the United States the importance of the struggle for peace and security in southeast Asia. Aggression by terror against the peaceful villagers of South Vietnam has now been joined by open aggression on the high seas against the United States of America. The determination of all Americans to carry out our full commitment to the people and to the government of South Vietnam will be redoubled by this outrage. Yet our response, for the present, will be limited and fitting. We Americans know, although others appear to forget, the risks of spreading conflict. We still seek no wider war. I have instructed the Secretary of State to make this position totally clear to friends and to adversaries and, indeed, to all. I have instructed Ambassador Stevenson to raise this matter immediately and urgently before the Security Council of the United Nations. Finally, I have today met with the leaders of both parties in the Congress of the United States and I have informed them that I shall immediately request Congress to pass a resolution making it clear that our Government is united in its determination to take all necessary measures in support of freedom and in defense of peace in southeast Asia. I have been given encouraging assurance by these leaders of both parties that such a resolution will be promptly introduced, freely and expeditiously debated, and passed with overwhelming support. And just a few minutes ago I was able to reach Senator Goldwater and I am glad to say that he has expressed his support of the statement that I am making to you tonight. It is a solemn responsibility to have to order even limited military action by forces whose overall strength is as vast and as awesome as those of the United States of America, but it is my considered conviction, shared throughout your government, that firmness in the right is indispensable today for peace; that firmness will always be measured. Its mission is peace."

After the broadcast, Johnson would privately admit to one of his advisors, "For all I know, our navy was shooting at whales out there." Johnson knew that the reports on the torpedo boat attacks on the Maddox and

Turner Joy were sketchy at best. And yet, he used that event to expand a war that would last eleven years, cost over a million lives, and tear America apart.

August 5, 1964 - North Vietnam Coastline

It was early the next morning when American warplanes from the aircraft carriers Ticonderoga and Constellation reached their targets on the coast of North Vietnam. During "Operation Pierce Arrow" sixty-four sorties were flown from the two warships over a five-hour period. It was the first time American warplanes were to publicly bomb targets in North Vietnam.

Through a series of low-level attacks on the Hon Gay, Loc Chao, Phuc Loi, and Quang Khe PT boat bases, the US fighter-bombers destroyed over half of the North Vietnamese Navy in just a few hours. In addition, the American pilots took out multiple shore facilities including the Vinh oil depot that held ten percent of North Vietnam's petroleum supply. A thick column of black smoke rose 14,000 feet from the burning storage tanks. No civilian population centers were targeted during the assault.

Two American aircraft were shot down by North Vietnamese anti-aircraft guns during the raids. During his after-mission briefing with the press, McNamara reported that both pilots were believed to be lost when their jets plunged into the sea. No bodies were ever recovered. Two more aircraft were heavily damaged but made it back to their ships. All other aircraft were recovered safely.

What McNamara failed to mention in his press conference was that one of the downed pilots,

Lieutenant Everett Alvarez, had survived when he ejected from his A-4 Skyhawk before it crashed into the sea. Landing in the water, he was taken prisoner by the crew of a local fishing boat and turned over to the North Vietnamese military. Since there was no declaration of war, Alvarez was branded a criminal and sent to the Hoa Lo prison compound, later to nicknamed, "The Hanoi Hilton." He was tortured and almost starved to death by his North Vietnamese captors. Imprisoned for over nine years, Alvarez would be the longest POW in the Vietnam War. Alvarez was the recipient of numerous awards, including the Silver Star and the Distinguished Flying Cross.

Undeterred, the USS Maddox and USS Turner Joy returned to their electronic surveillance patrols in the South China Sea. It was now North Vietnam's turn to respond.

August 6, 1964 – Hanoi, North Vietnam

After months of training at Mengzi airfield in Yunnan province in China, the North Vietnamese 921st Sao Dao Squadron arrived at Phuc Yen Air Base near Hanoi. They brought thirty-six MiG-17 and MiG-19 fighters with them creating for the first time a viable Air Force to counter the American and South Vietnamese bombing threats.

The government in the North did not believe Johnson when he said that he did not want a wider war. The members of the politburo believed that America's escalation of the war including the use of US combat troops in Vietnam was inevitable. They resolved to increase their efforts in the South and win the war before the United States troops were deployed. Their thinking was that if the South fell, it would be a fait du compli and the US would no longer interfere. For the first time, Hanoi sent large numbers of North Vietnamese regulars into the South by way of Laos on the Ho Chi Minh trail.

August 7, 1964, Capitol Hill – Washington DC, USA

Two days after the first aerial attacks on North Vietnam, the US Congress passed the Gulf of Tonkin Resolution giving President Johnson unrestricted authority to protect US troops and interests in Southeast Asia. The unanimous affirmative vote in the House of Representatives was 416–0 and the Senate conferred its approval by a vote of 88–2.

Few of the Congressmen that voted for the resolution were aware of Johnson's and McNamara's doubts concerning the second attack. Even fewer of the senators and representatives knew of the connection between the North Vietnam bombing missions and the U.S.-sponsored raids on the islands in the North or that the USS Maddox was on an intelligence mission when it was first attacked on August 2nd. America's temperament was clear and the congressmen could easily see the direction the political wind was blowing. South Vietnam had to be saved to stop the dominos from falling and to keep America safe in the long run.

Only Senator Wayne Morse of Oregon and Senator Ernest Gruening of Alaska opposed publicly American military involvement in South Vietnam. The senators strongly disagreed with McNamara's evaluation of the situation in Vietnam. To repudiate McNamara's position that America was fighting communism in South Vietnam, Senator Morse said, "There are no Chinese soldiers in South Vietnam. There are no Russian soldiers in South Vietnam. The only foreign soldiers in South Vietnam are US soldiers."

At that point in time, none of the other Congressmen were interested in siding with Senators Morse and Gruening. Political will would change over the years as more American soldiers were killed and arrived home in coffins.

Three days later, Johnson signed the bill into law and it became effective. The immediate result of the president's actions was an outpouring of encouragement. Johnson's support for the war jumped from forty-two to seventy-two percent overnight. Having shown a firm hand in dealing with America's enemies, the issue of Vietnam was effectively removed from the election campaign and Senator Goldwater, Johnson's Republican opponent, had no other issue to run on. In November Johnson would be re-elected by a landslide. But in the meantime, he had a war to manage.

Saigon, South Vietnam

Concerned about growing opposition to his government from Buddhist monks and their followers, Prime Minister Khanh declared a state of emergency and suspended the South Vietnamese constitution.

The declaration had the opposite effect that Khanh had hoped to accomplish, and large protests broke out all over Saigon, mostly among Buddhist monks, nuns, and students.

To Ambassador Taylor it seemed like déjà vu of the Diem era. He demanded that Khanh reverse his declaration and reinstate the constitution. But to Khanh, the demonstrations only proved the need for strong action. He refused and the demonstrations continued.

August 13, 1964 – Hanoi, North Vietnam

Watching events spin out of control, Chinese leader Mao Zedong sent a cable to Le Duan. He told Duan that he did not believe that the American provocations in the Tonkin Gulf meant war. The Americans, North Vietnamese, and Chinese did not want war. Therefore, because nobody wanted to fight a war, there would be no war.

THE PAPER TIGER

August 16, 1964 – Saigon, South Vietnam

Responding to pressure from the American embassy, Prime Minister Khanh approved a new constitution with a sixty-two-member revolutionary council that had the right to veto any of Khanh's decisions. Khanh became the new president of South Vietnam, replacing the figurehead chief General Minh.

August 20, 1964 – Okinawa, Japan

As a result of the Gulf of Tonkin Incident and the US bombing campaign of North Vietnam, the White House grew more concerned about Chinese intervention in Vietnam. The Pentagon ordered surveillance overflights of Southern China near the North Vietnamese border using new technology – Lightning Bugs.

The Ryan Model 147 Lightning Bug was a jet-powered pilotless reconnaissance aircraft or drone built by Ryan Aeronautical. Originally developed from an unmanned target aircraft, the reconnaissance drones were plagued with problems. The drones were controlled by a Lockheed DC-130 that also served as an aerial launcher that carried the Lightning Bugs on underwing pylons. To save on weight and simplify the design, the Lightning Bug was built without landing gear. Once its mission was complete, the drone would fly back to friendly territory and deploy a parachute to land. The film payload would be recovered and processed for intelligence analysts. The Lightning Bug would be recycled and prepared for a new mission.

The first two Lightning Bug missions were launched from Kadena Air Base on Okinawa. The engine on one of the Lightning Bugs failed to ignite and later was lost when it dropped off the DC-130's pylon. The second drone launched successfully and completed its mission landing by parachute in a rice paddy in Taiwan. The aircraft was dragged by its parachute by local farmers and was heavily damaged. While the navigation system was less accurate than hoped, the surveillance images did reveal several Chinese targets and the mission was declared a success. Over the next month, the Americans would launch five Lightning Bug missions with only two being successful.

In October, the drone reconnaissance operations were moved to Bien Hoa Air Base in South Vietnam. The increased number of flights over Southern China and Northern Vietnam was controlled by Strategic Air Command from a facility on Monkey Mountain.

The Chinese and North Vietnamese made a concerted effort to shoot down the Lightning Bugs and were able to destroy five drones in the next year. Because no American air crews were lost when a drone was shot down, the press paid little attention to the covert missions.

August 21, 1964 – Northern Mountains, Laos

Well past midnight, the Laotian jungle was dripping and steaming from a recent thunderstorm. It was pitch dark except for the flicker of a campfire surrounded by Pathet Lao trying to keep warm from the cool, damp mountain air. A barbed-wire prison held their prisoners forced to survive without any shelter from the hot sun and the daily downpours common in the mountains.

In the jungle thirty feet away from the prison fence, a small clump of foliage moved, then disappeared as it was pulled into a newly dug tunnel opening. Unseen by their guards, five Thai and Laotian prisoners climbed out the opening and crawled deeper into the jungle. The sixth escapee and last to leave the tunnel opening was US Navy Lieutenant Klusmann who had been shot down three months earlier over the Plain of Jars. It was the second time his aircraft had been hit by Pathet Lao ground fire. The first time he had been able to pilot his jet back to the Kitty Hawk aircraft carrier. But the second time the lieutenant had not been so lucky and he was forced to eject before his RF-8A Crusader crashed into the jungle. He had been captured a short time later.

As he slipped deeper into the dark jungle, Klusmann became one of only two naval aviators to escape captivity during the war. He was rescued two days later by CIA officer Terrence Burke and taken to Bouam Long, a Royal Laotian enclave deep within communist territory. Klusmann arrived back in the United States a few months later when he was finally smuggled out of the enclave and taken to Vientiane where he caught a flight to Bangkok and then back to the states.

August 27, 1964 - Saigon, South Vietnam

With the death of South Vietnamese President Diem and his brother during a coup, most South Vietnamese thought things would calm down and the country would stabilize under a new government. The Americans would finally get what they wanted – an ARVN military focused on defeating the Viet Cong and the NVA. Nothing could have been farther from the truth. If anything, things steadily got worse.

The majority of the South Vietnamese people had hated Diem and his family. But Diem did keep the various factions throughout South Vietnam under control. The generals that replaced Diem were not politicians and had no interest in the factions that truly ruled Saigon. The generals were used to ruling by dictating without anyone's permission. This was a grave mistake and brought about an enormous amount of discontent. The Buddhists didn't want to be ruled by the Catholics and the Catholics didn't want to give up the power that they had attained under Diem. The labor unions wanted more respect and higher wages for their members. Teachers and civil servants wanted laws that protected them and higher wages. Everyone wanted something, but the generals ignored them all.

And if that wasn't enough, the generals plotted against each other as they grabbed for power and control. Factions within the military sprang up supporting the generals that led them.

General Khanh had taken power when he overthrew the head of state after Diem, General Minh in an almost bloodless coup. Minh had originally been popular with the South Vietnamese people, but his inability to get things done quickly turned the people and the other generals against him. The Americans didn't care who was in power as long as they fought the Viet Cong and stopped communist expansionism.

When Khanh came to power, he moved forward quickly with many plans and seemed to be making headway. He also sent his troops to fight the Viet Cong. But Khanh was unreliable and did not follow through with the plans that he had made. He changed his mind like the wind whenever he came up against significant opposition. His desire to remain popular was more important to him than ruling the country.

When labor unions went on strike, he gave them what they wanted. When the Buddhists protested, he gave them what they wanted. The same was true with anyone that opposed him. He was great at negotiating by giving away more and more of the country's wealth and refused to take a stand against his opposition. The people loved him for his leniency. The generals hated him for his showboating. The Americans were concerned that there would be nothing left to govern if Khanh kept giving in to the opposition.

Even when Khanh gave concessions to his opposition, it only made them want more. The Buddhists demanded that the Catholics be removed from government positions, then threatened to stop supporting the war effort if they didn't get their way. The Catholics protested that they had been persecuted because of their religion since Diem's death and wanted laws that protected them.

Accused of being a "Paper Tiger," Khanh knew that he needed to show strength. With the Buddhist far outnumbering the Catholics, Khanh chose a show of force against a Catholic protest against his government and the United States that supported the coup that led to President Diem's death. ARVN troops were called in to confront the demonstrators outside the National Military Headquarters in Saigon. Even unarmed, the 3,000 protestors were a real threat as they hurled bottles and rocks at the soldiers. The soldiers were ordered to open fire. Several protestors were killed, and many more were wounded. This only exacerbated the problem.

The Buddhist leader, Thich Tri Quang was concerned that the unreliable Khanh would now swing in the opposite direction and give more power to the Catholic leaders to compensate them for their losses. Quang went to the US embassy and warned the Americans that the Buddhists would withdraw from the war leaving the Americans and the Catholics to fight the communists if he did not get his way. When Ambassador Taylor reminded Quang that the communists would most likely kill the Buddhist leaders and arrest their followers if they took power in the South, Quang said it was better to be ruled by Vietnamese than foreigners.

Street fighting broke out between Buddhists, Catholics, and students that supported both sides of the conflict. The Americans were concerned about the Viet Cong taking advantage of the instability in the capital.

Facing a growing number of protests, Khanh resigned and fled to Da Lat where he had his support base to protect him. The Americans were surprised by Khanh's actions and realized that he was the only leader available that could quell the violence spreading like a wildfire. No other general wanted to step up and lead with the protests growing out of control. Without leadership the government was helpless. Mayhem ruled.

Nguyen Xuan Oanh, a popular politician, was appointed as prime minister and charged with forming a caretaker government until domestic unrest and rioting could be brought under control. It didn't help. A strong hand was needed against the factions and Oanh, known for his ability to find a compromise, was not that kind of leader.

Desperate to solve the situation, Ambassador Taylor traveled to Da Lat and persuaded Khanh to return to power by agreeing to make a public statement that the United States supported Khanh.

Although it was not a perfect solution, Taylor's plan did work. Khanh returned to Saigon and sat down with the leaders of the various factions. Once again, he made concessions. More and more Khanh was siding with the Buddhists who he needed more than the Catholics. The Buddhist leader Quang was opposed to foreign influences such as the United States and Catholicism. But at least there was once again peace in the capital.

In September, the Khanh government was forced to step down and succeeded by a baffling array of unstable coalitions, some of which stayed in power for less than a month. During that time, even the best ARVN units seemed incapable of defeating the Viet Cong. The South Vietnamese troops had once again been demoralized and lost their will to fight as the confusion in Saigon continued. Not even their American advisors could shake them from their malaise. With little opposition, the communists were now deliberately targeting US military personnel and bases. Unable to stop them, the South Vietnamese military seemed paralyzed by politics.

September 9, 1964 – White House – Washington DC, USA

Meeting with Ambassador Taylor and the National Security advisers for the first time since the Gulf of Tonkin incident, President Johnson asked, "Does anyone doubt that Vietnam is worth fighting a war over?"

At that point, everyone at the meeting agreed that it was necessary to fight in Vietnam to protect the credibility of the United States worldwide. Taylor said, "The United States can not afford to let Hanoi win, in terms of our overall position in the area and the world."

The Chairman of the Joint Chiefs of Staff, General Earle Wheeler said, "If we should lose in South Vietnam, we would lose southeast Asia. Then, country after country on the periphery would give way and look toward Communist China as the rising power of the area."

It was not what Johnson had hoped to hear. He wanted a way out of an impossible situation with dire consequences. None was offered. He was stuck.

As a result of that meeting, President Johnson approved National Security Action Memorandum 314 which authorized the immediate resumption of naval patrols in the Tonkin Gulf and clandestine operations against North Vietnam under Operation 34A, limited military and covert actions in Laos, retaliatory actions if American personnel were attacked, and continued economic and military aid to South Vietnam. And then things went from bad to worse…

September 10, 1964 - Saigon, South Vietnam

To quell growing protests by the Buddhists over the unequal treatment of South Vietnamese religions in participation in governing, Prime Minister Khanh offered concessions to the leaders. Khanh promised the Buddhists an end to military rule and true democracy in the near future. This was seen as a sign of weakness among the South Vietnamese generals sitting on the military council. In response to more pressure from the Buddhist monks, Khanh removed Catholic generals Lam Van Phat and Duong Van Duc from their posts as Interior Minister and IV Corps commander, respectively. This did not sit well with either of the generals and other catholic officers that supported them. Once again, trouble was brewing…

Within a few days and with little forethought, the two generals and a third Catholic general Tran Thien Khiem, who had helped Prime Minister Khanh to power, executed a coup d'etat using the ten battalions around Saigon under their command. They quickly captured key government and communications facilities including the radio station. Phat then broadcasted throughout the capital promising a return to deceased President Diem's policies.

Khanh narrowly evaded capture. There was little fighting since the majority of the senior military officers refused to support either side. As was the case of post-Diem politics, most everyone was sitting on the sidelines waiting to see how things played out.

Although angry that another coup was underway, the Americans in the embassy were supportive of

Prime Minister Khanh and his administration. As usual, the Americans would not participate militarily in resolving the outcome in Khanh's favor but wished him luck. He would need it. Behind the scenes, the American advisors embedded in South Vietnamese units, encouraged the ARVN officers not to participate in the coup. The Voice of America broadcast a message emphasizing ongoing US support for Khanh and opposition to the coup. Khanh asked General Westmoreland to use US Marines to come to his aid. Although no US forces were involved in the coup, several Marine elements were placed offshore near Saigon and Da Nang in readiness to evacuate Americans if things got ugly. Westmoreland did contact the generals in charge of the coup and informed them in no uncertain terms that the United States government did not and would not support them even if their coup was successful. The American general advised the coup leaders to get their forces out of Saigon immediately before they did more damage to the South Vietnamese military effort against the Viet Cong and the North.

Throughout the day, Khanh contacted the leaders of various factions and rallied them to his side. Air Force Commander Nguyen Cao Ky and Generals Nguyen Chanh Thi and Nguyen Van Thieu sided with Khanh. Ky, Thi, and Thieu were the most prominent of the Young Turks, who gained increasing power in Saigon junta politics.

The next morning, Ky ordered a squadron of heavily armed jets to fly over Saigon at top speed as a warning to coup forces of what was to come if they didn't back down. Having been alarmed at Phat's strong statements on the radio and faced with the annihilation of his men by Ky's air force, Duc was the first to fold. He ordered his battalions to leave Saigon and return to their headquarters at My Tho. Khanh with the help of the Young Turks was able to force the remaining coup leaders to capitulate and the coup ended.

To placate the Americans, Duc, Ky, and Thi appeared at a media event where they proceeded to deny that a coup had taken place and claimed that nobody would be prosecuted over the events since they never happened. The Americans were not amused.

In addition, Khanh was now indebted to Ky, Thi, and Thieu due to their intervention in putting down the coup. In an attempt to maintain his political power, Khanh courted the support of Buddhist activists, who supported negotiations with the communists to end the war. Since the Americans were strongly opposed to this policy, the embassy's relations with Khanh began to decline as military opposition against him increased. He was truly between a rock and a hard place.

September 19, 1964 – Central Highlands, South Vietnam

For centuries, the Montagnard had been treated as second-class citizens in Indochina, then Vietnam. Montagnard complaints included: encroachment on tribal lands; no legislative representation; shabby treatment by local magistrates; refusal to allow their languages to be taught in schools; and promises of aid that never materialized.

Even when the Montagnard volunteered to fight the Viet Cong and NVA, they still garnered little respect from their South Vietnamese Special Forces commanders who regularly referred to the Montagnard as Moi, a pejorative term meaning barbarians or savages.

Having seen the protests in Saigon and the concessions offered by the government to civilians that were not even fighting for their country, the Montagnard had enough. Unimpressed with Saigon's ability to control the nation, the Montagnard wanted autonomy if they were to continue to fight the communists. They believed they deserved it.

In 1962, the Montagnard army in a single province in the Central Highlands was 10,000 strong with over 1,500 warriors organized into Mike forces that protected over 200 villages. Their leaders were South Vietnamese Special Forces officers accompanied by American Green Beret advisors. Their main mission was defensive, protecting their territory and villages from Viet Cong raids.

Considered to be wildly successful, the hill tribes program was expanded all across South Vietnam stretching from the DMZ on the northern border down to the southernmost part of the Mekong Delta.

Unhappy that the CIA was commanding such a large number of combat troops, MACV pleaded its case to the White House and took control of the program. Confusion increased when Khanh took over the government in a bloodless coup and issued a flurry of orders directed toward the Montagnard forces. The Montagnard were not happy with their new leaders which changed their role from defensive to offensive. With large groups of warriors ordered to attack the Viet Cong bases, the Montagnard villages were left shorthanded and under-protected. The Montagnard had been trained in defensive methods and were ill-prepared to carry out offensive assignments.

To exacerbate problems even further, supplies earmarked for Montagnard villages were being skimmed by corrupt provincial administrators. It seemed to the Montagnard like the government was not following through on its promises to the hill tribesmen. Hearing of the shortfalls, the US Special Forces logistics team made up the difference. It became clear to the Montagnard that the Americans were the ones giving them aid, not their own government. The loyalty of the soldiers in the Montagnard units shifted from the South Vietnamese commanders to the American advisors. This made Saigon angry at the foreign influence intervening in domestic affairs. It was a tangled mess.

On September 16th, 1964, problems came to a head, when five Montagnard camps attacked their command posts killing dozens of South Vietnamese soldiers and taking others hostage. The American Special Forces commanders tried to stop them with little success. The Montagnard had been pushed too far and were now taking their revenge. In some villages, the American advisors were taken hostage, although none were harmed.

As the Montagnard warriors set out to overthrow the provincial capital, the US advisors threw themselves in front of the warriors and pleaded with them to stop their futile revolt. The Americans knew that if the revolt spread to other Montagnard villages, the country would descend into civil war. With the local garrisons abandoned, the Viet Cong could very well take control of the local government and potentially bring the Montagnard villages under their control. When that happened all bets were off…

Saigon, South Vietnam

News of the revolt reached Saigon the next morning. Khanh ordered the military to put down the revolt and sent forces to the Central Highlands to reinforce the Army and the abandoned Montagnard garrisons.

General Westmoreland was concerned the battles between the ARVN and Montagnard might spark a countrywide insurrection that could topple the unstable South Vietnamese government. The MACV commander sent his operational commander, Brigadier General William DePuy, to straighten things out between the Montagnard and the ARVN. Before leaving for the highlands, DePuy met with Khanh's commanders and asked them to show constraint. He needed time for his plan to work. He also asked that they straighten out the supply problems to the Montagnard, his way of saying they should stop stealing them.

One of DePuy's biggest problems was that Khanh had made promises to the Montagnard but failed to keep them. This created mistrust and was one of the reasons for the revolt. He asked Khanh not to make pledges that he couldn't or wouldn't keep in the future. DePuy and Westmoreland wanted long-term stability in the Central Highlands. In addition to protecting their villages, the Montagnard had become a blocking force against North Vietnamese weapons and supplies being carried on the Ho Chi Minh trail. The Americans wanted that to continue. Khanh and his commanders agreed to DePuy's requests.

DePuy told Westmoreland that he felt Khanh and

his commanders acted as if they were doing the Americans a favor and would want something in return at a later date. Westmoreland believed that kind of thinking was what was wrong in Vietnam, but suggested DePuy disregard it and get the job done.

Central Highlands, South Vietnam

DePuy arrived in the highlands and immediately met with the elders of each village and the chiefs of the Montagnard camps. He listened to their complaints and asked intelligent questions that showed he meant to do something about their grievances. The general showed them a letter from Khanh that declared immunity for the Montagnard if they returned to camps and released the hostages without further bloodshed.

DuPuy's diplomacy worked. By September 28th, all of the hostages had been released and the Montagnard warriors had returned to the camps. It was an uneasy peace with the Montagnard wary of anything promised from Saigon. But DePuy had assured them the United States would its best to see that the South Vietnamese government and military would keep their word. The Montagnard knew that the South Vietnamese were dependent on American aid and therefore the Americans had strong leverage to ensure promises were kept.

To Westmoreland and DePuy it felt like the United States was being asked more and more to interfere with the internal politics of South Vietnam, yet little was being done by the ARVN forces to fight the Viet Cong and save their country. It was beyond frustrating. DePuy said that the American advisors were often perceived by the South Vietnamese unit commanders as helpers to call in air and artillery strikes when needed and nothing more. The South Vietnamese commanders made it abundantly clear that the Americans were not in charge and often disregarded their advice.

Within weeks of the end of the revolt, South Vietnamese commanders complained that the Montagnard had become more loyal to the American advisors than to their South Vietnamese unit commanders. They accused the Americans of stealing the Montagnard's loyalty by using bribes of more weapons and supplies and offering them jobs to rebuild their villages and garrisons. The Americans were taking the tribesmen's side whenever there were disputes between the ARVN and Montagnard. The US Advisors could do nothing but shrug, then promised to be more firm and less charitable with the Montagnard so the South Vietnamese commanders would look good. It was like raising siblings that were always fighting.

Originally opposed to any additional troops in Vietnam, Westmoreland told DePuy that he felt things would be far easier if they fought the war and the ARVN troops were used for support and to protect the major population centers as they were currently doing. DePuy agreed. Westmoreland's thinking was evolving and he was building support with his commanders for a new strategy.

September 25, 1964 – New York, USA

During a campaign stop at New York's Central Station, President Johnson addressed a group of reporters and said, "There are those that say you ought to go north and drop bombs, to try to wipe out the supply lines, and they think that would escalate the war. We don't want our American boys to do the fighting for Asian boys."

Nearby at the United Nations building, UN Secretary-General U Thant had secured an agreement with the North Vietnamese to engage in initial talks with the United States on ending the war. He immediately passed on the news to US UN Ambassador Adlai Stevenson. Stevenson was surprised and conveyed the information to Secretary of State Rusk.

But after several weeks, the White House had not responded to the invitation for talks. When Stevenson inquired, he was told that President Johnson was too busy with his re-election campaign to respond. When word of the slight reached Secretary-General Thant, he wondered if the invitation for talks was even shared with President Johnson. A stickler for protocol, Thant made no attempt to contact Johnson directly or even through back channels. The talks were dead before they even started. Instead, a war would decide the fate of Vietnam.

September 25, 1964 – Saigon, South Vietnam

To placate the continued pressure from the American officials at the embassy and the Buddhist community, Prime Minister Khanh and the senior officers in the military junta created a High National Council. The new council was staffed by civilians and served as a national legislature. It gave the impression that the Khanh and the military junta were moving toward civilian rule. The Americans and Buddhists saw it as a step in the right direction, but after the recent coup attempt, nobody was holding their breath.

BARREL ROLL

Vientiane, Laos

As part of President Kennedy's "Country Team" directive in 1961, all government agencies including the military were placed under the direct command of the country's US ambassador. As a consequence, newly arrived US Ambassador for Laos William Sullivan was heavily involved in the planning of covert military actions. So much so that Westmoreland nicknamed him, "The Field Marshal." Sullivan took seriously the interdiction of supplies and weapons on the Ho Chi Minh trail. He supported and encouraged the SOG commanders as they organized the hill tribesman into hatchet forces to fight the North Vietnamese and Pathet Lao rebels. But it still wasn't enough in his mind. His first major directive was named "Operation Barrel Roll."

The secret war in Laos was never intended to be an all-out effort by the United States. Instead, it was more of a holding action while the war in South Vietnam was carried out to a positive outcome in one or two years. Nobody thought the war would last as long as it did in either country.

Unlike the war in South Vietnam, which was mostly public, the war in Laos was one of the best-kept secrets in Southeast Asia. It had to be.

In 1962 in Geneva, Switzerland, the international community, and the warring sides in Laos agreed to a Declaration of the Neutrality of Laos. Although all sides could have been sincere at the time of signing, it soon became a big farce. The North Vietnamese were not about to give up their access and defense of the Ho Chi Minh Trail while the war continued to be fought in South Vietnam. And the Americans and their allies were not about to give the North Vietnamese and their allies a free pass to smuggle supplies and weapons to the Viet Cong.

The solution was for both sides to publicly deny that a war in Laos existed. While both sides would have loved to uncover the misdeeds of their opponents in Laos, the politicians found it more prudent to just not mention anything about hostilities or foreign troops in the country. Both sides were cheating, so silence became golden.

For the Americans, Laos evolved almost exclusively into an air war. The United States Air Force used conventional air power to support unconventional ground forces fighting to cut off the Ho Chi Minh Trail while protecting the fragile government in Vientiane and insulating Thailand from communist aggression. The generals in the Pentagon knew very well that the war in Laos could not be won by air without taking the ground below which was almost impossible since it was covered with steep mountains and jungle. The main objective of the secret war was not to win but rather to keep access open to Laos while the war in Vietnam was being fought. When the war in Vietnam was finally won, the Americans would deal with Laos and kick out the communists that were sure to hide across the border.

In Hanoi, Laos was also a holding action to keep the Ho Chi Minh Trail open. The leaders in North Vietnam needed to keep up the cover story that the war in the South was a popular uprising and not directed by the North. As long as supplies and weapons could be shipped covertly through Laos the lie was credible.

The CIA directed covert military efforts in Laos using the Royal Lao military and the Montagnard tribesmen led by their SOG advisors. The CIA established Headquarters 333 at Udon Thani in northeastern Thailand which served as a joint command center for covert military and intelligence activities in Laos. Logistical airlift to supply the Montagnard and SOG were provided by Air America, Bird and Son, and Continental Air Services, all of which were CIA-owned or sponsored airlines. Under Project Waterpump, the CIA provided a squadron of North American T-28Ds for use by American-trained Laotian, Thai, and Montagnard aircrews to support ground forces. The covert program produced the world's only guerrilla army with air superiority.

Hanoi principally used the Pathet Lao and their own troops to protect the logistical trail and fight off the American allies. The jungle canopy concealed the real story of what was going on in Laos.

Barrel Roll was conceived and planned during several secret meetings which included Sullivan, the Laos CIA station chief, the MACV commander, the SOG commander, the Air America commander, the USAF Seventh Air Force Commander, Lao Prime Minister

Souvanna Phouma, and Lao General Van Pao. Together they laid out an aggressive air campaign designed to cut off the Ho Chi Minh Trail and diminish the Pathet Lao by supporting allied ground actions codenamed "Tiger Hound" in the mountains of northeastern Laos. Command and control of the area of operation were handed over to Westmoreland in Saigon, but Sullivan was still ultimately in charge since the operations were in Laos. He watched Westmoreland like a hawk and often offered suggestions and strategies. Westmoreland was unamused and at times threatened to toss the whole thing back in Sullivan's lap.

Barrel Roll targets could be requested by the CIA, MACV, or the Royal Lao government. But it was decided at a Honolulu Executive Conference that Laos was not to become a priority of American air assets. US aircraft could be used for interdiction efforts in Laos only after close air support needs in South Vietnam had been met. Westmoreland also retained veto power on any bombing, interdiction, or reconnaissance air missions in Laos. As a stepsister of the Vietnam operations Rolling Thunder and Steel Tiger, this policy limited Barrel Roll's effectiveness in Laos. Most USAF aircraft would take off from Thailand, land in South Vietnam, then take off again to fly their missions in Laos before returning to Thailand. This extra step appeased the Thai who did not want to be accused of attacking Laos directly.

The aircraft utilized as part of Barrel Roll was an eclectic mix of vintage propeller-driven attack aircraft and fast-moving fighter jets. There were also cargo and transport planes left over from World War II. The majority of the close air support missions were conducted by Douglas A-1 Skyraiders and AT-28 Trojans. These propeller-driven Korean War-era aircraft came into their own in Southeast Asia. Their heavy ordnance loads, long loiter times, and high maneuverability at low altitudes made them more efficient than the more modern jet Air Force in the mountains of Laos.

Many of the bombs dropped in Barrel Roll were originally meant for North Vietnam targets, but for whatever reason were not dropped during their missions. As the bombers returned to Thailand, their aircrews released their bombs on designated targets in Laos. The commanders in Laos didn't care that the bombs were leftovers. The more bombs dropped meant more damage to the enemy and the Ho Chi Minh Trail. They would take whatever they could get.

Electronic tactical air navigation (TACAN) became an absolute necessity in Laos, where mountain peaks and unexpected inclement weather made flying extremely hazardous. This problem was solved by establishing unmanned Air Force stations that broadcast continuous radio transmissions, allowing navigation from fixed geographic reference points.

To support the Montagnard and SOG teams, the Americans established over 200 Lima Sites throughout Laos. The sites were made of rough landing strips and rudimentary supply depots. In the mountainous areas, the sites were compact and could only accommodate smaller aircraft with short landing and takeoff capabilities. Some were built at the top of mountain peaks where the planes would plop down and almost immediately stop because of the angle. Reeving the aircraft's engine until rocks could be placed behind the wheels kept it from sliding back down the mountain. Once unloaded, the pilots would turn around and then let mountain updrafts lift the lighter plane into the air with almost no runway. The small plane acted more like helicopters than fixed-wing aircraft.

For the Barrel Roll bombing campaign to be effective the aircraft need forward air controls to pinpoint targets in the rugged, jungle-covered terrain of Laos. The problem was a lack of reconnaissance aircraft and pilots capable of navigating in the mountains. As a solution, the USAF dispatched "sheep-dipped" Air Commandos from Combat Control Teams. They would parachute into the mountains of eastern Laos and find the bombing targets on foot. Although it worked, this method was ineffective and time-consuming. There simply were not enough Air Commandos to make a real difference in the campaign.

Air Commando Sergeants James Stanford and Charles Larimore Jones set out to solve the problem. To make the commandos more effective, the CIA assigned Air America and Continental Air Services aircraft to transport the commandos and identify the targets from the air. Stanford and Jones updated forward air controller (FAC) manuals to train more soldiers and expand the FAC program. O-1 Bird Dogs, U-17s, T-28s, and eventually, more O-2 Skymasters and OV-10 Broncos were sent to Laos and used by the FAC to mark targets. Each reconnaissance flight included a Laotian soldier to approve the target. The idea was to expedite mission approval before the target moved. The FAC teams used the call sign Butterfly. While everything seemed to be assembled with tape and glue, the ingenuity and dedication of the original

FACs in Laos made the program a huge success. Due to their unconventional backgrounds, most were not officers or even certified pilots, the Butterflies were eventually replaced by more experienced pilots using the call sign Ravens.

The aerial rules of engagement described the limits of the offensive action of pilots and the locations and circumstances under which offensive actions could be taken. They were created to protect the civilian population in Laos. To the American and allied pilots, the rules of engagement became complex to the point of absurdity. Nobody understood them and many were impossible to follow even when understood. And to make matters worse, the rules were constantly altered by the politicians in Washington and Vientiane. Most of the time, they bore little resemblance to the reality on the ground. There were different rules for every type of action, for each branch of service, and each military region throughout the country.

The rules that controlled the aerial operations stipulated that there would be no napalm used in Laos, that no enemy trucks could be attacked more than 200 meters from a road, and that no enemy forces could be bombed within 1,000 meters of a pagoda. Although these restrictions were often altered or removed, there were always others to take their place. There were "no bomb zones" that unintentionally created sanctuaries for PAVN and Pathet Lao forces. As the enemy studied American actions and adjusted to them, Pagodas and suspected PAVN hospitals were simply turned into ammunition dumps, supply caches, and anti-aircraft sites.

The strategic Plain of Jars was a plateau covered with grass and small hills spread over an area of approximately 500 square miles. Only sixty miles north of Vientiane, the Laotian capital, the area was hotly contested between the Montagnard forces, PAVN, and the Pathet Lao.

It was evident that the cyclical pattern of the monsoon weather would dictate the timing and pace of military operations in the northeast. During the dry season, North Vietnamese and Pathet Lao forces advanced out of Sam Neua Province along Route 6 and out of the Barthelemy Pass-through Ban Ban. Their target was the Plain of Jars and then Vientiane. The primitive state of the few roads in the area forced the communists to stretch their lines of communication taut and they were unable to create parallel supply routes. This invited counterattacks once the dry season had passed, and the communist forces could no longer maneuver. During the wet season, Vang Pao's Montagnard forces utilized air power, air mobility, and guerrilla tactics to push the communists back to their starting places.

Barrel Roll lasted eight long years. Although it was not the most effective program, it did accomplish the main goal to keep Laos open and drive back the communists. The pilots that flew their missions over the treacherous mountains and jungles of Laos became some of the best in southeast Asia. Because of the covert nature of their missions, few knew of their heroism.

October 14, 1964 – Moscow, Russia

Shortly after Stalin died in 1953, Nikita Khrushchev

replaced his mentor as First Secretary of the Communist Party of the Soviet Union. Khrushchev stunned the communist world with his denunciation of Stalin's crimes and embarked on a policy of de-Stalinization. Khrushchev could be charming or vulgar, cheerful or sullen. He was given to public displays of rage which were often contrived and to soaring embellishment in his rhetoric. He came across as more human than his predecessor or even than most of his foreign counterparts, and that made the USSR seem less mysterious or menacing. He was responsible for the Soviet space program and sought to ease tensions with the west wherever possible. He feared a nuclear war that he knew his country would lose. Although he had done much to help the North Vietnamese to reunite their country under a communist government, Khrushchev was also cautious and often put conditions on the aid offered by the USSR. After his success in helping Fidel Castro defeat the Bay of Pigs invasion of Cuba, Khrushchev stumbled during the Cuban Missile Crisis. The leaders in the Kremlin saw his waffling as a sign of weakness and his rival and protégé, Leonid Brezhnev, began planning Khrushchev's overthrow in the politburo.

Brezhnev was fifty-eight in 1964. He was described by many as caring and sensitive, but more importantly stable. He lacked the mood swings of Khrushchev. He had a strong sense of humor and a love of fast cars. He was a dedicated family man and while he had affairs with other women, he kept them private. He was a chain-smoker with a passion for Marlboro cigarettes. More than anything, Brezhnev loved his country and was a party man dedicated to the expansion of communism. His comrades in the politburo realized he was what Russia needed after Khrushchev's explosive nature.

Brezhnev considered having Khrushchev arrested as he returned from a trip to Scandinavia in June, but instead, he spent time persuading members of the Central Committee to support his removal of Khrushchev.

Khrushchev's downfall was not a coup, because it followed the Central Committee procedures for naming leadership that Khrushchev had himself introduced. There were no show trials, no ritual attacks, no public confessions, and no executions. For most members of the Central Committee, there was a growing annoyance with Khrushchev's arbitrary decision-making. In the end, he was too old and tired. In his last years as party leader, he had paid less attention to maintaining his political base, while his enemies carefully and systematically assembled a coalition in the Party's Central Committee.

While Khrushchev was on vacation at Pitsunda, Brezhnev called to notify him of a special Presidium meeting to be held the following day, ostensibly on the subject of agriculture. Even though Khrushchev suspected the real reason for the meeting, he flew to Moscow taking no precautions. When he landed at Vnukovo Airport, Khrushchev was arrested and taken to the Kremlin, to be verbally attacked by Brezhnev. Khrushchev had no stomach for a fight and put-up little resistance. The next day, the Presidium and the Central Committee each voted to accept Khrushchev's "voluntary" request to retire from his offices for reasons of "advanced age and ill health." It was done. Brezhnev was elected First Secretary and Alexei Kosygin was appointed premier.

The new Soviet leadership increased military aid to the North Vietnamese without tying it to preconditions. With this support and no external pressure to negotiate peace, Le Duan and the North Vietnamese leadership were free to carry on the war as they saw fit.

October 16, 1964 – Lop Nur, China

While Khrushchev was still in power, he had intended to help the Chinese become a nuclear power. In the USSR, a nuclear device was made as a prototype along with a slew of manufacturing, testing, and operational documents that would allow the Chinese to develop their nuclear technology even further.

After a falling out with Mao over his nonchalant view of nuclear war, Khrushchev got cold feet and ordered the device and documents destroyed. Over 1,400 Soviet advisors and scientists were withdrawn from China. The Chinese scientists were on their own. The Chinese named their new nuclear development effort Project 596 and built a huge development and testing facility at a location near Lake Lop Nur in Xinjiang Province. It took tens of thousands of laborers and prisoners four years to construct the facilities and surrounding site.

Once the Chinese had enough fissionable U-235 from their enrichment plant in Lanzhou, they prepared their own device – a uranium-235 fission implosion device weighing 1550 kilograms. The device was hoisted up a 102-meter tower and detonated. The results produced a yield of 22 kilotons, similar in size to the Soviet's first nuclear bomb in 1949 and America's Fat Man bomb dropped on Nagasaki, Japan in 1945. China was the fifth nation with nuclear capabilities. The Chinese would go on to complete forty-five successful nuclear tests over the next two years.

Hanoi saw China's new weapon as a strong deterrent to any potential invasion of North Vietnam by South Vietnam and its American allies. Nobody wanted nuclear war and even the threat of it would alter a nation's policies and military strategies.

White House – Washington DC, USA

President Johnson was understandably concerned, but not completely surprised when he was informed about the Chinese nuclear test. The CIA had given him an advanced warning of the Chinese progress in developing the device and the testing facility. There wasn't much he could do about it. There was a discussion with the Pentagon about the possibility of bombing the Chinese enrichment facilities or the test site to slow them down, but that was just wishful thinking mixed with bravado, and nobody wanted to start World War III. What was done, was done. The world would just have to live with a nuclear China.

It did have some influence on the American strategy for North Vietnam, but it didn't change the fact that the war was expanding, and the USAF continued to bomb the North. There were discussions about a Chinese reaction, but the Pentagon and the CIA believed Chinese fighter aircraft entering the theatre was a far more likely response than using a nuclear bomb. The Chinese had few options when it came to delivery. They didn't have bombers big enough to carry a nuclear bomb and their missile technology was not advanced enough to carry a nuclear payload and accurately target a city, even in South Vietnam. The only real way to deliver a nuclear weapon to a target was to borrow a bomber or missile from the Soviet Union and they were in no mood to help China.

Hanoi, North Vietnam

The Americans had bombed the north and in so doing had expanded the war just as Le Duan had hoped. He could now point to the American actions and claim that Ho Chi Minh's policy of tolerance to keep the Americans out of the war was a failure. Duan respected Ho, but he did not agree with him and often went behind his mentor's back to accomplish the tasks that needed to be done.

Duan now had the full support of the politburo and few questioned his decisions when it came to executing the war on the south. Armed with the latest Russian and Chinese weapons, North Vietnamese troops used the trails in Laos and then poured over the border into South Vietnam at various points. There was little the ARVN and their American advisors could do to stop them. There were too many passes to guard them all and when they tried to stop the flow of soldiers and supplies, they were often overwhelmed by the mass of enemy troops descending from the mountains. It was much more difficult to accurately target the enemy with artillery and air power when it was traveling through the jungle or in the mountains.

The more North Vietnamese troops that entered the south, the more options became available to Duan. His priority was to show the Americans that they and their air force were not invulnerable. He wanted to hit them hard before they decided to put boots on the ground. Duan knew that odds were slim of deterring the Americans to the point where they would not choose to fight in Vietnam, but he thought he might be able to delay them until he and his troops gained more of a foothold in the south. He wanted to strike and show his enemy the true ability of the North Vietnamese forces and their Viet Cong allies. The gloves had finally come off and Duan meant to take full advantage of his new muscle.

October 24, 1964 – Anlong Chrey, Cambodia

Cambodia was in flux. Under the leadership of Pol Pot, the newly formed Khmer Rouge was slowly, but steadily rising to power. With the help of local communists, the NVA were expanding the Ho Chi Minh Trail to include parts of eastern Cambodia. More weapons and supplies were pouring into South Vietnam and into the hands of the Viet Cong.

In an attempt to interdict the communist weapons and supplies, the South Vietnamese used multiple surveillance aircraft to keep an eye on the border. When a caravan was spotted, a squadron of fighter-bombers was sent to destroy the porters, their cargo, and the NVA that escorted them. The problem was that the border was not visible from the air making it difficult to know which territory the caravan was traveling in – Cambodia or South Vietnam.

On October 24th, the RVNAF aircraft were hunting a large caravan that had been reported moving toward the border between Cambodia and South Vietnam. The jungle canopy in the area of the report was thick making it extra difficult to identify the caravan. One of the pilots spotted a group of people carrying sacks on their heads and shoulders. The squadron strafed and rocketed the people as they ran to the nearby village of Anlong Chrey located on the Cambodian side of the border. The South Vietnamese pilots continued their attack as the people ducked into their huts for cover. As often happened in war, the pilots' blood ran hot, and they continued their attack.

When the air assault was finished, seven villagers were dead and a dozen more were seriously wounded. The warplanes returned home, their pilots not knowing that they had attacked a group of farmers returning from the mountains with a harvest of wild fruit.

Saigon, South Vietnam

Hearing the reports of the attack on a Cambodian village, Ambassador Taylor was furious. He had explicit instructions not to allow the war to expand into Cambodia. He went to the new Prime Minister's office and read him the riot act for not consulting with the United States Embassy about the attack. The Prime Minister tried to explain that it had been a simple mistake and the pilots did not know they were in Cambodia when the attack was executed. Taylor did not want to hear the Prime Minister's excuses and told him that if American-supplied aircraft were used to attack Cambodia again, the United States would cut off military aid.

Things got even worse a few days later when the Cambodians retaliated by shooting down a USAF C-123 aircraft that was flying over the Cambodian border village of Dak Dam in the Mondulkiri Province. All eight American crew members on board were killed. Since the aircraft that had previously attacked the village Anlong Chrey was American-made, the Cambodians saw this as a fair exchange and did not seek additional restitution. For the time being, the Americans and the South Vietnamese had averted another war.

October 25, 1964 - Saigon, South Vietnam

Johnson had made it crystal clear to Ambassador Taylor his feelings on recent events when he said, "No more of the coup shit."

In turn, Taylor echoed Johnson's demand to the generals in charge of South Vietnam. If they wanted America's continued aid and support, the leaders had to get their act together and transfer power to a civilian government. The generals' solution was Phan Khac Suu. Suu was nobody's first choice, but he was someone that all the generals could accept. A trained agricultural engineer, Suu was a founding member of the Cao Dai religion which combined Buddhism, Christianity, Taoism, and Confucianism. Its tolerance for different religious ideas made Cao Dai perfect for Vietnam where religion was often a point of contention. He was a member of Emperor Bao Dai's political cabinet. Under President Ngo Dinh Diem, Suu was briefly jailed for mild dissidence but then released early when Diem was assassinated. His brief time in jail gave credibility that he was not part of the pre-coup government and that made him acceptable to the generals that overthrew Diem and his family.

As far as the Americans were concerned, as long as he prosecuted the war against the communists and didn't cause too much upheaval among the public, Suu was acceptable. He lasted one year.

November 1, 1964 – Bien Hoa Air Base, South Vietnam

Le Duan wanted a retaliatory strike for the bombing in the north that would show the Americans that the communists were not to be crossed without repercussions. Fifteen miles northeast of Saigon, Bien Hoa Air Base was the main jumping-off point for the Republic of Vietnam Air Force (RVNAF) and the USAF. US Army, Air Force, Navy, and Marine units were stationed at Bien Hoa along with hundreds of aircraft and helicopters including HH-43 Huskie and A-1 Huey helicopters, C-47 Dakota cargo planes, U2 high-altitude reconnaissance jets, B-26 Invaders, T-28 Trojans, A-1E Skyraiders, and a recently arrived squadron of B-57 Canberras jet bombers.

As the war grew, so did the air base. By 1964 it was huge, encompassing two jet-capable runways and hundreds of buildings, including barracks, Quonset huts, hangers, headquarters, ammunition depots, and storage facilities. Miles of barbed-wire fencing, blockhouses, and gate sentries protected the perimeter of the base. There were almost 5,000 American airmen housed and working on the base.

Watching from several safe houses just outside the base perimeter, the Viet Cong had carefully planned their infiltration and assault of the air base. The VC commandos' mission was to destroy and damage as many aircraft as possible. Human targets and buildings were secondary. It was decided to use mortars to hit pre-targeted areas where the most valuable aircraft were being stored. Although the unit commander wanted to destroy the U2 reconnaissance jets, they were being stored in concrete bunkers along with other jet fighters and bombers. Easily identified by their highly polished skins, the B-57 Canberra bombers had just arrived from the states and were lined up on the tarmac outside a hanger waiting to be painted. The Canberras were a much easier target and represented a substantial part of the US arsenal of bombers that would soon carry out more raids in the north.

In the days before the raid, the company of commandos practiced with their mortars until they could fire eighteen rounds per minute. It was unlikely they could sustain that rate under battle conditions, but they were as prepared as possible. The commandos wanted to get at the airmen and their aircraft that had killed so many of their comrades over the years of fighting. They also wanted to make a good showing of their first encounter with the Americans on the base.

Just before midnight, the Viet Cong began their infiltration with sappers carefully belly-crawling to the perimeter and digging holes beneath the wire. The commandos followed on their bellies pulling the mortar tubes, base plates, and shells with them. They planned on attacking the air base until their mortar shells ran out. They brought just under 1,000 shells with them into the base making multiple trips. They carried rice balls flavored with fish sauce in their backpacks to give them strength as they shuttled the mortar shells into the base. Their bellies, elbows, and knees were raw before they were done.

As they entered the base undetected, the commandos moved behind the base bomb dump where hundreds of bombs were stacked two-high on sets of 4x4 wooden beams. The earthen berm that surrounded the ammo dump gave the commando mortar teams great cover from direct fire and disguised their firing positions. Defensive positions were set up using the berm as cover. It was like a mini fortress. The Viet Cong were nervous about locating their firing positions in the middle of a bomb dump until their commander explained that the American bombs could not explode without a detonator and that there was no risk of a bullet setting off a bomb - a calming detail that was mostly true… mostly. It was almost 2 AM before the Viet Cong were completely set up and ready.

Returning from a night test run, Coyle piloted the Convair C-131B gunship prototype as it neared the runway at Bien Hoa Air Base. He was tired and ready to call it a day.

Terry and Granier sat in the cargo area discussing possible modifications to the minigun mounts. Because of the availability of aircraft and replacement parts, it had been decided to use C-47s as test gunships instead of the Convair. Five more miniguns were on order with General Electric and were scheduled to arrive in-country at the beginning of the following month. Two C-47s had been secured as part of the development program and were undergoing badly needed maintenance.

As Coyle landed the Convair, the first Viet Cong mortar shell exploded just off to the side of the runway in an attempt to hit the landing aircraft. Coyle was completely caught off guard but didn't jerk the controls as most pilots would have. He had learned from experience that sudden reactions were a bad thing when taking off or landing an aircraft. He kept the plane in the center of the runway and touched down as Granier and Terry ran into the cockpit. "What the hell was that?" said Terry.

"I'm pretty sure the air base is under fire," said Coyle.

More explosions went off all around the base lighting it up. "Sounds like mortars," said Granier. "We've got to find the enemy's firing position. If they're M2s they've got to be fairly close to the base… within a mile."

"That's base security's job," said Terry. "We need to get my aircraft into its hangar and out of harm's way."

Coyle kept his eyes focused on the far corner of the air base away from the runway and hangars. He watched as dim flashes of light appeared over the air base ammo dump. The Viet Cong along the berm were purposely holding their fire so as not to give away their position. But Coyle saw through the ruse. "There," said Coyle pointing to the flashes.

"They're inside the perimeter," said Granier.

"That can't be a good thing," said Terry.

As Coyle turned off the runway onto the apron, a mortar shell hit a Huey helicopter and blew it to bits. The Convair's windshield went white blinding Coyle for a moment. Again, he didn't panic. He knew his eyes would adjust in a few moments. He could see more flashes and hear the explosions that followed.

Blast pressure from the explosions blew out the window in the control tower showering the air traffic controllers with broken glass. Another shell landed next to an A-1E Skyraider and ripped off its tail. A jeep with a 50-Cal machine gun sped along the parking apron when a mortar shell exploded directly in front of it. The jeep flipped end over end and landed in a lump of metal and flesh. The three soldiers inside the vehicle were crushed to death.

"They're kicking our ass. Where in the hell is base security?" said Granier.

"I don't think they know the mortars are located in the ammo dump. The blast berm is too high. How much ammunition do we have for the minigun?" said Coyle.

"None. We're out," said Granier. "Why?"

"We're gonna need some more."

"Whatever you're thinking forget it, Coyle. We are not authorized to engage the enemy," said Terry.

"You can't be serious," said Granier. "We're under attack. Fuck authorization. This is life and death."

"I mean it. This program has rules and if we don't obey them, we'll get our funding cut and the project will be put into mothballs. I've seen it happen plenty of times."

"So, don't tell anyone," said Coyle taxing toward the project hanger. "Granier, I'll keep her running. You and your guys get the ammo."

"I'm on it," said Granier disappearing through the cockpit doorway.

"You guys aren't listening to me. We're not doing this," said Terry.

"I think we are. Once we're done, you can fire us if it makes you feel any better," said Coyle. "Of course, we don't technically work for you. Let's just call it a mutiny and leave it at that."

"Goddamnit. This is no joke. If this aircraft gets damaged in any way, I'll make sure you both get court-martialed."

"Your plane will be fine. Just think of it as another test run."

A mortar shell exploded nearby, and a piece of shrapnel hit the co-pilot's side window shattering it. "Put that on my tab," said Coyle. "You might wanna get down… just in case."

Terry knelt on the cockpit's deck as more explosions went off nearby shaking the aircraft. "One thing's for sure… they mean business," said Coyle sliding down as low as possible in his seat.

A few minutes later, Granier and his assistant gunners loaded the ammunition into the cargo hold. A shell exploded ten feet away sending shrapnel into both legs of one of the assistants. The wounded airman collapsed to the ground screaming in pain. Granier jumped down from the aircraft and checked on the man. He was bleeding badly. Granier used his and the other assistant's belt as tourniquets. "You stay here and keep him from falling into shock, I'll radio for a medic."

The assistant nodded. After yelling for Terry to radio a medic on the aircraft's radio, Granier finished loading the last of the ammo and climbed back aboard. He went to work reloading the minigun and said, "Coyle, I'll have the weapon up in a couple of minutes. Go."

Coyle turned the plane and headed back toward the runway. Through the windshield, he saw more mortar shells explode and multiple aircraft burning darkening the night sky further with plumes of black smoke. Bodies of fallen airmen and security soldiers were scattered across the tarmac, some still moving, others not. Careful not to run anyone over, he taxied to the end of the runway and turned. More mortar shells exploded near the plane as it rolled down the runway and finally took off.

Once in the air, Coyle banked the aircraft hard and looked down at the air base. It was an inferno with fire and explosions everywhere. Once again, he saw the dim flashes of light coming for the ammo dump. That was his target. It would take time to ascend to 2,000 feet. More would die and more aircraft would be destroyed unless something was done immediately. He needed to hit the enemy hard now. "Granier, you ready?" said Coyle over the intercom.

"Gun's up," said Granier.

"We're gonna do a strafing run and let 'em know we're here," said Coyle.

"Why are we doing that? That's not how the weapon is supposed to be used," said Terry.

"We gotta throw them off now. Make 'em put their heads down. We need to buy time while we climb and get into normal firing position."

Coyle turned the gunship and lined up his run. The twin engines roared as he increased airspeed. He was only flying 100 feet off the deck as the gunship screamed toward the ammo dump. Seeing the approaching plane, the Viet Cong along the berm opened fire, finally giving away their position to the base security teams. At the last moment, Coyle rotated the aircraft and pulled the remote trigger on the minigun. The weapon's six barrels rotated for a brief moment, then opened fire. At 3,500 Rounds Per Minute, the noise from the discharging weapon was deafening. Granier covered his ears. The muzzle flashes lit up the cargo hold and the sky outside the aircraft doorway.

Nestled behind the safety of the berm, the Viet

Cong were surprised by the cargo plane they thought was harmless. It was spewing long fingers of reddish fire from the side. Anything the fingers touched was torn to shreds like a mythical monster. Seeing the fingers move toward them, most of the Viet Cong hit the deck, and those that didn't were ripped apart. Bullets ripped into the wooden 4x4 holding the stacks of unarmed bombs. The timbers collapsed and the bombs rolled off the stacks clanging into each other on the ground. Other minigun shells hit the bombs' outer casings and ricocheted on the metal but nothing exploded. It was over in less than a couple of seconds, but the effect lasted much longer. The Viet Cong seemed to be in shock as if fearing the beast's return.

With the strafing run completed, Coyle turned the aircraft and ascended into the sky above in a wide arc like a truck climbing a mountain road. The engines groaned at the strain. Coyle knew how far he could push the aircraft without causing a stall. Up and up it went. He looked out the side window and saw that the Viet Cong had recovered and were once again firing their mortars. He could also see the muzzle flashes of the South Vietnamese security teams and American airmen approaching the ammo dump and firing back at the commandos behind the berm.

In the cargo hold, Granier attached a second belt of ammunition to the links of the first belt. He would stand beside the weapon as it fired and make sure the new belt didn't jam when it reached the breach. He knew he would be pelted with hot empty cartridges and pieces of disintegrating shell links. He didn't care. He'd live.

When the Convair reached two thousand feet, Coyle put the aircraft into a pinion turn, rotated, and repositioned the fuselage until his homemade gun site on the side window lined up the enemy mortar positions. Satisfied, he pulled the trigger. The weapon fired.

The Viet Cong could hear the beast circling above them, but it wasn't until they saw the red streams from the tracer rounds descending upon them that they panicked. It was too much. They broke leaving their mortars and remaining unfired shells behind.

Seeing the retreating enemy below, Coyle realigned the weapon with a focus on the perimeter fence. He waited until the majority of Viet Cong reached the fence. Some waited for their turn crawling under the wire. Others climbed over the wire and got caught in the Constantine loops capping the fence. Coyle didn't care. They were the enemy and had destroyed American aircraft and killed airmen. He pulled the trigger as he used the aircraft to guide the weapon along the fence line like a sewing machine. The ground twenty feet on either side of the fence was chopped up, kicking up dirt clods, grass, rocks, and bloody pieces of Viet Cong into the air. Nothing survived in the weapons' path.

Coyle could see little movement below. He didn't kill everyone that had attacked the air base, but almost. He didn't want to press his luck and hit one of his own men which were giving chase to any survivors of the gunship's fury. He had proved his point.

But the retreat of the Viet Cong was hardly a victory. During the thirty-minute attack, the Viet Cong commandos had devastated the air base with hundreds of mortar shells exploding. The Viet Cong claimed to have killed and wounded hundreds of airmen and soldiers. Not wanting to encourage the Viet Cong, the

Americans and South Vietnamese reported far fewer causalities and aircraft losses. But those there that night knew the truth. It was a clear victory for the Viet Cong who had caught the Americans and the ARVN completely by surprise. Since the gunship's counterattack was not authorized, there were no reports filed of the weapon's first encounter with the enemy. But many on the base saw what really had happened and passed it on to their family and friends. The crew of the gunship had performed brilliantly and saved the lives of their fellow soldiers. They took no credit and the aircraft was stored back in its hangar before the news photographers arrived at the base to document the carnage and destruction.

In all, fifty-nine aircraft were heavily damaged or destroyed, including eighteen B-57s Canberra jet bombers, six UH-1 Huey helicopters, four Kaman HH-43 Huskie rescue helicopters, and two Douglas C-47s Dakotas. A number of Trojan T-28s and A1-E Skyraiders fighter-bombers were also destroyed but not reported to reduce the perception of defeat. Fortunately, most of the jet fighters were launched from American aircraft carriers off the coast or the losses could have been much worse.

White House – Washington DC, USA

Upon receiving reports of the attack, Johnson's cabinet and advisors were united in their counsel that America should immediately retaliate against the Viet Cong. Many in the White House and Pentagon were now ready to send in American troops to protect the US air bases and facilities.

With the election only two days away, Johnson was

hesitant to make any major announcements and therefore decided to err on the side of caution ordering his staff to make another list of airstrike targets and their suggestions for troop deployments. He was stalling. He had the election in the bag and didn't want any last-minute surprises. In the name of good military planning, retaliation could wait a few days.

Two days later, Johnson won the election by a landslide over his Republican opponent Senator Barry Goldwater. Goldwater quickly conceded after it became obvious that he had lost. Johnson now had what he craved – the mandate of the American people.

November 6, 1964 – Saigon, South Vietnam

The Bien Hoa Air Base was a shambles and would need months before it was back to normal operations. The Americans replaced the destroyed aircraft and repaired the facilities.

With their fighting capability temporarily reduced, the Americans used the South Vietnamese Air Force to exact their revenge on the Viet Cong.

The RVNAF squadron was led by Air Vice Marshal Nguyen Cao Ky. Thirty-two aircraft, mostly fighter-bombers were launched in a retaliatory strike. The target was a large VC base that had been discovered during reconnaissance flights over the area. The attack came without warning when the aircraft flew straight over the base strafing and bombing the VC. Rockets and napalm canisters were also used to destroy enemy anti-aircraft emplacements and take out clusters of resistance firing their rifles into the air as each warplane passed over. The camp was brutalized during the thirty-minute assault. For the Viet Cong, unaccustomed to so many aircraft in one raid, it seemed like an eternity. Smoldering bodies were scattered across the ground and left hanging on animal pen fences. There was little movement when the aircraft finally ran out of ammunition and returned to their air base.

The South Vietnamese claimed to have killed 500 VC during the air assault. The Viet Cong claimed far fewer were killed and they had shot down several RVNAF aircraft during the air raid. Both sides were very good at stretching the truth beyond recognition. Only those that participated in the air raid know what really happened.

THE PLAIN OF JARS

Xiangkhoang Plateau, Laos

Hewn from giant boulders, thousands of stone jars were scattered around the upland valleys and the lower foothills of the central plain of the Xiangkhoang Plateau in Laos. Lao legend told of giants under the command of King Khun Cheung that built the jars to brew and store rice beer called, Lau Hai. The liquor was used to celebrate the King's victorious battles against his enemies. The jars were arranged in clusters so they could be watched over during fermentation.

The Xiangkhoang plateau was at the northern end of the Annamese Cordillera, the principal mountain range of Indochina. Its location made the plateau strategically important, especially in the age of flight. The plateau had many level fields that were turned into landing strips. Because it was a plateau it was less susceptible than the valleys to flooding during the monsoons. Xiangkhoang was centrally located in northern Laos. It was the closest level area near the mountains that could be used to land large transport and cargo planes. It became a key supply hub for the mountain villages of the Montagnard. It was also the only way the villagers had of getting to market their key cash crop – opium.

The truth was that life in the mountains was more than difficult. The tribesmen needed hard currency to buy medicine, seed, and tools to plant their crops. They also needed protein. While the jungle provided plenty of fruit and tubers, it lacked in protein. As the population grew and thinned out the available prey, an entire village would often have to survive off a snake and a couple of monkeys for their daily source of protein. It wasn't nearly enough. The tribesmen needed to buy chickens, pigs, and cattle to survive. They needed the cash that their opium crops provided.

The Plain of Jars was also the closest weapon and ammunition supply point for the Montagnard warriors trying to cut off the Ho Chi Minh Trail. The North Vietnamese could not afford to lose their precious supply line into South Vietnam. They encouraged the Pathet Lao to attack and overrun the Plain of Jars between monsoon seasons. But while they were successful for a time, the Pathet Lao could not withstand the Royal Army counterattacks that always came when the rain returned and washed away their resupply roads through the mountains. And so it was, a seesaw of seasonal battles to claim the Plain of Jars.

That all changed during the 1964 coup in the Laotian capital of Vientiane. The generals throwing the coup pulled their mobile force from the Plain of Jars to help overthrow the government. With a reduced force guarding the Plain of Jars, the government troops were no longer capable of routing the Pathet Lao when the rains came. The Pathet Lao controlled the Plain of Jars and the landing strips through the monsoon season. The equilibrium was broken. Not only were the Montagnard's supplies cut off, but they also lost their opium revenue when they could not send their crops to market. It meant financial ruin for the Montagnard villages and made it difficult for the warriors to continue their fight against the NVA on the Ho Chi Minh Trail.

The biggest buyer of Laotian opium was the Corsican mob which originated in France but had branched out into Saigon where they could control the quality of their biggest product and deal with any competitors. The Corsicans would process the opium into heroin locally before distributing it throughout the world, including in Europe and the United States. The Corsican mob boss in Saigon was Mathieu Franchini, the mentor and longtime friend of Lucien Conein.

Conein had met Franchini in France at the beginning of World War II. Conein, a French soldier on the run and former printer, helped Franchini and his mob counterfeit German Reichsmarks. In exchange, Franchini taught Conein the art of creating chaos. Together they fought the Nazis until America entered the war and Conein left to join the American Army. The two would meet up again when Conein was sent to Indochina to fight the Japanese as the leader of a commando team. When the war ended, Franchini moved to Saigon to oversee the Corsican production and distribution of heroin among other nefarious businesses. The old friends met, drank pastis, and ate Corsican boar at Franchini's restaurant. It was just like old times. While Conein stayed out of the drug business, he was not above helping his old friend when a favor was asked. The same was true of Franchini. Now, it was Franchini's turn to ask a favor…

Coyle was concerned when he received a message from Conein that he wanted to meet him off-site at a coffee house near the paramilitary headquarters. He knew what it meant – Conein was ready to call in the debt that Coyle owed him for saving his former girlfriend Bian and her father from prison. He had no idea what Conein would want him to do, but he doubted it was authorized or legal. His mind raced trying to guess the task he would be asked but there were too many possibilities. It was Conein, after all, a man with few scruples and numerous connections with nefarious characters. Coyle felt he had truly made a deal with the devil to save Bian and in the end, she died away. Nevertheless, her death didn't erase the debt Conein was about to collect.

Coyle arrived at the coffee house early and Conein was already waiting. He was seated away from the other customers sipping his coffee and reading a French newspaper. Coyle sat. Conein said nothing. The waitress came over and Coyle declined to order anything. "Don't be rude, Coyle. Have a pastry. They're good here," said Conein still reading his paper.

Coyle ordered a coffee. Conein remained silent until the waitress served Coyle's coffee and left. It was Coyle that started the conversation, "Enough with the suspense. What do you want, Conein?"

Conein finished reading his article, set the newspaper down, and said, "You deliver supplies to the SOG and the Montagnard, right?"

"You know I do."

"So, from now on, whenever you drop off supplies, you're going to pick up a couple of packages and deliver them to General Pao at Long Tieng. He'll give you a different package that needs to go back to the Montagnard. It's safer if you don't open any of the packages."

"What's in the packages?"

"Does it matter?

"Of course, it matters."

"No, it really doesn't. A deal is a deal and I own your ass."

"For how long?"

"As long as I want. But if you do your job and don't ask a lot of questions, I won't be unreasonable. I may even pay you for each delivery."

"Why would you do that?"

"To keep you motivated."

"I don't want your damned money."

"You say that, but it could be a lot of money. Think of it as a retirement fund… I do."

"It doesn't matter, Conein."

"Okay, but what does matter is that you guard those packages with your life… literally."

"I'll make sure your drugs get delivered."

"Who said anything about drugs?"

"Like you said… it doesn't matter," said Coyle as he rose and left his untouched coffee on the table.

Leaving the coffee house, Coyle was enraged. He felt trapped. He had little choice but to do what Conein demanded if he wanted to keep breathing. Unhindered by morals, Conein was not a man to disappoint. Even beyond that, Conein was right… Coyle had made a deal to save Bian and Conein upheld his part of the bargain. Coyle was a man of his word, even if it meant delivering opium for Conein.

Northeastern Mountains, Laos

As the Montagnard tribes joining the war effort had grown, so had their need for supplies and weapons. Coyle had traded in his O-1 Cessna Bird Dog for a Swiss-made Pilatus PC-6 Porter. While both aircraft had good STAL capabilities, the PC-6 had a much higher cargo capacity – 2,200 lbs. Coyle had taken out all the seats except the pilot's chair giving the aircraft plenty of room for cargo and stretchers to airlift wounded soldiers. The PC-6 was an awkward-looking aircraft with its long nose and extra-wide wingspan. The extra-long nose provided high prop clearance that prevented the prop from digging in on a sloped landing, while the extra-wide wingspan gave the aircraft the lift it needed for short takeoffs and heavy loads. It had a three-blade prop that was fully reversible to help stop the aircraft during short runway landings. The PC-6 wasn't a helicopter, but it was close and didn't need much of a runway. It had been developed for mountainous terrain like Laos.

Coyle never knew exactly where he was going to land until Blackjack and other SOG team leaders radioed him the coordinates of the landing strip they had cut into the mountain range and cleared of large rocks, small trees, and large bushes. The SOG needed to keep the location of their bases secret and therefore changed the landing location every time a shipment arrived. Because of his skill and experience, Coyle was given the most difficult runway locations. As a result, Coyle had the landing gear and wing struts reinforced so that the occasional missed pothole or rock would not snap off anything of importance. He had made hundreds of landings and takeoffs in the mountains of Laos since the war had begun. The Air America pilots like Coyle were the lifeline of the SOG and Tribesmen. They kept the war effort in Laos running smoothly with only the sporadic snafu.

Coyle landed the PC-6 in a newly cut clearing near the top of a mountain. Coyle had grown accustomed to landing on the upward slope near the top of a mountain ridge, turning the aircraft around, and taking off on the downward slope. The PC-6 with its long nose and high clearance made it much easier to land in rough terrain than the Bird Dog aircraft that he used to fly. More than once his Bird Dog's prop had mowed the dirt. Coyle turned the plane around for takeoff on the downslope and shut off the engine while the aircraft was unloaded by the Montagnard.

Blackjack approached as Coyle climbed out of the cockpit. "Morning, Coyle. Have a nice flight?" said Blackjack.

"Any flight that results in me still alive is a nice flight," said Coyle.

"Do you have time for lunch? The Montagnard are cooking up some monkey. Good eating."

"I'm going take your word on that, but I think I'll stick to my beef jerky."

"Suit yourself. But you should really expand your palette."

"That's funny. McGoon used to say that too?"

"McGoon? Like the funnies?"

"Yep. Big as a mountain."

"He's a friend of yours?"

"He was. He died at Dien Bien Phu."

"That's a shame. He sounds like an interesting character."

"He was. Always the loudest man in the room."

"So, I hear you're gonna be the Montagnard's new

drug mule."

"Yep. That's me. Have drugs, will travel."

"Conein?"

"Yeah. You know him?"

"No, but I've heard of him."

"Yeah, he gets around that's for damned sure."

"I was surprised when I heard the news you'd be carrying the loads. Doesn't seem like your kinda thing."

"It ain't. I wasn't given much of a choice."

"I see. I won't pry. But if it makes you feel any better, the Montagnard really need the money. Their income's been cut off since the Plain of Jars fell to the Pathet Lao."

"So, you think all this is okay?" said Coyle angry.

"When I first arrived, I could see that there were a lot of things I would be forced to accept that didn't agree with my Christian upbringing. Since then, I've learned that the Montagnard are no different than most people. They just want to raise their families and keep their children safe. Yeah, they've got some pretty weird traditions and backward ideas. But all and all, they're good people just trying to get through life. I can't really blame them for that."

"Even if it means selling opium?"

"Well, technically they grow opium. But yeah, even if it means they gotta sell opium to make ends meet."

"I don't want to sit in judgment against the Montagnard or anyone else for the matter. But I never expected to be in this position when I joined the CIA. It's just wrong."

"I hear, ya. But I've seen things that are far worse than growing opium. Things I don't want to remember and I sure as hell don't want to talk about. Life is cruel and unjust, especially in the jungle. I just have to live with whatever comes my way. It's thc job I trained for."

"I suppose. Still, it doesn't feel right."

"And you should hope it never does. You're a good man, Coyle."

Coyle glanced at the Montagnard loading up the last of opium packages and said, "Well, I better get going. I still have a lot of flying to do before I head back to Vietnam. Enjoy your roasted monkey."

"Oh, I will. Safe travels, Coyle."

"Good hunting, Blackjack," said Coyle as he climbed into the aircraft and closed the cargo door.

A few minutes later, Coyle took off, banked the aircraft hard, and headed toward Long Tieng.

Long Tieng, Laos

When Coyle landed on Long Tieng's dirt airstrip, he taxied over to the building that served as a terminal and shut off his engine. He was immediately surrounded by a squad of Montagnard warriors, some pointing their rifles at him and others pointing their rifles away from the aircraft as if protecting it from potential raiders. Coyle raised his hands to show he meant no harm. Several Montagnard ran to the plane opened the cargo door, pulled out the packages of opium, then closed the door. A US Advisor carrying a canvas satchel walked over, took out his knife, and plunged the tip into one of the bags a Montagnard was carrying. He withdrew a small sample of the black gum, sniffed it, then took a taste. His expression showed that it was the real deal. The advisor walked to the plane and opened the co-pilot's door. "You, Coyle?" said the advisor.

"Yeah. Who are you?" said Coyle.

"No one," said the Advisor as he set the satchel on the co-pilot's seat. "You keep a good eye on that. We wouldn't want to see anything get misplaced, accident or otherwise."

"Right," said Coyle annoyed. "You want a receipt or something?"

"You're a funny guy."

"That's me… Mr. Shits and Giggles."

The advisor grunted, then closed the door and walked away. Coyle restarted his engine, taxied to the runway, and took off. He banked his aircraft and headed back the way he came.

Coyle didn't need to think much about the procedure of piloting a plane. He was a natural pilot and his instincts took over. It left his mind free to think about other things. He thought about what he had just done and what it would mean to the addicts hooked on opium and its derivative – heroin. Some would feel great relief when the drug entered their systems After a while, opiates stop having the desired effect of euphoria and become more of a Band-Aid covering the side effects – uncontrollable itching, severe cramps, cold sweats, and switching in and out of drowsiness - that make addiction so horrible. Coyle was no expert, but he had seen enough addicts in Saigon to know the brutality of using opium or heroin. And now, he was part of the problem… He tried to tell himself that it wasn't his fault. That he had tried to do the right thing in saving Bian and her father. He wondered about the consequences of defying Conein and the Corsicans. A death sentence for sure. But Coyle could choose to run. He had a plane and what he imagined was a large amount of money sitting next to him on the co-pilot's seat. They'd never find him… or would they? And what about his duty? He was an important cog in the CIA wheel and the fight against communism. In the end, would his contribution even matter? There was no way to tell until the war was won or lost.

As he approached the dirt runway on the mountain range, Coyle snapped out of his rambling thoughts and focused on preparing to land his plane. It was at that moment he heard several loud thumps and his windshield turned black from leaking engine oil. His aircraft had been hit. Oil pressure was dropping. His engine would soon seize. He was going to crash… again. If there ever was an expert at crashing and surviving, Coyle was it. He didn't panic. He let his experience and instinct take over as he used the plane's windshield wiper to clean away some of the oil. His view was lousy, but it was enough to find a good place to crash. He wanted a full canopy of leaves with no gaps. It was the gaps that could kill him. Just like landing in the ocean, he would use the canopy of leaves and branches to float his landing and hope he didn't flip over. But even if he did, the most important thing was to stop the plane's momentum, then avoid the fifty-foot drop to the jungle floor.

As he approached the jungle canopy, the black oil turned to flames. The aircraft's engine had seized and was on fire. "Great," he said to himself.

Coyle's crash-landing plans quickly changed. The idea of being trapped in the jungle's canopy while roasting alive was not a good option. He searched for a gap, then aimed the aircraft downward. A soft landing was no longer in the cards. He would dive into the canopy and take his chances of reaching the jungle floor alive and conscious. If he blacked out from a concussion, he would burn to death inside the cockpit. His odds of surviving were quickly falling as he glided into the gap in the jungle canopy. He tightened his seat harness.

The long nose of the PC-6 was the first to enter the canopy. The prop had stopped when the engine seized. Coyle had not bothered to release it so it could spin freely. It no longer mattered. The wings and cockpit were next as the aircraft plunged further into the green chaos. One of the wings hit a thick branch and spun the aircraft around. The tail hit another thick branch and snapped off. The aircraft's forward momentum had stopped. The cockpit and wings continued to turn as the aircraft dropped. The burning wreckage smacked into branches and caused an avalanche of falling leaves. To Coyle, it felt like an eternity as the cockpit shifted direction each it made contact with a branch. Finally, the cockpit tilted downward and slammed nose-first into the jungle floor at the base of a large tree. The tree's trunk supported what remained of the tail of the aircraft and kept it from falling over. It could not have stopped in a worse position for Coyle. The flames from the engine fire that had calmed for a moment as the plane was falling were now resuming their blaze engulfing the cockpit. Coyle pounded at his harness release, but his weight kept it from opening. He was going to burn alive. He pulled out his pocketknife and cut at the chest harness strap as the flames grew and the temperature rose. He could feel it. His skin was roasting. He sliced at the chest strap with all his strength. The strap broke free. He tried hitting the release again. Still nothing. He went to work on the bottom belt trying not to panic as fire crept into the cockpit and licked at him. His shirt caught fire. He let it burn as he continued to cut the strap. The bottom strap broke allowing Coyle to roll out of the harness. He grabbed the door handle and pulled. His hand sizzled. He ignored the pain. The handle didn't work. The door was jammed shut. He turned back into the cockpit's flames and kicked open the door. He rolled out of the cockpit and onto the jungle floor. He kept rolling putting out the fire on his shirt. His clothes were smoldering. A few more seconds and they would have burst into flames. Coyle had been lucky… again. With the door open, the flames in the cockpit found the oxygen they craved and grew quickly. "Oh, shit," said Coyle to himself. "The money."

Coyle moved around the co-pilot's door. It was slightly ajar, but the cockpit was now consumed with fire. He knew that if he opened the door the flames would leap out at him. He considered letting the money burn. It wasn't his fault. Had been shot down. But he knew he would be blamed anyway. They would think he set up the crash to hide the evidence. It was an absurd notion, but when it came to money people believed the stupidest things. Conein, General Pao, the Montagnard, and the Corsicans would want his head on a spear. "Fuck," said Coyle as he picked up a broken tree branch.

He plunged the end of the branch into the gap in the doorway and pried the door open. As he had expected, the oxygen again fed the flames as fire poured out of the doorway. Coyle could barely see inside the cockpit, but he spotted the satchel holding the money on the floor. It was burning. He used the end of the branch to scoop up the satchel's strap and pulled the burning canvas free. The end of the branch was on fire. He cast it aside and grabbed the burning strap burning his hand once again. He slammed the satchel on the ground several times and stomped on the satchel with his boot extinguishing the flames. The satchel was charred and smoking. Coyle opened it and looked inside – the cash was smoldering but okay. He moved away from the burning aircraft and sat against another tree. He was exhausted and coughing heavily from the smoke he had inhaled. He replayed the crash in his mind. It dawned on him that whoever shot his plane down would be looking for him. They would see the smoke sifting up through the canopy and into the sky. He wasn't out of danger.

There was no sign of the enemy, but that didn't mean much in the dense Laotian jungle. Coyle pulled out his pistol and chambered a round… just in case. He knew he was close to the landing strip on top of the mountain range. He figured it was three to four miles away, which didn't seem like much on flatland, but could a day or two to reach in the steep mountain jungle. He didn't know if anyone would still be there when he arrived. It also occurred to him that the enemy that shot him down would follow his trail and would find the landing strip. He would be leading them to the Montagnard and SOG if they were still there. He didn't have much choice if he was going to survive. He needed medicine for his burnt hand if he was going to prevent infection. Bacteria grew at an incredible rate in the hot jungle. He knew the airstrip was due East. He used the sun which was at his back to determine his direction. He couldn't see the top of the mountain range through the canopy, but he knew where it was… sort of. He didn't have any water which could be a problem if it didn't rain soon. But he liked his odds. It rained a lot in the mountains, plus there were always mountain streams.

He picked up the scorched satchel and started walking. He was heading downhill on a steep slope. He guessed that at the bottom of the valley, there would probably be a stream. He would need a long drink before he started up the opposite slope toward the airstrip. He had no machete or long knife to hack through vines and heavy foliage. He would have to find his way through the jungle without getting stuck. The jungle wasn't cognizant like a beast, but it sure seemed that way. One could die if one got stuck in the tangle.

After a few hours, the sun sunk below the mountain behind him, and things got very dark. After sunset, it would become pitch black. Coyle was going to need to sleep in the jungle and he didn't like the idea. He had crashed in the Laotian jungle before, but he was with others. Beasts tended not to bother humans when they traveled in groups, but Coyle had no such group. He was alone and that made him fair game. He started to wonder if maybe it was better to surrender to the enemy following him. At least he would be safe. He rejected the idea. He had heard too many stories of the way the Pathet Lao treated prisoners, especially Americans. They hated pilots most of all. Of course, he didn't know it was Pathet Lao that shot him down. He supposed it could have been NVA, but that was a long shot and no better if it was true. He hated the idea of living in a North Vietnamese prison.

As it grew darker, he could no longer see where he was walking. A twisted ankle would end him for sure. He could hear the sound of running water. A stream he imagined and probably the bottom of the valley. He kept going until he slipped and landed on his ass. He was close to the stream and decided it was safer to slide down the slope on his ass. It was demeaning, but at least he wouldn't twist an ankle. He reached the stream and had a long drink of the warm water. He splashed water over his head to cool down, then let his burned hand soak for a bit. It felt good. The burning sensation diminished. He looked around and could see very little. It was very dark and very still... not even a breeze.

A rifle shot cracked through the stillness and a bullet ricocheted off the rock next to him. The enemy had found him. He had no idea how many he was facing, but he was sure they were armed better than he was. He scrambled to his feet and headed up the slope on the opposite side of the stream. It was rough going. After the first minute of climbing, his leg muscles burned. His only solace was that his enemy would need to climb the same mountain slope if they were going to catch him. He imagined they would be in far better shape than he was. It wouldn't take them long to catch up to him, but he wasn't going to make it easy for them. Two more rifle shots zipped through the leaves around him. Coyle turned and fired two rounds from his pistol into the darkness downhill. He had no hope of hitting anyone, but it would make them think twice about their strategy knowing their prey was armed. He needed all the time he could get. His lungs were burning as he huffed and puffed his way up the slope. If he stopped to rest, they would capture him for sure. He didn't stop, but the going was slow. The mountain slope seemed to be getting steeper. The mind plays tricks when the body screams in pain. He kept pushing himself until his legs finally gave out and he was unable to take another step. He fell to his knees and finally to his hands. Another bullet chipped off the bark of a tree next to him. He crawled behind the tree for cover. He couldn't catch his breath. His legs were hungry for oxygen. He couldn't hear anything above his panting for air. He stopped for a moment and listened. He could hear the enemy climbing the hill. Their commander was shouting out orders in what he thought was Vietnamese, but he wasn't sure. He imagined he had flown his aircraft over an anti-aircraft battery manned by NVA when he was shot down. There weren't that many anti-aircraft guns in the Laotians mountains. Most protected the Ho Chi Minh Trail which could be anywhere in these parts. It was bad luck for sure.

Coyle peeked around the tree trunk to see if he could spot anything. He saw shadows coming up the mountain slope just a dozen yards away. That was it. He was going to be captured or die. He wasn't sure which he preferred. He turned back behind the tree and took a few more breaths. He would fire until he ran out of ammunition, then whatever was going to happen would happen. It was out of his hands. He readied himself and turned toward the enemy. He squeezed the trigger. To his surprise, the gunfire was far louder than he supposed. Bullets whizzed over his head from behind. The enemy shadows turned into muzzle blasts returning fire. He was in the middle of a firefight. His pistol's chamber locked back signaling that he was out of ammunition. He turned back behind the tree and saw dozens of shadows racing down the slope. They charged past him and crashed into the enemy below in a fierce hand-to-hand battle. The enemy was outnumbered and quickly retreated across the stream and up the opposite mountain slope.

A tall shadow stood before him and said, "Coyle, is

that you?"

"Blackjack?" said Coyle hoping.

"Yeah. Are you okay?"

"My hands are a bit roasted, but besides that I'm fine. What are you doing here?"

"When you didn't show up, we saw the smoke and figured something had happened. We came to look for you."

"Awfully damned nice of you. You saved my ass."

"Ass saving is part of the service we SOG offer."

"Don't you need to supervise?"

"Naw. The Montagnard have them outnumbered. They'll finish them off in a few minutes. It's best I stay out of their way."

Blackjack offered Coyle his hand. Coyle used his unburned hand and Blackjack pulled him to his feet. "Oh, God, my legs," said Coyle almost falling back down.

"Maybe you should rest for a spell?"

"Sound advice. Here's your money," said Coyle handing Blackjack the burnt satchel.

"It ain't my money, but I'll see that the chief gets it. Why does it smell like smoke?"

"The satchel got a little toasty inside the cockpit after I crashed. None of the cash burned. I checked."

"I'm sure the Montagnard will be grateful."

"Yeah, I figured."

"I'll radio for another plane to pick you up once we get back to the airstrip."

"You think that's wise… using the same airstrip?"

"The Montagnard will hold anyone off until you get picked up. They're in a fighting mood."

"I appreciate it. You got any water?"

Blackjack handed Coyle his canteen. Coyle drank

heavily. "Not too much. Your legs will cramp up," said Blackjack.

"Too late," said Coyle.

"So, I guess we are going to see a lot more of you."

"I suppose you are. It wasn't such a bad trip…except for that last part."

Blackjack laughed.

MONSOONS RISING

November 9, 1964 – Quang Nam Province, South Vietnam

Even without war, Southeast Asia was not easy. There were jungles, mountains, dangerous diseases, and a plethora of poisonous snakes, frogs, and spiders. Some rivers overflowed their banks and avalanches that took out entire villages during the monsoon season. But aside from war, the event that the Vietnamese feared most was typhoons, especially for those living along the extraordinarily long coastline.

In addition to the war expanding between the North and South, 1964 was an especially bad year for typhoons. In all, six cyclones had developed into typhoons hammering the western villages and cities bordering the South China Sea. Three of those typhoons made landfall during a twelve-day period in November – Iris, Joan, and Kate… one right after the other. The problem with sequential storms was that the soil became saturated, and the water could not be absorbed. Instead, the excess rainfall sat in giant puddles that soon became lakes and eventually overflowed causing massive floods throughout the lowlands. Roads and paths were submerged. Rice paddies broke their dikes. The force of the overflowing rivers caused pylons to wash away making the bridges they were supporting collapse.

While many of the Vietnamese knew the basics of how to swim, they were not strong swimmers. Dog paddle was the most common swimming stroke but lacked the power needed to navigate a rushing river. Adults would drown trying to save the elderly and the young. Seven thousand Vietnamese, mostly in Central South Vietnam, were killed by the three typhoons. Thousands of farms were destroyed when dikes broke, and the topsoil was washed away by the fast-moving water. Water buffalo and horses were drowned in many villages destroying the farmers' ability to plow and plant their fields. Famine would follow the floods when harvest time arrived.

Hostilities between the North and the South were brought to a temporary halt when combat operations were no longer possible, and troops were needed to help civilians. Military trucks with their powerful engines and high ground clearance were used to carry people across raging rivers and out of harm's way in flooded areas. But even a truck loaded with villagers could be washed down the river if the water was strong enough. Many died as they thought they were being saved. The soldiers were often powerless to save civilians as they were carried away by the brown water full of fallen trees and drowning animals.

When possible American and South Vietnamese helicopter crews attempted to save stranded individuals and families that had climbed onto their roofs to escape the floods. Even during the storms and high winds, the crews risked their lives to save whomever they could, but it was often hopeless as the villagers exposed to the elements were too weak to hold on to the ropes and ladders tossed out the helicopters' doorways.

It would take months and even years before some villages and cities fully recovered from the damage caused by the typhoons. In some places, the mud was deeper than a man and had to be removed with bulldozers and dump trucks. Some farms would never recover and were abandoned by their owners. Over one million civilians were left homeless. The government's aid was massive but not nearly what was required. The United States helped with more aid, but as always, its priority was the war. American aid workers helped the people rebuild their villages and farms. The effort was massive and still fell short of what was truly needed.

To circumvent the Geneva neutrality agreements, the Americans used the disasters to bring more covert operatives into Laos disguised as aid workers designated to rebuild villages and bridges. Many worked for a few days to keep up appearances, then disappeared into the jungle and mountains to join their fellow SOG team members. This had the unfortunate side effect of NVA and Pathet Lao targeting foreign aid workers that they suspected might be SOG. Most were not and were there to help the Laotian people.

November 10, 1964 – Saigon, South Vietnam

US Ambassador Taylor cabled Washington with his current views on the war. Taylor's opinion on US involvement had evolved since becoming the ambassador of South Vietnam earlier that year. It had been his previous opinion that the South Vietnamese government needed to get their act together before America committed any further resources in the fight against the Viet Cong and NVA. He had come to realize through the latest series of coups and government musical chairs that the South Vietnamese government and military may never become competent and stable.

But the fight against the communists had more importance to America and its western allies beyond saving South Vietnam. Southeast Asia was at stake and possibly the world if the communists could not be stopped. Taylor advocated removing the American prerequisite that South Vietnam become stable and efficient at fighting its own wars before America's commitment was expanded. The way Taylor saw it was that the American military needed to take charge of the war to ensure it was won in short order and southeast Asia was safe. He favored expanding the war to North Vietnam, and if needed, that meant US troops committed to Vietnam.

November 20, 1964 – Laos – North Vietnam Border

For the first time, Le Duan ordered three PAVN regiments to march south along the Ho Chi Minh Trail. At almost 12,000 troops, it was the largest commitment of Northern troops to date. Their job was to train and assist Viet Cong rebels in their fight against ARVN and American forces in South Vietnam. The PAVN troops were well trained with many being veterans of the Indochina War and other being trained by the Chinese and Soviets. They were brave, experienced, and resourceful. Without fear of attacking large ARVN forces, the PAVN soldiers set a strong example for the Viet Cong troops. Knowledge and experience were power.

With the new influx of allied troops, the Viet Cong would increase their attacks against villages and military facilities. They were not yet strong enough to attack the well-protected southern cities, but the time was coming. Training and more modern weapons were required to take on the ARVN forces and American airmen.

As always, Le Duan was impatient and pushed the politburo and North Vietnam's allies to supply the necessary weapons and supplies the Viet Cong needed. Both the Chinese and the Russians sent more supplies and more modern weapons. China and the USSR competed to win influence over North Vietnam as it prepared to unite the country. While the Russians tended to have better and more modern weapons, China supplied the advisors to train the Northern military. The Chinese also sent some troops to replace PAVN troops needed to guard infrastructure and operate anti-aircraft guns. And of course, money from either ally was always welcome by the North Vietnamese.

It took the PAVN troops the rest of the year to travel the Ho Chi Minh Trail and enter South Vietnam. It took another six months to train Viet Cong rebels to fight in well-organized units and stand their ground against the ARVN military and American Air Force. But when the training was finally done and their new weapons had arrived, the Viet Cong and PAVN troops were confident and looking for a fight to prove themselves.

November 25, 1964 – Vientiane, Laos

A career foreign service officer, William Sullivan became US ambassador to Laos, replacing Leonard Unger. With over thirty years of foreign service under his belt, Sullivan had vast experience dealing with difficult situations and less than stable governments. He spoke his mind with candor and force which was exactly what President Johnson wanted in Laos – plain talk and no bullshit. Under former President Kennedy's executive order, Sullivan took over supervision of all US military operations in Laos. This did not make him any friends at the Pentagon or with the local military forces. He didn't care what they thought or said behind his back. He had a job to do and was determined to do it.

December 1, 1964 – Bien Hoa Air Base, South Vietnam

Working inside a large hangar, Granier, Coyle, Terry, and their work crews finished the final installation of six GE miniguns into two C-47 gunships. Neither of the planes had nose art with nicknames. The odds of getting any new weapon approved by the Pentagon were very slim, so it was best for the development team not to get too attached to their projects.

But for Terry, Coyle, and Granier, it was already too late to keep their emotions in check. All three deeply wanted the project to succeed. Having seen a lot of combat in both the air and on the ground, they knew of the weapons' potential for saving South Vietnamese and American lives. Before the project was originally funded by the Pentagon, Terry had used his personal

American Express credit card to purchase needed tools and parts. Later, after the development part of the project was approved, the government reimbursed him for his expenses.

The well-worn planes looked less than impressive with sheet metal patches from enemy gunfire covering large sections of their outer skins. Neither plane had been painted in years and with their cargo doors removed looked to be destined for the scrap heap. But Terry and his team didn't care. The project wasn't about entering a beauty contest. It was about developing a new weapon to kill the enemy while keeping the villagers in the hamlets and the soldiers in the outposts safe. The twin FC-47D's had a loiter over target time of seven hours each. The planes had been given the call signs, "Spooky One" and "Spooky Two."

"So, what's next?" said Coyle tightening the last mounting bolt at the base of one of the miniguns.

"Well, we need to align and site the guns in both aircraft. Then, we'll need about a week of flight tests and practice runs," said Terry. "After that, I'll apply for official permission to carry out field tests during an actual battle."

"How long will that take… official permission?" said Granier.

"I have no idea. It could be a few weeks, a year, or never."

"Never?"

"It's a possibility. They can stop funding at any time because they don't feel the weapon is needed or the eventual cost will be too high to be practical. And even if the weapon makes it past its final field tests, it can still get shit-canned if a congressman gets a bug up his ass."

"Why would they do that?" said Coyle.

"New weapon manufacturing contracts are a big deal. They can bring hundreds or even thousands of jobs to a state. You can bet they'll be a line of politicians fighting for their state to get the contract. And if it doesn't go their way, they could hold up funding."

"That's just stupid," said Coyle.

"No. That's Congress," said Terry.

It didn't take long for official permission to be granted. As Terry had hoped, the Pentagon was excited by the possibility of side-firing gunships. It was a new approach to air-to-ground support. The C-47s to be modified were cheap and plentiful which made the entire weapon system affordable. Plus, the C-47s had already proven their battle worthiness in three previous wars – World War II, Korea, and Indochina. They were tough and reliable aircraft.

On the 15th of December 1964, both newly designated AC-47 gunships were assigned to the 1st Air Commando Squadron for combat testing. There were still no guidelines as to when and how to use the gunships, but the commanding officer in 1st Air Commando could see the potential and was anxious to give them a try. All he needed was a battle close enough to the air base to send out one of the gunships. He didn't have to wait long.

December 20, 1964 – Saigon, South Vietnam

In a twisted turn of events, General Khanh led a group of officers called the "Young Turks" in yet another coup against the civilian High National Council that was governing South Vietnam at that moment. Khanh dissolved the council and arrested a large number of civilian and military officers who he felt were undermining the war effort. After creating an Armed Forces Council to take the place of the High National Council, Khanh asked Huong to stay on as Prime Minister in hopes of providing a sense of stability. It didn't work.

On reading the cable from Taylor that reported the coup, President Johnson replied, "This latest stunt is over the top. I told them no more coups! It's like it goes in one ear and comes out the other."

Reading Johnson's angry reply, Taylor felt he had his marching orders in no uncertain terms. When he met with Khanh and his Young Turks, Taylor berated them, saying, "You have acted without consulting the United States representatives in South Vietnam. You have disregarded our advice on important matters."

Khanh was outraged at Taylor's audacity. Two days later, in an address over military radio as a veiled threat against Taylor and the Americans, Khanh said, "We make sacrifices for the country's independence and the Vietnamese people's liberty, but not to carry out the policy of any foreign country. It would be better to live poor but proud as free citizens of an independent country rather than in ease and shame as slaves of the foreigners and Communists. I pledge my support and that of my followers for both Huong and Suu's civilian rule, and we condemn colonialism."

Reading a transcript of the broadcast, Taylor was livid.

The next day, in an exclusive interview published in the New York Herald Tribune, Khanh stated, "If

Ambassador Taylor does not act more intelligently, Southeast Asia will be lost. Taylor's attitude during the last forty-eight hours as far as my small head is concerned-has been beyond imagination."

That evening, Khanh convinced his fellow officers to join him in an attempt to get Huong to declare Taylor persona non grata which would expel him from South Vietnam. It was the CIA, tipped off by an informant in the Junta, that warned Taylor what was about to happen. US officials at the embassy lobbied individual South Vietnamese officers to change their position and allowed Taylor to stay. The American officials also informed Prime Minister Huong that if Taylor was expelled, all US funding would stop immediately.

The next day, the South Vietnamese generals officially changed their minds. They asked Huong to formally denounce Taylor for his behavior in his meetings with Khanh and the Young Turks. After denouncing Taylor, Huong said, "I will take appropriate measures to preserve the honor of all the Vietnamese armed forces and to keep national prestige intact."

While hurtful to the pride on both sides, disaster was diverted, and Taylor remained as US Ambassador in South Vietnam just as General Khanh remained in control of the new Armed Forces Council. But Khanh was not done. He issued a declaration of independence from foreign manipulation and condemned colonialism directly accusing Taylor of abusing power.

Concerned that Khanh might act against the US Embassy, General Westmoreland requested CINCPAC to station a Marine Landing Force at the mouth of the Saigon River in case the embassy had to be evacuated quickly. He also informed the American Marine commander stationed at Subic Bay in the Philippines that his battalion might be needed on short notice to defend American installations in South Vietnam. Although there was little a battalion of Marines could do against the entire South Vietnamese military, they still were a serious deterrent should Khanh try anything underhanded. For the first time, America was concerned that the South Vietnamese military might attack Americans in-country. Even with the perceived threat, the American military stayed true to its mission and stayed in South Vietnam.

December 23, 1964 – Mekong Delta, South Vietnam

Built in the shape of a triangle, the RVN Special Forces outpost near Tranh Yend in the Mekong Delta was well-protected. Commanded by VSN Captain Huong, the company-sized unit had one American advisor, Lieutenant Shattuck. Huong liked Shattuck but felt he was too pushy at times. The Vietnamese commanders had their way of doing things and often saw their advisors as tools to call in American air support and artillery strikes. The relationship worked as long as the American officer kept his cool and didn't overstep his authority. Together for over a year, they worked things out and had killed a lot of Viet Cong. Trust was the key.

Special Forces were often put in harm's way and this outpost was no exception. It was in a remote area known to have high Viet Cong activity. The camp defenses were designed to cover all 360 degrees around the site and had two perimeters – outer and inner. The fighting positions within the outer and inner perimeters were encircled with trenches and barbed wire to prevent any enemy breach from attacking from the rear or flanks. Trenches fronted with Constantine wire and foot-tangle wire connected everything. Mines surrounded the outer perimeter and fougasse canisters protected the most vulnerable places along the wire. On each corner, there was a reinforced bunker with a .30-cal. Machine gun. In the center of the outposts was the below-ground mortar pit surrounded by an earthen berm and layers of sandbags. The M29 mortar fired an 81-millimeter shell and was the key defense for projecting firepower beyond the outer perimeter. It had a range of three miles and a good crew could fire an average of twelve rounds per minute at a consistent rate.

Shattuck shared intelligence reports with Huong. The latest batch showed a large buildup of Viet Cong in the area. The advisor and the commander had little doubt that their outpost would be the target. This wasn't the first time the VC had tried to overrun the outpost. The South Vietnamese had been lucky and were able to fight the VC off with the help of American air power. But reports that the VC had been armed with modern Soviet and Chinese weapons were a cause for concern.

The morale of the Special Forces company was also a problem. Political turmoil in Saigon had taken its toll on the South Vietnamese military. Even though the generals were in charge, they didn't seem to have much interest in fighting the war. General Khanh, now in power, was no exception. He spent his energy consolidating his political base and had little time to plan an overall military strategy for the country. He didn't trust any of the other generals with such an important task, so it languished, and the military was left unguided. The head of government had switched so many times, the soldiers did not know if the government would be around for another year or even next month. It was difficult psychologically to fight for a country so unstable as South Vietnam.

Both Huong and Shattuck knew that the morale of the troops was the biggest factor in both victory and defeat. Things did not bode well for the Special Forces outpost. Huong put out more patrols beyond the perimeter. He kept the number of soldiers in each patrol to a minimum, so he did not lose too many men if they were overrun in a firefight. He did not want to be caught off guard if the Viet Cong attacked. But if the VC didn't engage with the RVN patrols there was no way to determine where they might be. An RVN could walk right by a VC platoon hidden in the thick vegetation that was common in the Mekong Delta.

When the Viet Cong finally attacked the outpost after dark that evening, Huong immediately radioed and ordered his patrols back into the fortress. As they folded back into the outpost, they entered special corridors through the wire and entryways that were heavily guarded. Huong was able to recover all his patrols during the initial stages of the assault. It was a good thing… he would need every man he could get.

The Viet Cong probed the outpost's defenses looking for weak spots. There were none. The Special Forces engineers were experts at building outposts and made sure the defenses were the best possible with the limited resources they were given. Huong and Shattuck could already see that the company in the outpost was vastly outnumbered. Hearing the rate of fire, Shattuck could determine that the VC's weapons had been upgraded. There were far more automatic rifles being fired than ever before. The explosions from the enemy's mortar rounds were more powerful too, most likely coming from captured American-made 81 MM mortars. Huong and Shattuck knew they were in trouble. With Huong's okay, Shattuck got on the radio and called in for air support. The American lieutenant knew that it would take some time before the fighter-bombers arrived and by then the outpost could be in deep shit. It was always better to put in an air support request before it was needed and call it off if the enemy broke off the attack. He knew he would catch hell for canceling an air support request once the planes were en route, but he and Huong would be alive along with most of the soldiers in the outpost. He was willing to take the heat if it came.

Bien Hoa Air Base, South Vietnam

Coyle and Granier were at the officer's club on base. It was a nice place with a surfing theme but lacked go-go dancers and loud rock and roll. On standby, they were drinking Cokes while munching on peanuts and potato chips. Terry came running through the club entrance. Coyle and Granier didn't need to be told. They jumped up and ran toward the entrance. "Special Forces outpost near Tranh Yend is under attack. 1st Air Commando wants us to try out the weapon," said Terry as they all left the club together.

"Any idea the size and configuration of the enemy?" said Granier.

"Sounds like it could be as big as two battalions. If

it wasn't big, they wouldn't have radioed us. We'll take Spooky One."

"Why not both?"

"This is still a field test. One at a time. Besides, if it is as good as we think it is, one should be enough."

The project hangar was only a couple hundred meters away from the officer's club and they covered it at a dead run. Their biggest fear was not the enemy or even death, it was arriving too late to properly test the gunship. They needed a lot of targets to prove its usefulness. The flight crew, loadmaster, and gunnery assistants were already on board as well as the ammunition. Coyle climbed in and sprinted through the cargo hold to the cockpit. He had already performed his preflight check. His co-pilot was already going through the startup procedure when Coyle strapped himself in.

Terry and Granier climbed in and checked over the three miniguns one last time. The weapons were already loaded with the long belts of 7.62 mm bullets connected by disintegrating ammunition links. There wasn't much to do. The miniguns had a fairly simple design - a six-barrel, air-cooled, electrically-driven rotary machine gun. While one barrel was firing, two more were in different phases of reloading. Since only one of the six barrels fired at any one time, the other barrels were able to cool off before firing again. Overheating wasn't a problem even with the weapon's extreme rate of fire.

After the gunship took off, the loadmaster attached lanyards to two parachute flares beside the doorway. The flight would be less than thirty minutes and everyone wanted to be ready. This was the moment they had worked so hard to see. The final test against a real enemy. For the development team, everything was on the line.

From the cockpit, Coyle could easily identify the battlefield. There were already Four T-28s firing rockets and buzzing around the outpost like bees around a hive. They would need to break off their attack before the gunship could begin to fire at the enemy. There was too much risk of fighter aircraft flying through the gunship's stream of bullets which would be disastrous. Coyle would wait until his aircraft was in position 2,000 feet above the outpost before calling the commander of the T-28s.

Below, the Viet Cong could hear the low thrum of the AC-47's twin engines but could see nothing. It was a strange sound during a battle. The VC commander wondered if the South Vietnamese were dropping paratroopers to reinforce the outpost. The VC could not see the aircraft in the night's sky because Terry had the bottom of the aircraft painted black a few days before the mission.

In the outpost, Shattuck received a radio call that "Spooky was approaching and for the men in the outpost to keep their heads down for the next five minutes." The lieutenant told Huong. Because of the warning to keep their heads down, Huong wondered if it might be a napalm drop. Neither was familiar with the call sign Spooky, but by the end of the night, they would never forget it.

In the gunship, the loadmaster threw the two parachute flares out the doorway a few seconds apart. He watched each of the flares ignite as the parachutes popped open a hundred feet below the belly of the AC-47. As they drifted downward, they lit up the battlefield in an eerie green light. Granier poked his head out the doorway and studied the ground below. He identified the outpost and the positions of the VC forces attacking it. He ran into the cockpit and gave Coyle a description of the enemy's positions. Coyle put the aircraft into a pylon turn above the outpost. Even with the flares, he could barely see the enemy. The VC muzzle flashes helped. It was enough to place the enemy within the crosshairs of his site. "Guns up," he called through the intercom to warn the crew.

He flipped all three-gun selector switches, checked his site one more time, and pushed the button used as the trigger.

In the cargo hold, everyone watched and listened to the gun barrels as they started to whirl "Brrrr…" then mayhem as the weapons fired. The noise from the three miniguns was ear-piercing and fire lit up the cargo hold. Terry thought one of the guns had exploded, but it was just fire escaping from the six barrels as they turned from one position to the next and coming from the gun's opening and closing chambers as the empty casings were ejected. Terry and the crew had been aligning the weapons during the day and had forgotten the bright bursts of fire at night from the original minigun. All three miniguns firing in sync created a light show like no other. Each flash was like a strobe light catching the movements of the crew like some weird movie that was loud as hell. The combined guns poured three hundred rounds per second into the enemy below. Every fifth round was a tracer meaning a three-second burst from the three miniguns put out one hundred and eighty tracers into the night sky.

From the ground, the red steams seemed to appear from nowhere and licked the ground. After a brief burst of red streams, the sky would suddenly go dark again as the last of the tracers sped to the earth. Then, it would start again repeating. It seemed the hungry beast never ceased for more than a few seconds. It was an unnerving sight for the petrified Viet Cong. Many were peasants before joining the revolution. They were superstitious and believed in magical beasts.

Huong and Shattuck watched wide-eyed as red tracer round came out the side of the cargo plane in three streams. They descended through the darkness and touched down just a few hundred meters away just outside the outer perimeter wire where the VC had formed their front line. "My God. What the hell is that?" said Shattuck.

"You're asking me?" said Huong. "I'm just glad it's on our side."

It wasn't the strafing runs of fighters sweeping across the enemy lines for a brief moment. It was accurate pools of bullets being laid down on the enemy positions, tearing them apart. There was a burst of red streams from the sky wiping out anything in its path, then it would stop for a moment, move position slightly, then begin again, chewing up its prey, destroying everything it touched. Again and again without let up, the overhead beast fired its weapons. "I can't even imagine what it must be like to be under that," said Shattuck awestruck. "The poor bastards."

Shattuck turned to Huong and they both started laughing as if realizing the irony in Shattuck's observation. Whatever it was in the sky above, it was wiping out the enemy that wanted to kill them. It was saving their asses. They could hear the shouts of their men cheering from the trenches and blockhouses. They joined them hollering up to the sky in a rebel-like yell.

In the gunship above, Terry ran into the cockpit and yelled, "Nice shooting, Coyle. Don't oversaturate an area. It'd be a waste of ammo. Three-second bursts should do the trick."

Coyle gave Terry a thumbs up as he remained focused on the side window gunsight. He fired another three-second burst and said, "Like that?"

"Perfect," said Terry before moving out of the cockpit and closing the door.

There was nowhere the Viet Cong could turn for safety. Red tracers were everywhere, ripping up the very earth beneath them. Terrified, the Viet Cong broke as they yelled, "Con Rong" and ran back into the jungle. The few wounded that had survived a barrage from the gunship crawled back into the darkness of the foliage as their comrades were too frightened to carry them. The dead were left behind.

With grins on their faces, Shattuck and Huong watched the enemy retreat.

"What does that mean, Con Rong?" said Shattuck.

"Dragon," said Huong.

With the enemy retreating the mission was over. Everyone in the gunship was ecstatic. As with all warriors, the stories of a victorious battle would be told again and again. There was little doubt the field test was a success. Nobody knew how many of the enemy soldiers they had killed in the ten-minute engagement with the gunship, but they were sure it was a lot. "First rounds on me," said Terry with the biggest grin of all.

"Top shelf?" said Granier referring to the best and most expensive liquor on the top shelf of most bars.

"Top shelf."

Everyone cheered. Coyle called Terry into the

cockpit and said, “How much ammunition do we have left?”

“About half. Why?” said Terry.

“We just got a radio call from 1st Air Commando. There’s another outpost in Trung Hung under attack. They are asking if we could help out.”

“So, what are we waiting for?”

“That’s what I told ‘em. We’ll be over the site in about seven minutes.”

“We’ll be ready,” said Terry as is disappeared through the cockpit door on his way to reload the weapons.

Trung Hung, South Vietnam

The Special Forces outpost at Trung Hung was similar in size to the Tranh Yend outpost, but the layout was different. It was shaped like an hourglass and had four machine gun positions. The mortar pit was in the middle of one of the bulbous shapes while the other spherical area had the command post and hospital. An inner and outer perimeter surrounded the entire outpost with plenty of mines, fougasse, trenches, and Constantine wire.

When the gunship arrived, the outpost was in deep trouble. The Viet Cong had already penetrated the outer perimeter and were making attempts to penetrate the inner perimeter. Once that happened, there wasn’t much the gunship could do. Terry was not about to risk killing South Vietnamese troops with a broken arrow air assault. Tracer rounds streaked across the battlefield from both sides, but the VC fire was heavier and seemed to be coming from everywhere. The outpost troops ignited the final fougasse emplacement near the entrance to the compound. The entire area lit up for over a minute while the fougasse burned off. Burning Viet Cong bodies littered the outer perimeter and wire.

With the additional light from the fougasse, Coyle had a good view of the enemy as they began repositioning their forces for the final assault. He put the aircraft into a pylon turn and placed the side window site on the area he wanted to attack first. "Guns up," he said over the intercom.

This time everyone in the cargo hold backed away from the three miniguns and covered their ears. The barrels began to whirl and just like before the cargo hold lit up as the guns began to fire. The bright flashes were blinding. The strobe effect created a macabre ambiance as death was dealt to the enemy below. Having seen the last battlefield, the gun crew knew of the human destruction they were generating. It was more somber this time as they imagined the men being torn to shreds from a hail of bullets from above. They realized that the gunship they had helped to create was a weapon of mass destruction like napalm canisters and cluster bombs. Yes, they were the enemy, but they were also human beings with families and friends. Their lives were being snuffed out by something mystical that they feared and did not understand.

Knowing his ammunition was limited, Coyle fired shorter bursts, then moved on to fire again and again. He was caught up in the moment of battle and did not think about the consequences beyond saving the lives of the soldiers in the outpost.

Below, after just a few minutes, the Viet Cong, who could see the streams of fire from the beast above consuming their comrades, broke just as they had done at the previous outpost. They ran for the protection of the jungle canopy leaving their dead and wounded behind. The garrison cheered as they watched the enemy rout.

In the gunship, the celebration was more subdued. The air and gun crews were exhausted. The overwhelming emotion that accompanies battle had taken its toll. Still, it was another clear victory that proved what they all knew – they were flying a beast that could change the outcome of the war.

Saigon, South Vietnam

Terry sat in the reception area of General Moore's office sipping a cup of coffee. It was his third. He felt like a fidgeting child that didn't know what he had done wrong but was about to be taken out to the woodshed for a beating. The phone rang and the receptionist answered. It was time. Terry rose and entered through the doorway.

General Moore was sitting at his desk reading the after-action report that Terry had submitted. It was preliminary and a more detailed report of the entire project and the field tests would soon follow. As Terry snapped to attention and saluted, Moore said nothing but saluted back and pointed to the chair across from his desk. Moore finished reading the report for the third time and said nothing. It took all the captain's willpower not to fidget while he waited. Finally, Moore set the report down and looked at Terry with an angry expression that would make most men cry. "This is bullshit," said Moore.

"My report?" said Terry.

"Damned right your report. Why in the world

would you sacrifice your career putting this exaggerated crap in writing?"

"Sir, it is not exaggerated. Every word is true."

"Bullshit! You are telling me that your little gunship prototype broke not one but two regiment-sized VC assaults on Special Force's outposts?"

"Yes, sir. That's exactly what I was saying."

"How do you know the VC weren't ready to give up by the time you arrived? Those outposts were manned by elite troops with the best weapons."

"The RVN troops were doing their best to fight off the VC. But when we arrived, the VC were not giving up. In one case they had already broken through the outer perimeter and the outpost was close to falling."

"And you could see this from 2,000 feet above the battlefield in the dark?"

"Yes, sir. We had launched flares and the commander of each outpost was radioing for help."

"This is the biggest bunch of malarky I have heard since I arrived in the country."

"With all due respect, General, you're wrong. The weapon system works and it would be a great disservice to our allies and troops to ignore its potential to save lives."

"We are not in the business of saving lives, Captain."

"Fine. Then killing the enemy, sir."

"You're not going to retract your report?"

"No, sir. It's the truth and I am willing to stand by it."

"Even if it means your career is down the shitter?"

"Yes, sir."

"I see."

There was a long pause as Moore considered, then

picked up the phone, and said, "Get me, General Greenberg."

Terry wondered if he had made a big mistake not retracting his report. Generals were talking and that was always dangerous for a lowly captain. Moore just stared at Terry with a disgusted expression and said nothing until his phone rang again. He picked it up and said, "Joe, you know that gunship project AFSC has been working on? Right, well… they just finished their field tests and I've gone over the preliminary results. It's incredulous, to say the least. I've never seen anything like it. I want a full squadron of the damned things and I want it now. I know there's a shortage of miniguns. We can use .30-Cals until we can swap them out with the miniguns when they arrive. But this needs to be a priority. We can break their backs with these things."

Terry was stunned. The team's gunship project was going into production. He relaxed and leaned back in his chair trying to keep from smiling. He suddenly realized he had consumed too many cups of coffee while waiting and needed to pee badly. Smiling was no longer a problem.

BOB HOPE

December 24, 1964 – Bien Hoa Air Base, South Vietnam

Whooping and hollering, two thousand airmen crowded around a recently built wooden stage in front of a hangar. Bob Hope was entertaining the troops as he had done in World War II and the Korean War. Hope was a strong believer in American efforts to stop the expansion of communism and he was even a stronger believer in the US military. He and his troop of sixty USO singers, dancers, warm-up comedians, and a four-piece band plus staff would tour across South Vietnam at bases and camps. Being asked to tour with Hope became a badge of honor among celebrities and there was no lack of famous volunteers willing to drop everything and go overseas with Bob. Movies and television stars including Phyllis Diller, Raquel Welsh, Jim Nabors, Ann-Margret, Jerry Colonna, Anita Bryant, Red Foxx, and Brooke Shields accompanied Hope all over Vietnam and did their best to personally connect with individuals in the crowd of soldiers. Hope began his first Christmas show in South Vietnam by joking, "Hello, Advisors. Here I am in Bien Hoa... which is Vietnamese for 'Duck!!'"

The troops roared and clapped. Already on a roll, Hope continued, "My military handlers told me I was coming to Sniper Valley. As I flew in today, they gave us a twenty-one-gun salute... Three of them were ours." Tickets were given and sometimes secretly sold to the troops that wanted to attend. Tickets to a USO show were always a hot item. Coyle and Granier didn't need tickets. The stage had been built near the front of the gunship project hangar. They rolled out a scaffolding tower and sat on the top platform with their legs dangling, watching the performances, and sipping cold beer. The two gunship prototypes were loaded with ammunition and parked a few hundred yards down on the apron just in case they were needed. Armed guards protected the two aircraft which were quickly becoming legends as gossip spread about what they did to the enemy that attacked two Special Forces' outposts.

Earlier that morning, a Vietnamese artist had painted a cartoon of a dragon on the nose of one of the gunships along with the words Puff, the magic dragon. The original painting of the creature had Asian-looking eyes and was changed later to look more American.

Although kept to a minimum, military aircraft continued to take off and land during the USO's performances. The war didn't stop for entertainment, even if it was Bob Hope. When a B-26 fighter bomber came in for a landing, he made a joke of it and said, "I sure hope that's one of ours. My nose is an easy target."

American troops came to rely on the USO shows. They were a reminder of home and that even as they served miles away, the folks back home in America still remembered and cared about them. The shows and

entertainers, many of which were attractive dancers and singers, reminded them of what they were fighting for. For soldiers and airmen on the front lines who were dealing with the daily pressures and hazards of being in a war zone, the USO shows provided a brief moment of levity and fun in otherwise dark and challenging times. Hope said during the performance, "I know you guys serve in some pretty remote areas and it can get pretty lonely. I met a GI who was so lonely he was going steady with his tattoo. And his buddies kept asking him if she's got a sister!"
Hope would do anything to make the troops laugh. Even generals were fair game. Always researching his next stop, Hope would build his monologues around the officers and the situation in the area. He would also poke fun at himself: "Working in a war zone is great for a comedian. You can always blame the bombs on the enemy."

Hope loved the American soldiers, which he proved by willingly going just about anywhere to perform for them even if it meant endangering his life and those that traveled with him. Hope's USO career lasted a half-century during which he headlined fifty-seven times. He was so beloved by the troops he entertained; that the United States Congress passed a bill that made Hope an honorary veteran of the U.S. Armed Forces. During an interview, Hope said, "Believe me when I say that laughter up at the front lines is a very precious thing — precious to those grand guys who are giving and taking the awful business that goes on there. There's a lump the size of Grant's Tomb in your throat when they come up to you and shake your hand and mumble 'Thanks.' Imagine those guys thanking me! Look what they're doin' for me. And for you."

December 24, 1964 - Saigon, South Vietnam

By 1964, there were 24,000 American military personnel in South Vietnam serving as advisors and airmen. The Viet Cong saw the Americans as colonizers that wanted to take over both South and North Vietnam as the French had done. The VC saw the South Vietnamese government as a puppet controlled by the Americans. Leaders in Hanoi wanted to show the Americans that the Viet Cong could strike whenever they wanted and wherever they wanted. Nobody in South Vietnam was safe. Hanoi had its agents in the South constantly looking for vulnerable targets that could demonstrate America's weakness in keeping their own people safe. They found such a target in the Brinks Hotel in downtown Saigon.

Four years previously, the Brinks had been converted into Bachelor Officer Quarters for U.S. Army officers. It was six stories with 195-rooms plus meeting halls, administration offices, and common areas such as a rooftop lounge and restaurant. After several bombings of American entertainment venues and bars in Saigon, the Army engineers build a six-foot concrete wall around the entire hotel and installed two guard gates – guest and delivery, to control entry into the facility.

The North Vietnamese intelligence assigned two covert Viet Cong agents, Nguyen Thanh Xuan, and his comrade, to analyze the Brinks and determine if an attack on the facility was possible. The two agents spent almost a month reconnoitering the Brinks and the South Vietnamese guards that protected the

American officers inside. They immediately noticed that South Vietnamese officers were allowed into the facility and freely mingled with the American officers.

To get a closer look, Xuan stole a South Vietnamese officer's uniform. Dressed as an ARVN major, Xuan passed through the main gate claiming to meet an American officer already inside the hotel. It was surprisingly simple to deceive the guards with only the name of an American officer. While inside, Xuan got a good look at the building's layout and took special attention to examine the parking garage below the hotel. The hotel was decorated for the upcoming Christmas holiday and there was a party in the lobby that Xuan was able to join. It gave him the time he needed to make mental notes of needed details.

Leaving the hotel, Xuan quickly devised a plan to destroy the hotel and kill its occupants using a car bomb parked in the garage. He hoped to create a large enough explosion to take out the support columns and cause the hotel to collapse in on itself. After consulting with a North Vietnamese engineer, Xuan settled on 400 pounds of explosives with a timed detonator.

Xuan presented his plan to his Viet Cong commander and received approval to carry out the mission. The VC commander had two goals in mind for the mission. The first was for revenge against the Americans for air strikes against North Vietnamese bases and facilities in the North. The second was to prove to the public in the south that the Americans were incapable of protecting themselves let alone the South Vietnamese people.

In the weeks leading up to the attack, South Vietnamese military intelligence had captured documents indicating that the Vietcong were planning to increase the number and ferocity of their attacks against the Americans in Saigon in hopes of demoralizing the civilians in the United States and turning them against the war in Vietnam.

Xuan entered the hotel again to observe the mannerisms of the South Vietnamese officers including how they held their cigarettes and the procedure of getting a car into the garage.

It took a week for the Viet Cong engineer to gather the explosives that Xuan needed. A few more days were required to place the explosives in the car's trunk and to rig the timer. In the meantime, Xuan observed the comings and goings of the American officers and determined that the bomb should detonate between five and six in the early evening when the lobby was filled with Americans coming back from their daily assignments. The lobby was directly over the garage and would suffer the most damage of any floor thereby being the most effective means of killing Americans. He also decided on Christmas Eve as the day of the attack because he felt the officers would most likely gather around the huge Christmas tree in the lobby for a holiday drink.

When Christmas Eve arrived, Xuan wore his officer uniform while his comrade wore a chauffeur's uniform and drove the vehicle with Xuan in the back. The explosives in the truck noticeably weighed down the back of the car, but there was nothing they could do about it except hope the guards at the main gate didn't notice. Before arriving at the hotel, they pulled the car over and set the timer on the bomb giving themselves plenty of time to escape.

When the Viet Cong duo arrived at the gate, Xuan's comrade informed the guard that Xuan was there to see Lieutenant Colonel Torrent. The guard informed the chauffeur that the colonel had left earlier for the Bob Hope show at the air base and had not returned. Xuan jumped in and said that he was to meet the colonel when he returned and had been asked to wait in the lobby. The guard said the major would have to wait outside until the colonel returned. Xuan berated the guard and ordered him to open the gate. The guard not wanting any trouble phoned his unit commander and asked what to do. Xuan pulled out his sidearm hoping he wouldn't have to use it on the guard. If needed, Xuan had already told his comrade they would sacrifice their lives to kill the Americans and would become martyrs of the revolution. The guard hung up the phone and opened the gate. They drove through and down into the parking garage.

Inside the garage, Xuan spotted a delivery truck dropping off gas canisters to the kitchen. Xuan ordered his comrade to park the car next to the truck in hopes of increasing the explosive effect. With no parking space available, the agent parked the car behind the truck preventing it from leaving before the detonation of the explosives.

Since he didn't have a watch and there was no clock in the garage, Xuan stepped out and moved to the back of the car. He took a look around to ensure nobody was close enough to see what was in the trunk, then opened the lid until he could see the timer. There wasn't much time. He closed the trunk lid and ordered his comrade to follow him out of the garage by way of the ramp.

When they again came to the gate, Xuan informed the guard that he and his comrade were going to get something to eat at a nearby café and that when the colonel arrived to inform him that they would be back shortly and meet him in the lobby as planned. The guard agreed and the two agents walked out the gate and down the street. When they reached the corner, they turned down the intersecting street and disappeared from view. Their mission was complete... as long as the bomb worked as planned. Whatever the result, there was nothing they could do at that point. What was done, was done. They were more nervous than giddy. The mission was the most important thing they would ever do in their lives. It gave their lives meaning.

Escorted by a squad of South Vietnamese soldiers in jeeps, Bob Hope and his entourage were on their way back from Bien Hoa Air Base where they had just concluded their performance. The convoy had left quickly in hopes of avoiding the crush of traffic from the crowd. Hope was feeling good about the show. He got in a few zingers and that was as much as a comedian, even one as famous as Bob Hope, could hope to achieve. The group was staying in a hotel across the street from the Brinks. Pulling onto the boulevard less than two hundred yards from their hotel, the car bomb in the garage beneath the Brink's exploded with such force it cracked the windshield of

Hope's vehicle. Stunned, Hope was wide-eyed as he saw the smoke and flames pouring from the hotel.

Moments later, as a result of two concrete supports compromised by the explosion, the bottom four floors within the hotel collapsed trapping officers and civilians in the debris. But the hotel did not collapse entirely as Xuan had wanted. Two American officers were crushed in the rubble while another sixty were seriously wounded. Twenty-five Vietnamese civilians were also injured during the bombing. The Americans had been lucky that so many of their officers housed in the facility had not yet returned from the USO show at the Bien Hoa Air Base because of the heavy traffic. Unknowingly, Bob Hope and his entourage had literally saved American lives.

Xuan and his comrade escaped uninjured and were never captured. The US officials could not immediately determine if the bombing was instigated by the Viet Cong or disgruntled South Vietnamese officials fed up with the American's meddling in the government.

December 25, 1964 - White House – Washington DC, USA

In response to the bombing, Ambassador Taylor, General Westmoreland, and the Joint Chiefs of Staff backed by every other senior military officer in Saigon and Washington urged President Johnson to retaliate with an all-out air assault against ninety-four targets in North Vietnam. But Johnson sensed that the bombing of the Brinks hotel was a convoluted scheme to blame General Khanh and his administration as a pretext for another coup by dissatisfied South Vietnamese generals. He sent a cable to Taylor that read - Tell the generals in the high council no more coups will be tolerated by this administration and if any of the generals attempt a coup, America will not recognize their new government and all American aid will be immediately terminated. Make sure the generals in Saigon understand the importance of unity and stability in the government in these perilous times.

Dumbfounded by Johnson's response, Taylor responded that he would deliver the message. In his return cable, Taylor asked if there were to be any consequences for the North Vietnamese. Johnson understood what Taylor wanted – a further expansion of the air war. But Johnson did not see the value in bombing the North and responded - "The final responsibility is mine and the stakes are very high indeed. I do not wish to bring such heavy apprehensions on the American people during the Christmas season. Let them have their holiday and we will deal with North Vietnam at the start of the New Year. In the meantime, I suggest we tighten up security for our advisors already in-country before we poke the tiger any further than we already have. An overwhelming reaction from the enemy could put our entire mission in danger if we are not ready for it."

December 28, 1964 – Binh Gia, South Vietnam

After a year of political instability in South Vietnam, the Viet Cong and the People's Army of Vietnam (PAVN) were ready to take advantage of their position.

Although the members of North Vietnam's Politburo disagreed on the best strategy, they were united in their belief that the time had come to overthrow the south and reunite the country under the communist flag.

In sharp contrast to the political unrest in South Vietnam, the communist leaders in Hanoi were much more focused on developing a strategy to overrun the South Vietnamese forces. The members of the politburo were divided between the Chinese strategy of supporting national liberation movements throughout the world and the Soviet strategy of peaceful co-existence. But the members preferring the Chinese strategy were much more aggressive and took control of the politburo when Ho Chi Minh stepped back from politics because of health concerns. It was decided that North Vietnam would fully support the Viet Cong in their struggle to liberate the South.

Toward the end of 1964, with pressure mounting from all sides against Saigon, the VC began a series of large-scale operations to defeat the ARVN. The spearhead of the North's Winter-Spring Offensive was the newly created 9th division designed to fight large battles against the South Vietnamese forces and their American advisors and air force. The two enemies met at Binh Gia, a South Vietnamese village in Phuoc Tuy province forty miles southeast of Saigon.

Six thousand South Vietnamese civilians lived in Binh Gia. They were Roman Catholic refugees that had fled North Vietnam during Operation Passage to Freedom in 1954 at the end of the Indochina War. They were staunch anti-communists and had feared persecution by the new northern government.

The Viet Cong attack on Binh Gia was a key part of Le Duan's plan to win a quick and decisive victory. It was meant to send a strong message to the Americans and South Vietnamese that North Vietnam and its Viet Cong allies meant business.

Ordered to block and destroy any enemy units attempting to reinforce Binh Gia, Colonel Ta Kham was the commander of the VC 272 Regiment. It took weeks for the 1,000 VC soldiers to skirt around Saigon undetected. They traveled in small groups using VC-friendly villages for food and shelter. They stayed off the roads trekking through the jungle and across rice paddies. Fresh supplies and new weapons were smuggled by sea from North Vietnam, then transported and distributed to the VC soldiers as they arrived at their destination.

The South Vietnamese troops had many advantages – tanks, armored personnel carriers, artillery, aircraft, and helicopters flown by American pilots. But the superior equipment and weapons made them complacent. There was a tendency to let technology do all the heavy lifting whittling down the enemy while keeping the troops at a safe distance. And that strategy often worked when the ARVN knew where the VC were located and caught them off guard. But when the VC had time to prepare their defenses and set up ambushes for the ARVN reinforcements that they knew would come it was a different story. The average Viet Cong soldier carried far less equipment and supplies than their ARVN counterparts making the VC far more flexible and faster. And the VC didn't need to wait for their armored vehicles to catch up with their troops or their aircraft to arrive because the Viet Cong didn't have any of those things. If things went bad, the VC could disappear into a nearby jungle at a moment's notice. As the Battle of Binh Gia would prove, the VC's strategy was not to fight toe-to-toe with the ARVN in a set-piece battle, but rather fight through a series of quick engagements, mauling their enemy, then breaking off hostilities before aircraft or artillery could be called in.

Once all of his troops arrived at the rendezvous point, Kham positioned his units southwest of the village on Inter-provincial Roads No. 2 and 15. Leading up to the main battle, Kham's forces ambushed and destroyed an entire ARVN mechanized rifle company including 16 M-113 APCs. One week later, the 272nd ambushed another ARVN company and destroyed an additional six armored vehicles.

In the early morning hours, the VC 271st Regiment and the 445th Company moved silently through the countryside outside of Binh Gia. Once in position, the Viet Cong began their assault with a mortar and recoilless rifle barrage as the Viet Cong soldiers advanced toward the village. Binh Gia was defended by sixty-five members of the South Vietnamese Popular Force militiamen. The village defenses were quickly overwhelmed by the Viet Cong's superior firepower and the village was captured. The surviving militiamen retreated into hidden underground bunkers where they radioed the district headquarters for help.

Colonel Kham established his command post in the

village church and called for reinforcements to fend off the counterattack that he knew would come. Time was short and resources were few. Kham's scouts had already determined the most likely routes of approach to the village and potential landing zones for enemy helicopters carrying reinforcements. As his reinforcements arrived, he ordered his men to dig trenches and bunker at key locations around the village protected by barbed wire and landmines. In a network of defensive fortifications, the regiment set up their heavy mortars, machine guns, and recoilless rifles.

In response to the village militia's pleas, the district chief sent two Ranger battalions to retake Binh Gia and destroy the Viet Cong. Concerned that the Viet Cong would flee before his troops arrived, he ordered the battalion commanders to move quickly. He did not know the size of the enemy force that his battalions would face.

Once the South Vietnamese forces arrived and surrounded the village, reconnaissance patrols informed the commanders that they were outnumbered, and the enemy was dug in like a tick. The battalion commanders held off their attack beyond a few probing skirmishes and radioed for reinforcements.

The next morning, two more Ranger battalions were airlifted by helicopters to the battlefield by the US 118th Aviation Company. As the 30th and 33rd Ranger battalions arrived at the landing zone, they came under attack from a well-planned VC ambush. The 30th

Ranger battalion took a heavy beating as they attempted and failed to break through the Viet Cong front line. Even with their heavy losses, the Rangers continued their attack when several more companies for the 33rd Battalion joined their ranks allowing enough manpower to attack the enemy from multiple directions.

One of the companies from the 33rd Battalion reached the village but failed to penetrate the Viet Cong defensive perimeter. A second company from the 33rd moved to outflank the Viet Cong but was ambushed on open ground by three VC battalions with machine guns, mortars, and recoilless rifles. It was a kill zone. After a brave defense, the company of Rangers was wiped out suffering a seventy percent casualty rate. The few survivors escaped and made their way to the nearby Catholic church.

The 30th Ranger Battalion assaulted the Viet Cong front line from the west and had more success. With the help of local civilians, the rangers were able to fight their way through the enemy perimeter and into the village. But it was at a heavy cost with the battalion commander and his American advisor seriously wounded. The villagers picked up the fallen rangers' weapons and ammunition and hid the wounded government soldiers from the Viet Cong.

The helicopters carrying the 38th Ranger Battalion landed with no opposition. Once the entire battalion was on the ground, the rangers advanced on Binh Gia from the south. When they met the enemy, the rangers fought for an entire day trying to break through the Viet Cong defensive perimeter. The rangers in the 38th were unable to link up with the surviving and wounded rangers hiding in the village church. As the sun began to set, the VC attempted to encircle the ranger battalion and forced them to fall back, but not before calling in mortar fire that annihilated the Viet Cong trying to trap them. It was welcome payback for their fallen comrades.

The next morning, the 4th South Vietnamese Marine Battalion was airlifted by helicopter to the outskirts of Binh Gia. The Marines had a fierce reputation and called themselves the "Killer Sharks." They were tough and experienced fighters. Many of the battalion's officers were Da Lat Military Academy graduates, the South Vietnamese equivalent of America's West Point. The Marines were anxious to "get at the enemy."

Once the entire battalion had landed, they cautiously advanced toward the village to relieve the besieged Rangers in the church. When the Marines reached the VC front line, the fighting began. The two sides fought furiously for one and half hours. With the help of villagers armed with weapons from fallen Rangers attacking the enemy positions from the rear, the Marines finally broke through the perimeter and entered the village. They linked up the 30th, 33rd, and 38th Ranger Battalions. Greatly outnumbered, the Viet Cong began their fighting withdrawal to the northeast leaving their fortified positions in the village. Within a few more hours, the Marines and Rangers had completely recaptured the village. As usual, the Viet Cong forces disappeared into the nearby jungle.

Later that evening, the Viet Cong, reinforced and resupplied, returned to Binh Gia and once again attacked from the south-eastern side of the village. The ARVN forces immediately called in for air support as they engaged the enemy trying to keep them from overrunning the village. It was fierce fighting with the villagers joining the ARVN forces defending their village. As the last of the daylight faded, American helicopter gunships from Vung Tau airbase arrived and hammered the Viet Cong positions with rockets and machine guns. The Viet Cong broke and fled back toward the jungle.

Pursing the fleeing Viet Cong, an American gunship from the 68th Assault Helicopter Company was shot down by gunfire from the tree line and crashed in the Quang Giao rubber plantation. All four of the American aircrew were killed in the crash. The crash site was two and a half miles from Binh Gia.

The next morning, the 4th Marine Battalion was ordered to locate the crashed helicopter and recover the bodies of the dead airmen. The commander of the 4th Marine Battalion, Major Nguyen Van Nho sent one of his companies to the Quang Giao rubber plantation to find the wreckage and retrieve the crewmen's bodies. After one hour, the company commander radioed that they had found the crashed helicopter and had recovered the bodies of the American aircrew.

While he was on the radio, his men came under attack from all sides. Unknowingly, the Viet Cong 271st Regiment had been using the plantation as an assembly point for their troops. The South Vietnamese Marines were vastly outnumbered and attempted to pull back out of the plantation but were cut off.

Having heard the assault over the radio, Nho ordered the rest of the 4th Battalion to advance toward the plantation and rescue the trapped company. As the South Vietnamese Marines approached the plantation tree line, they came under heavy and accurate artillery fire. This was something new. For the first time in the war, the Viet Cong used artillery before attacking with their troops. Following the enemy barrage, the Marines were hit by multiple waves of Viet Cong.

Hearing the distress calls of their battalion commander over the radio, the trapped company of Marines fixed bayonets and fought their way out of the plantation. There was no ARVN artillery support because the plantation was out of range of the 105mm guns based in Ba Ria and Phuoc Tuy. After fighting hand-to-hand with the Viet Cong, the surrounded Marine company linked up with the rest of their battalion. American aircraft and helicopters once again pounded the Viet Cong positions and drove them back from their pursuit of the Marines. With a lull in the fighting, the Marines quickly made their way back to the safety of the village and its fortified defensive positions now occupied by the villagers and Ranger forces. They had left their dead behind which demoralized the Marines.

The next morning as the sun rose, the entire Marine Battalion headed back to the plantation to retrieve the American crewman and their own fallen. In the afternoon, a single American helicopter landed next to the plantation and picked up the bodies of the four American crewmen. The American aircrew did not pick up any of the South Vietnamese dead which left a bad feeling between the Marines and the Americans. The American advisors that had worked with the Marines for months were ashamed of the callous demonstration by the American airmen. They assured the South Vietnamese that more helicopters would be sent to retrieve the corpses of the dead Marines.

Surrounded by the enemy, the South Vietnamese waited for over three hours for the American helicopters. They never came. Lieutenant Brady, an American advisor told Nho that they were losing the light and the battalion needed to get out of the plantation immediately before the Viet Cong attack. Nho ordered his men to carry the bodies of their comrades back to the village. As the Marines began their march, they were suddenly assaulted by three VC battalions and mauled by enemy artillery. The battalion's commanding and executive officers were killed by gunfire and artillery. The battalions' radios were destroyed preventing the Marines from calling in air support. They were surrounded and on their own.

Two of the Marine companies fought their way out of the ambush and made it back to the village. The third Marine company was overrun and almost completely wiped out. The fourth Marine company fought its way to a nearby hilltop and took up defensive positions. They were battered by enemy artillery shells and fought off multiple Viet Cong assaults. They fought off the Viet Cong all night long. When they ran low on ammunition, the Marines fixed bayonets and fought the assaulting Viet Cong hand-to-hand.

At dawn the next day, the fourth Marine company slipped through the enemy lines and back to the safety of the village. When the fighting was finally done, the 4th Marine Battalion had lost 117 soldiers, thirty-five of which were officers, with another seventy-one wounded and thirteen missing. All four of the American advisors attached to the battalion were seriously wounded and were evacuated leaving the battalion already short on officers almost leaderless and combat ineffective. It was a devastating loss.

Hanoi, North Vietnam

The leaders in Hanoi were overjoyed. Le Duan and his followers were convinced more than ever that their strategy was working. "The liberation war of South Vietnam has progressed leaps and bounds," said Duan. "After the Battle of Ap Bac two years ago, the enemy knew that it would be difficult to defeat us. After Binh Gia, the enemy realized that they are in the process of being defeated by us." Ho Chi Minh called the Battle of Binh Gia 'A little Dien Bien Phu.' Binh Gia demonstrated the Viet Cong's new military strength and fighting abilities. It was the largest battle to date where the Viet Cong had launched a large-scale operation. They had held their ground for four days against elite government troops and American airpower. The battle showed the leaders in Hanoi that when well-supplied the Viet Cong could fight and inflict heavy damage on even the best ARVN forces.

Saigon, South Vietnam

The results of the battle came as a shock to Westmoreland and the South Vietnamese generals. The biggest question they had was how one thousand Viet Cong could travel through the countryside so close to Saigon and not be noticed. Even with all the American military and financial aid that had poured into Saigon, it was clear that if the US military did not intervene, South Vietnam could be lost before the end of the coming year. If nothing was done soon, there would be no South Vietnam to save and the communists would have achieved their goal of expanding their global revolution into southeast Asia. Once again, everything was on the line.

December 30, 1964 - White House – Washington DC, USA

Ambassador Taylor again cabled President Johnson asking him to expand the bombing campaign of the North in retaliation for the bombing of the Brink's Hotel and the Battle of Binh Gia. What Johnson wrote in his reply cable, completely surprised Taylor and was an ominous declaration – "I am contemplating more than ever a US combat commitment. I have never felt that this war will be won from the air, and it seems to me that what is much more needed and would be more effective is a larger and stronger use of rangers, special forces, and marines, or other appropriate military strength on the ground and on the scene. I know that it might involve the acceptance of larger American sacrifices but I myself am ready to substantially increase the number of Americans in Vietnam if it is necessary to provide this kind of fighting force against the Viet Cong."

That was it. After winning the election by a landslide and feeling that the American people were behind him, President Lyndon B. Johnson had finally picked up the gauntlet and was ready to commit American combat troops to war.

Letter to Reader

Dear Reader,

I hope you enjoyed When War Dawns. As America entered the Vietnam War, I feared what I already knew would happen. It was a strange emotion. I will admit, the historical research phase of writing this book was fascinating.

The next novel in the Airmen Series is A Savage Joy. Based on true events - When the North Vietnamese and Viet Cong are undeterred by American bombing campaigns and continue their attacks on South Vietnam, President Johnson finally calls in the Marines and puts American combat boots-on-the-ground in Vietnam.

Like all books in the Airmen Series, it's full of action, suspense, and historical facts. It's available as eBook and Paperback. Here is the link:

A SAVAGE JOY
https://www.amazon.com/Savage-Joy-Vietnam-Novel-Airmen-ebook/dp/B0B1WWXDKN

Sign-up for my never-boring newsletter and you will receive a free ebook – Prophecies of Chaos (one of my favorites) in addition to new release updates, special offers, and my thoughts on history. Here's the sign-up link:

Newsletter Sign-Up
https://dl.bookfunnel.com/5tl2favuec

Reviews and recommendations to friends and family are always welcome. Thank you for your consideration, and I hope to hear from you.

In gratitude,

David Lee Corley

LIST OF TITLES WITH READING ORDER

The Airmen Series

1. A War Too Far
2. The War Before The War
3. We Stand Alone
4. Café Wars
5. Sèvres Protocol
6. Operation Musketeer
7. Battle of The Casbah
8. Momentum of War
9. The Willful Slaughter of Hope
10. Kennedy's War
11. The Uncivil War
12. Cry Havoc
13. When War Dawns
14. A Savage Joy

The Nomad Series

1. Monsoon Rising
2. Prophecies of Chaos
3. Stealing Thunder

Facebook Page:
https://www.facebook.com/historicalwarnovels

Shopify Store: https://david-lee-corley.myshopify.com/

Amazon Author's Page:
https://www.amazon.com/David-Lee-Corley/e/B073S1ZMWQ

Amazon Airmen Series Page:
https://www.amazon.com/dp/B07JVRXRGG

Amazon Nomad Series Page:
https://www.amazon.com/dp/B07CKFGQ95

Author's Website: http://davidleecorley.com/

DAVID LEE CORLEY
A SAVAGE JOY
THE AIRMEN SERIES

Author's Biography

Born in 1958, David grew up on a horse ranch in Northern California, breeding and training appaloosas. He has had all his toes broken at least once and survived numerous falls and kicks from ornery colts and fillies. David started writing professionally as a copywriter in his early 20's. At 32, he packed up his family and moved to Malibu, California, to live his dream of writing and directing motion pictures. He has four motion picture screenwriting credits and two directing credits. His movies have been viewed by over 50 million movie-goers worldwide and won a multitude of awards, including the Malibu, Palm Springs, and San Jose Film Festivals. In addition to his 24 screenplays, he has written fourteen novels. He developed his simplistic writing style after rereading his two favorite books, Ernest Hemingway's "The Old Man and The Sea" and Cormac McCarthy's "No Country For Old Men." An avid student of world culture, David lived as an expat in both Thailand and Mexico. At 56, he sold all his possessions and became a nomad for four years. He circumnavigated the globe three times and visited 56 countries. Known for his detailed descriptions, his stories often include actual experiences and characters from his journeys.

Made in the USA
Las Vegas, NV
02 June 2023

72871760R00184